THE FIGHTING COCK

THE THREE COMMANDERS
Generals Hawthorn, Roberts and Savory at the Nasik parade

The Fighting Cock

BEING THE HISTORY OF THE
23rd INDIAN DIVISION
1942-1947

BY

LIEUT.-COLONEL A. J. F. DOULTON

O.B.E.

With a Foreword

by

LIEUT.-GENERAL SIR REGINALD SAVORY

K.C.I.E., C.B., D.S.O., M.C.

late G.O.C. of the 23rd Indian Division

DEDICATED TO

ALL WHO WORE THE
''FIGHTING COCK''
OFFICERS AND MEN
BRITISH AND INDIAN
LIVING AND DEAD

Contents

Contents

Illustrations

Maps

Foreword

THIS is an excellent history. All of us who belonged to the 23rd Indian Division must be grateful to the author for having written it. He has recaptured the atmosphere. To read the book is to be transported back to the days about which it was written—days of great obstacles, great efforts, great spirit and great comradeship.

I finished reading the final draft only an hour or two ago; and on casting my mind back, I find that one sentence in it stands out more clearly than all the rest. It is an extract from a war diary and it will be found in Chapter 18. Here it is:

> "The men were incredible: we never heard a moan or a grumble. They worked harder than I believed men could work: and all in such a cheerful spirit that *we, their officers, felt very humble.*"

The italics are mine. The author of that war diary went to the root of the matter and expressed thoughts which must so often have been with those of us who held command in whatever rank or capacity: thoughts of deep lasting and humble gratitude to the men we led.

R. A. SAVORY.

Preface

THIS book is the story of a Division which had as long and honourable a record of service as most war-raised formations, but had no chance to attract the public eye through some conspicuously fine feat of arms. The obscurity of the 23rd Indian Division has persisted; one official account implies that the only action it fought as a concentrated unity was carried through by other troops, and another publication consigns it to the Arakan, the one part of the Assam–Burma front in which it was never found.

Hence this story has been written first for the men of "The Fighting Cock," that their deeds may be known. As I wrote, the old Indian Army disappeared for ever and the book took on a wider purpose, for there can be no questioning the quality of that Army or Britain's indebtedness to it. It is right that we should not forget the Indian sepoy and his officers, and this book is in its small way a tribute to some of them.

I have been helped by many, but there is no room to mention them individually, and I hope those who sent accounts, orders and photographs will accept this general expression of thanks for their assistance. I am especially grateful to Lieut.-General Sir Reginald Savory for writing the foreword, and to him, to Lieut.-General Sir Ouvry Roberts and to Major-General D. C. Hawthorn for reading and commenting on those parts of the book which cover their several periods of command; nor can I forget Mr. Owen of the Historical Section of the Cabinet Offices, who, with his staff, endured me for many hours as I delved into the War Diaries they guard. I owe the excellent maps and diagrams to the skilful execution and kindness of Lieut.-Colonel L. F. A. "Busti" Maddocks, designer of the original "Fighting Cock."

Mr. A. L. Kipling, Assistant Sales Manager of Gale and Polden, who has long made the production of military histories his special province, has been continuously patient and helpful and this brief acknowledgment can only suggest the value of his advice and assistance.

A. J. F. DOULTON.

UPPINGHAM, RUTLAND.
18*th February*, 1950

Abbreviations

FORMATIONS and units have been given in full the first time they occur in the story; thereafter the normal Army abbreviations have been used. Readers not fully conversant with these will find that appendices A and B form a glossary for units in the 23rd Indian Division; other units can be easily traced in the index. A few abbreviations of staff officers' titles and the like are covered by short footnotes.

The 24-hour clock system has been used throughout.

RANKS IN THE INDIAN ARMY

There are three main divisions in the old Indian Army. These are:

(*a*) N.C.Os., corresponding exactly to their counterparts in the British Army though the nomenclature is different: Lance-Naik (L./Naik), Lance-Corporal; Naik (Nk.), Corporal; Havildar (Hav.), Sergeant; Company Havildar-Major (C.H.M.), Company Sergeant-Major (C.S.M.); Subedar-Major (Sub.-Maj.), Regimental Sergeant-Major (R.S.M.), the senior Warrant Officer in a battalion.

(*b*) Viceroy's Commissioned Officers (V.C.Os.), a class peculiar to the Indian Army coming between N.C.Os. and officers. They are normally N.C.Os. promoted for long service. The junior rank in this class is Jemadar (Jem.), the senior Subedar (Sub.). V.C.Os. take the place of junior officers in British service and command platoons; in action many took over companies when the commanders became casualties. In Gurkha units, V.C.Os. are styled Gurkha Officers (G.Os.).

(*c*) Commissioned Officers, originally all British but with an increasing proportion of Indians as the policy of introducing Indian officers became effective. It was not due to this policy that 1 Patiala, whose exploits feature frequently in this book, was entirely officered by Indians; they were a battalion belonging to one of the major states, loaned for the war to the Indian Army, of which they were not strictly a part though they had been trained under British guidance.

CHAPTER 1

Early Days

THE 23rd Indian Division was a child of the war. Our birthday, January 1st, 1942, is easy to remember and takes the reader back to those days of turmoil, uncertainty and confusion following the Japanese entry into the Second Great War. True, we had an earlier, a kind of pre-natal, existence in the closing months of 1941 when we were styled 34 Indian Division, but it is to that New Year's Day that we must trace the start of our story.

There was not much of a Division at Jhansi in January, 1942. There was our commander, Major-General R. A. Savory, who had led a brigade of 4 Indian Division at Sidi Barrani and Keren and had subsequently been appointed military governor of Eritrea; there was the skeleton of a staff, though a journey to Lucknow was necessary if anyone wished to find the C.R.E.[1]; but there were few troops to command and these few were at Delhi, where 98 Indian Infantry Brigade and the Hyderabad Lancers were stationed, the latter being the proud possessors of one armoured car.

From time to time we were given newly raised formations to equip and train for war in a remarkably short space of time. One such was 63 Indian Infantry Brigade, which we were ordered to have ready a month after it was raised at the end of January. There was never a chance of replacing in the time equipment thirty-five years out of date, but so ill was the war going that this Brigade left for Madras in little over a fortnight, and small boats were used to ferry out to the transports equipment which had arrived at the last moment. Similarly, 64 Indian Infantry Brigade came under our care for a brief period.

These were birds of passage and cannot be considered as integral parts of the Division. In fact, we were an insignificant

---

[1] Commander, Royal Engineers, the senior Engineer officer in a Division with rank of Lieutenant-Colonel.

child until we reached Ranchi, where we were forced, after barely a month of adolescence, to come hastily to full maturity as a fighting formation, ready to face the Japanese threat on the borders of Assam and Burma.

As the formations and units that were to form the Division began to gather at Ranchi early in March, few could have foreseen how short the time for overcoming teething troubles was to be. When 158 Field Regiment, R.A., arrived on the 9th, they were greeted by the A.D.M.S.,[2] who was the Division in Ranchi! The rest of Div. H.Q. was on the move from Jhansi. 37 and 23 Indian Infantry Brigades, the latter shortly to be renumbered 123 Brigade, though already in the Ranchi area, were part of 14 Indian Division and were not transferred until after the arrival of Div. H.Q. Many units had been hastily mobilized, all were short of equipment and few had trained with modern weapons. Though 1 Indian Infantry Brigade was not yet under command, an extract from a letter written by its commander, Brigadier F. V. R. Woodhouse, on March 27th, five days after it had orders to mobilize, sums up the position: "It must be remembered that both the battalions going with this Brigade have received no training with modern weapons" or "in the technique of modern warfare against a first-class enemy."

All through the month of March, units were arriving at Ranchi, and by the end the diverse identity of the Division began to appear. We were, from the outset, predominantly a division of Indian troops, volunteers one and all. Punjabis, Gurkhas from the hills of Nepal, Mahrattas from the Western Ghats, these were some of the races that had made the name of the Indian soldier famous and they were all to be found among our ranks. Equally well known for their fighting qualities were the Rajputs, Patialas and Kumaons who joined us in Assam; nor must we omit the Bengalis and Madrasis who, if they could point to no such distinguished past, under the stress of war rendered fine service in the engineer, signal and administrative units. Apart from a short acquaintance at the start with 82 Anti-Tank Regiment, R.A., the Seaforths and the Field Regiment were the only two British units in the Division.

---

[2] Assistant Director of Medical Services, the senior medical officer in a Division with rank of Colonel.

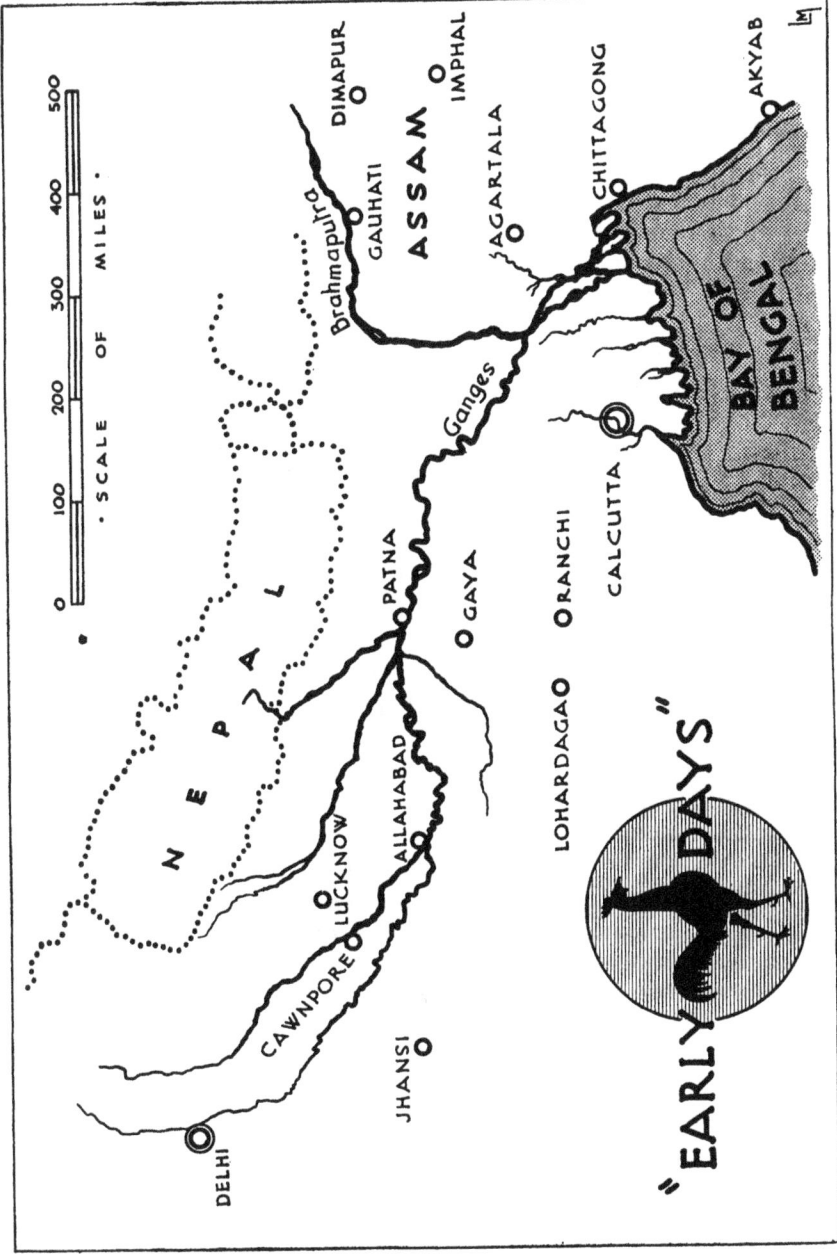

"EARLY DAYS"

SCALE OF MILES

DELHI
JHANSI
CAWNPORE
LUCKNOW
ALLAHABAD
NEPAL
PATNA
GAYA
LOHARDAGA
RANCHI
CALCUTTA
Ganges
Brahmaputra
GAUHATI
DIMAPUR
ASSAM
IMPHAL
AGARTALA
CHITTAGONG
AKYAB
BAY OF BENGAL

At the end of March we left Ranchi for Lohardaga, where we pressed on with training. The Division, at this time mobile reserve for Eastern Command, was fully mechanized and each Brigade had its troop-carrying transport. Though there was a hint on April 12th that we might be bound for Burma if that front needed reinforcing, our task of providing columns to harry the Jap if he landed on the coast of Bengal and Bihar was not altered. No one's eyes were turned to the jungles of Assam and when, on the 24th, 123 Bde. were ordered to move next day to Calcutta, the order came not unexpectedly as the logical conclusion to our training and to the far-ranging reconnaissances that the General and other officers had made along the coast.

But the course of a war is not wholly subservient to principles of logic, as the events of April 25th, an interesting day, were to illustrate. The D.A.Q.M.G.[3] was visiting the newly arrived 4 Corps H.Q. to discuss details of the 123 Bde. move when he was told the move was postponed for twenty-four hours. There was no time to be lost and the news of the postponement reached the Brigade only when they were loaded and ready to start. At 2000 hrs. that night this move was finally cancelled and another ordered, but it did not concern merely one brigade. The whole Division was bound for Assam and the battalions were to use animal transport.

It is worth recording that at this point, with a major operational move due to take place within three weeks, the D.A.Q.M.G. was the only A.Q. staff officer in Div. H.Q., as the A.Q.[5] was away on sick leave and the D.A.A.G.[4] had fallen ill. He was to receive very early reinforcements in the persons of three chaplains who reported for duty on the 27th, when the D.A.Q.M.G. may have felt that he was a fit subject for their ministrations.

---

[3] Deputy Assistant Quartermaster-General.
[4] Deputy Assistant Adjutant-General.
　Both these officers, rank Major, were under the Assistant Adjutant and Quartermaster-General (A.A.Q.M.G. or, as here, A.Q.[5]), the senior administrative staff officer in a Division. The D.A.A.G. is concerned mainly with discipline, morale and casualties, the D.A.Q.M.G. with supplies.

CHAPTER 2

Into Assam

On receiving orders for the move to Assam, General Savory only stayed long enough at Ranchi to attend the Army Commander's conference and issue his instructions so far as this was possible. He left on April 30th with his A.D.C., a G.S.O.3[1] and a few I.O.Rs.,[2] and was followed on May 5th by an advanced party under the C.R.A.,[3] Brigadier Goulder.

Meanwhile the battalions were wondering how they would fare after their reorganization on an A. and M.T. basis. For the benefit of the uninitiated who may chance to read this book, the A. in this abbreviation stands for animal; M.T. explains itself, and the essential point to remember is that "animal" in this particular instance means the mule. He is a wonderfully patient beast, without whose aid we should not have survived; but he is an obstinate creature and a damned awkward customer for those unused to handling him, as many who were unversed in his delightful peculiarities were to discover.

It was not simply a matter of saying good-bye to all ideas of motoring into battle at thirty miles an hour and of learning how to handle a new method of transport. All load tables had to be revised, the distribution of weapons and equipment worked out afresh and tactical ideas readjusted at the last moment, though there was little time for thought about the last of these problems. The conversion, forced upon us by the terrain in which we were to fight, had been ordered on April 29th; G.H.Q. in New Delhi was clamouring for the staff tables from which to organize the move and these were dispatched on May 7th, when the staff allowed themselves the suspicion of a sigh of relief. They could have spared themselves the effort. On the 8th there were two

---

[1] General Staff Officer, Grade 3; a junior "operations" staff officer (Captain).
[2] Indian Other Ranks.
[3] Commander, Royal Artillery, the senior artillery officer in a Division.

important events—the first mules arrived and rapidly made their presence felt, and fresh orders were received putting other units besides the battalions on to an A. and M.T. basis, which meant that some of the groundwork must be done again and did not increase the chances of a smooth send-off. These were hectic days with the staff engaged in a battle against time while units were handing in stores and vehicles that were now surplus to establishment and hoping to draw their new requirements before leaving for the front. On the 12th orders came through that the move would start on May 18th.

In the early hours of the 15th, there was a large pile of saddlery several feet high and some yards long in front of the 3/10 Gurkha Rifles' quarter guard and similar heaps were to be seen all over the divisional area. As no one piece of equipment was fitted on to its neighbour, a considerable number of men had been employed sorting out the muddle and fitting together the jig-saw puzzle; but there was not to be much progress on the 15th. At 0530 hrs. Div. H.Q. received a warning order to be prepared to move at midday to Calcutta fully motorized. Fully motorized! Minds that were just beginning to adjust themselves to bits and bridles, hocks and withers had rapidly to revert to clutches and brakes, spanners and oil cans. With all respect to the magnificent qualities of the Indian soldier, that was asking much of him. And what of the vehicles? Mercifully, these had not yet left the divisional area so the change-over was miraculously accomplished to time, mules were forgotten, vehicles restored to their owners, and by 1200 hrs. the Division was ready to move off, albeit a little breathless. Two hours later the original order was cancelled and we were told to stand down. Someone had thought that he had seen forty Japanese ships sailing up the Hooghly. He had erred and it was as well, for India was not in a fit state to receive the contents of forty Japanese transports.

After this alarm, the departure of the Division continued with tolerable smoothness. An urgent signal from the General summoned to his presence the G.S.O.1,[4] A.A.Q.M.G. and heads of services, who left on the 18th, the first trains left on

---

[4] General Staff Officer, Grade 1 (Lieutenant-Colonel), the senior "operations" staff officer in a Division.

the 20th, and 37 Bde. were away complete by the 25th when Adv. Div. H.Q.,[5] Div. Sigs.[6] and 123 Bde. started to move. It was the day before this that such of the staff as remained were set a further problem when they were told to make all arrangements to receive the remnants of the force which had struggled out of Burma. When busy moving house, it is not a particularly easy task to care for an incoming family of 15,000 tired, battle-worn troops, though all possible was done to extend a hand of welcome to the parties who began to arrive from the 28th.

It was about this time that the move out became an affair of fits and starts owing to difficulties forward which led to a halt on all movement from May 29th to June 2nd. A further, if minor, encumbrance was caused by the large quantities of urgently needed ordnance stores which continued to arrive at Lohardaga after the bulk of the Division had left. India is a vast country; it was not by April, 1942, geared up to compete with the speed of modern warfare, nor were the main depots sited for a war in Assam. Delays in answering demands for equipment were inevitable even if the equipment was in the country; only too often it was not, as the theatre remained at the bottom of the priority list until the end of the war in Europe.

The "difficulties forward" were due to the defects of the Bengal and Assam Railway up which all traffic had to pass. This railway was designed to serve the tea estates of Assam and was in peace-time a leisurely system of the sort that is sometimes met in the remoter parts of England where the driver has his friends in each wayside station. That is not conducive to speed and, if the driver happens to be an Indian, the exchange of gossip is likely to be protracted. Nor did the nature of the system make for speed. The traveller from Calcutta had to change from broad to narrow gauge at Parbatipur or Santahar, wander up the north bank of the Brahmaputra to Pandu, and there cross to the south bank in a ferry always liable to interruption when the snows melted in the Himalayas and the river became a turbulent mass of seething water. The whole of this narrower metre-gauge section was still one-way except at the stations.

---

[5] Advanced Divisional Headquarters.
[6] Divisional Signals.

It was no wonder that the railway rocked under the sudden strain placed upon it in May, 1942. The traffic it was called upon to handle had not, could not have, been foreseen. Remembering the purpose for which the system had been designed, no one could expect to transform it in the twinkling of an eye into an efficient L. of C.[7] feeding a battlefront, for that would be like expecting a dormouse to move freely one minute after waking from its winter's sleep. Hitches, and they were many, were inevitable with the Burma Army and thousands of refugees filling the trains in one direction while another force with all its equipment, transport and stores was moving in the other. Before the war the daily express from Calcutta took twenty-five and a half hours to reach Manipur Road. 158 Fd. Regt.'s seventeen days may not be a record for the run, but it is a very, very long time to linger on this stretch of line. Others were more fortunate than this, but it was a matter of degree as times varying between seven and ten days were common. The worst hold-ups were at Pandu, where the sidings were full of trains that had been stationary for days, and on the section on the south side, which sometimes took four days instead of the normal eight hours.

Conditions on the journey beggar description. With the approach of war to the frontiers of India, many of the railway staff had fled in fear of their lives, and among them all the sweepers. In their absence, the urinals and lavatories at the stations became clogged with refuse and many, shunning this filth, went farther afield and made the evil more widespread. The stench rose up into the heavens, mingling with the sickly odour from the putrefying corpses of refugees who lay unburied where death had overtaken them.

When the units at last arrived at Manipur Road their troubles were far from over. By the end of May, the monsoon had broken and the troops were greeted by the sight of rain ceaselessly pounding the earth. Though they may have longed for shelter, there was none to be had. Soaked through and through, the men were shown stretches of virgin jungle and told to make the best of it. Surveying the scene, one Gurkha rifleman was heard to remark "What a

---

[7] Line of Communication.

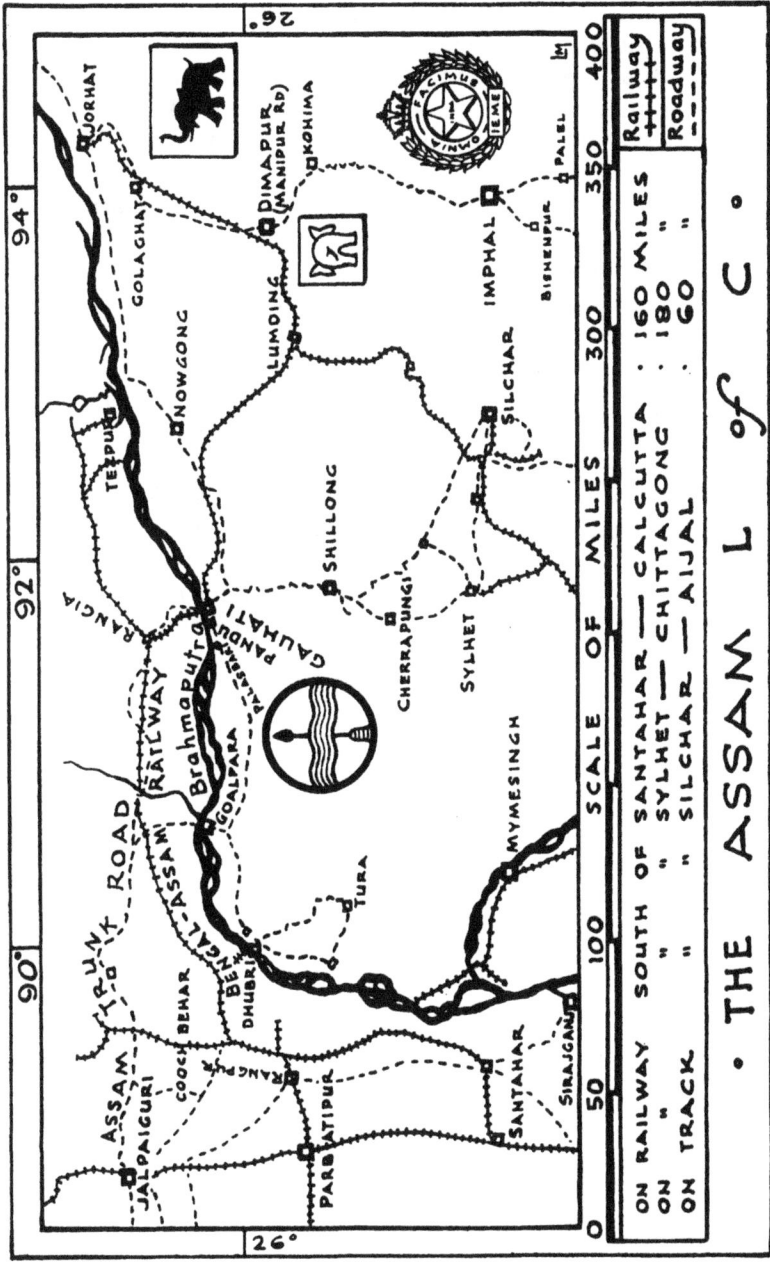

· THE ASSAM L of C ·

Railway +++++
Roadway -----

ON RAILWAY SOUTH OF SANTAHAR — CALCUTTA : 160 MILES
ON " " " SYLHET — CHITTAGONG : 180 "
ON TRACK " " SILCHAR — AIJAL : 60 "

SCALE OF MILES
0   50   100   200   300   350   400

JORHAT
DIMAPUR (MANIPUR RD)
KOHIMA
GOLAGHAT
NOWGONG
LUMDING
TEZPUR
IMPHAL
BISHENPUR
PALEL
SILCHAR
SHILLONG
CHERRAPUNGI
SYLHET
RANGIA
PANDU
GAUHATI
Brahmaputra
ASSAM — BENGAL RAILWAY
GOALPARA
TURA
MYMESINGH
ASSAM TRUNK ROAD
COOCH BEHAR
DHUBRI
RANGPUR
JALPAIGURI
PARBATIPUR
SANTAHAR
SIRAJGANJ

90°   92°   94°
26°

bandobast![8] If things are as bad as this down here, will we get any rations when we get up the line?" It was no fault of the staff at the Manipur Road base that conditions were as bad as they were. The Rest Camp was packed out with troops evacuated from Burma, there was no time to build other accommodation, there was an unending movement programme to supervise and all the troops in the area had to be provisioned. The wonder is that the staff contrived to do as much for us as they did.

Part of the art of soldiering is to make yourself as comfortable as the conditions permit. There was not much scope at Manipur Road for anything approaching Ritz standards, but the men, with the natural resource of soldiers, soon contrived to make themselves shelters which warded off some of the fury of the tempest. These were no protection against the mosquitoes which droned throughout the night and zoomed to the attack to batten on unguarded bodies. The battle against malaria was on, an enemy quite as formidable as the Jap until science came to the rescue.

So the 23rd Indian Division gathered piecemeal in Assam at a pace more befitting a funeral procession.

---

[8] "Arrangement."

CHAPTER 3

Into the Breach

GENERAL SAVORY, after hastening away from Ranchi, reached Jorhat on May 3rd. He pushed on the next day by car to Manipur Road, found the route impassable forward of Golaghat, returned to Jorhat, reached Manipur Road by train at half-past nine that night, was in Imphal on the evening of the 5th and rushed on the next morning to Palel and Tamu. That day he found time, though without his staff, to produce an operation order of which the intention paragraph read:

"23 Ind. Div. will (a) stop the Japanese invading
INDIA, and
(b) defeat them if they do."

That paragraph and the urgent haste of his movements were characteristic of the man. Possessed of moral courage in the highest degree, he remained undaunted despite the frightening prospect that confronted him, and he instilled his fearlessness into all those who served under him. These were dark days. The Japs had gained overwhelming successes, Singapore had fallen and our army had been chased out of Burma. As a result, a legend of invincibility attached to the Japanese name—they were masters of the jungle, had abnormal powers of endurance, and fought savagely, as though they were a race of supermen lacking normal human feelings. Tough as they proved to be, they were to be outfought in Burma and sent reeling back the way they had come, but that was two years ahead of these days when the 23rd Indian Division took up its station, naked and alone, on the frontiers of Assam and Burma. The Japanese bogy had not been exploded.

There was need of a man of General Savory's quality at the head. You cannot account mathematically or in any other way for the work that a "big" man does when confronted with a task that would make lesser beings quail.

You sense the presence of your leader, you take confidence from him, you try to live up to his standards. This is not to underestimate the quality of the brigade, battalion and other commanders who did their appointed tasks right royally. But the lead came from General Savory and it is to him that tribute is first due for heightening the combative spirit in all ranks until they knew that they were superior to the foe.

It was not for nothing that he had chosen the "Fighting Cock" as the Divisional sign, with the emphasis in his mind very much on the "fighting." That was to be the spirit required of us by our commander, a man without fear and a soldier who understood that discipline and efficiency are the foundations of his profession. He was to gain the liking of all —except, perhaps, the inefficient.

As the General moved forward on May 6th, he found nothing but chaos and weakness. At Palel the garrison was formed of the H.Q. and one company of a Nepalese battalion, the H.Q. of a second regiment, some sappers, a couple of A.T. companies, a few pioneers and a company of M.T.; a motley collection this, ill suited to the task of resisting the Japanese Army. At Lokchao he met the head of the Burma Army and intermingled with its ranks the first of that stream of refugees who were to come staggering in search of safety during the next month. Sensing the confusion there would be when this column met troops coming up from Imphal, he sent his A.D.C. back to stop all forward movement before he pushed on down the long, straggling column to Tamu. There he found the H.Q. and two battalions of 1 Ind. Inf. Bde. under Brigadier Woodhouse awaiting his orders. At this moment, 1900 hrs. on May 6th, apart from the rearguards of the Burma Army, there stood as organized forces between the Japanese and India General Savory and 1 Ind. Inf. Bde.

This Brigade, starting earlier than the Division, had had an easier passage up the L. of C. to Manipur Road. After mobilizing at Abbottabad, their peace station, where they had been training in mountain warfare, they began to leave from April 10th and had concentrated in Assam by the end of the month. Though they came complete with tommy-guns, Brens and mortars, none was trained in their use, and their commander's opinion on the fitness of his units for war has

THE
ORIGINAL
FIGHTING COCK
GEN. SIR R. SAVORY

"DON'T FIGHT WITH ONE
EYE LOOKING OVER
YOUR SHOULDER"

already been recorded. But when Brigadier Woodhouse arrived at Manipur Road on April 14th, his immediate concern was to find out the task of his command, and this was not an easy discovery to make. He was told that he must press on to Kalewa with all the speed he could muster, but what he was to do at this obscure village on the Chindwin none could say. As it was unsatisfactory to launch the only fresh brigade in Assam far into the blue with its role undetermined, a signal was sent on May 18th to G.H.Q.,[1] at this stage still in New Delhi, seeking for enlightenment. As the only answer was silence, the signal was repeated on the 22nd.

Meanwhile all arrangements were made for the forward movement of the Brigade. Despite the urgent need for haste, this could only be a slow business as the units had arrived without their transport and the few local resources were committed to other purposes. Some slight relief was provided by the appearance of 1 Assam Regiment, which had been ordered under command 1 Bde. on its arrival in Assam in place of a battalion left behind in India. Where there was so much confusion, it was no small relief to find the unit in position at the appointed time, and the discovery that it was complete with transport made its appearance doubly welcome. Though this transport was at once impressed into the brigade service, it was a mite when it came to moving a brigade group, and it was soon found that three-ton ten-wheeled Studebakers were not fit vehicles for the road to Imphal, which was in these early days more a mountain track than a road. The track was narrow, the surface loose earth, the bends in the hill sections sharp, the gradients severe. It was not pleasant driving by day with nothing to prevent a slightly errant vehicle from disappearing over the side into the jungle, when the fall might be a few feet or hundreds; by night, when lights were forbidden, there must be accidents to heavy vehicles which had to reverse on many of the corners.

But this was no time to worry about the condition of the road. The move must go on and the bulk of it had to be done on foot. This was an infantryman's slog, a route march perhaps, but exhausting when repeated day after day and devilish uncomfortable if it had to be done in the monsoon.

---

[1] General Headquarters.

The first stage was to reach Palel, twelve marches away, and the plan divided the Brigade into nine echelons, each limited to eight hundred men and two hundred and thirty animals owing to the size of the staging camps on the way. The first echelon hit the trail on May 19th, the day after the first signal had been sent to G.H.Q., and succeeding echelons followed at regular intervals, the only hindrance being an outbreak of serious disease among some of the mules. The Brigadier and his staff, unable to delay further, left on the 25th, still in ignorance about the future.

You cannot control operations from a H.Q. thousands of miles away. In this case the answer came on the 28th, ten days after the first signal, and the orders were that the Brigade should concentrate at Tamu. So it was that on the evening of May 6th, when General Savory reached Tamu, he found there H.Q. 1 Bde. with two of its battalions, 7/14 Punjab and 1 Assam, while its third battalion, 1 Patiala, was still on the road. Actually the Brigade had acquired a fourth battalion on that day as 1 Seaforth, then in the Kohima area, had been put under command. The connection of 1 Seaforth with 1 Ind. Inf. Bde. and of the Brigade with the Division, begun in the turmoil of May, 1942, remained unbroken until we left Java.

As the General had left the Imphal plain at Palel and climbed up to Shenam, ten miles away, he had been struck by the great natural strength of the position. Straddling the easiest line of advance from the Chindwin, the Shenam ridge, 4,500 feet above the sea, with Laimatol Hill and its twin peak beyond, stood out like a bastion of an ancient fortress, glowering defiance at the east. A further advantage was that the L. of C. up from the plain was short and unlikely to be cut unless the ridge itself fell. Here, then, General Savory had resolved that he would stand even before he reached 1 Bde. We were to know this place very, very well ; we were soon to christen it "The Saddle" and nickname Laimatol "Gibraltar" and its twin "Malta"; and there were to be "Recce Hill," which dominated the "Saddle" and was the key to the whole feature, Patiala and Punjab ridges and others; for many of us this was to be our home for months on end; we were to know all its moods, tasting the fury of its storms and the bitterness of its early morning chill; and we were to hear the whine of bullets overhead and the thump of shells; but on this May 6th the ridge was a stranger to us and all was quiet. Advance parties were at work on the 8th siting and digging slit trenches, the Patialas arrived from near Imphal on the morning of the 9th, and the battalions from Tamu marched in that evening, having covered thirty-three miles over a road turned into cloying mud by the rains. Besides manning part of the main defences, 1 Assam were called on to find an outpost screen on the Chindwin.

As the troops worked on the 8th, they were watched by other high-ranking officers besides the General, for there were also present the C.-in-C., H.E. Field-Marshal Sir Archibald Wavell, and the G.Os.C.-in-C. of Eastern Army and 4 Corps. The need, already noticed, for closer control of the front had been met by putting H.Q. 4 Corps under Lieut.-General N. M. S. Irwin, in command of all troops in Assam. The immersion of this H.Q. in the jungle was hardly less abrupt than our own. In February they had landed in Iraq from the United Kingdom, on March 1st they found themselves clambering on board ship again at Basra, on April 2nd they had moved from the Poona area to Ranchi, where we had first made their acquaintance, and here they were rejoining us early in May for the defence of India. We were to have a long and friendly partnership, starting with our mutual apprenticeship in the jungle of Assam and lasting to the days of the Imphal siege.

During their meeting, the Generals had mounted Recce Hill to scan the country to the east, deeply conscious of the scanty resources at their disposal, of the precarious L. of C. which served the front and of the confusion on the roads. Their overriding concern was clear—whatever other approaches into the Imphal plain by tracks and paths were open to a determined enemy, the main route from Tamu must be blocked. To this end, immediate approval was given to the plan to hold the Shenam ridge. The L. of C. was more a matter for prayer than military science, the deities to invoke being those in control of the railway and the monsoon, and to prayer it had to be consigned. Control of the roads was established by putting troops of the Burma Army under command 4 Corps as soon as they passed Tamu and by deploying a large part of 1 Seaforth for police work, that at a time when the bayonets ready for action could be counted by hundreds. Where more and more troops were desperately needed, the only reinforcements anywhere near at hand were 49 Indian Infantry Brigade at Agartala in south-east Bengal. This Brigade, commanded by Brigadier R. D. Whitehouse, was now three months old and had moved shortly after mobilization from Secunderabad to Bengal; as it had the good fortune to be on the railway that runs from Chittagong to Manipur Road, it missed the horrors of the L. of C. when it began to move up to Assam on May 7th.

Up to this point, the natives of Imphal had gone about their daily pursuits apparently undisturbed by the sudden threat to their peaceful existence. Though troops were marching and counter-marching through their midst, some to the east, others to the north, they paused only to watch, little sensing the drama of which they were a part. When our advance party arrived on the 9th, the bazaars were in full swing, the shops were stocked, children played in the streets. On the 10th they heard a strange drone overhead and they looked up into the skies to see some fifteen shapes, packed close together, coming towards them. As though guided by an unseen hand, these wheeled away to the north-west and, while the people watched, came back. Whines in the air, suddenly growing louder, the crash of breaking timber, dark smudges rising from the ground tinged with the ominous red of incipient fires. Once more the hammer of war had fallen on the innocent, who fled panic-stricken from their flimsy homes. Within four hours Imphal was a place of the dead, save for convicts who broke free from the gaol in the confusion that followed the bombing. When the second raid occurred on the 16th, the bombs fell on an empty town. It was as well that the inhabitants had fled. Nothing is easier to fire than a flimsy native house and there was almost no one to aid the wounded and maimed. In the emergency hospital one Medical Officer worked alone with the aid of three native helpers, whose nerves might overcome them at any moment, until two Anglo-Burmese girls, who had walked out from Burma, came in of their own will to

c

take on the task of nursing sisters. In those raids we suffered our first casualties, an Indian batman being killed in the first and Major Callan, a L.O.,[2] in the second, when Munro, the General's A.D.C., who was with Callan, had a very near escape.

On the evening of the 10th, while fires were still breaking out over Imphal, the General held in the Residency a conference attended by all officers of his staff who had reached Assam. The next day we moved out five miles down the Palel road to the village of Langthoubal, for Imphal, unprotected by A.A.[3] guns, was not the place for a divisional H.Q. There was nothing attractive about the four or five huts which we first occupied and they were not in the best of repair, but they provided a roof of sorts for the small staff.

At that time, as the H.Q. began to settle in, no one knew whether we might not be fighting a desperate battle a few days ahead. The Jap had the whip hand and was on the heels of our retreating forces up to the Chindwin; it might be that, despite the great length of his communications, he would find the means to cross the river and resume the pursuit. A message from the Burma Army on the 19th, in which they said that the final stages of their withdrawal had not been opposed, gave ground for some hope that there might be a breathing space. We were right to hope, for our lack of strength was transparent, but if the clash came some were there ready. By the evening of the 22nd, a party formed by 1 Assam and 1 Patiala was in position on the left bank of the Lokchao river to cover the dismantling of the bridge and the withdrawal of the Burma Army rear-guard. These troops passed through at the appointed time on the night of May 22nd/23rd. When dawn broke on the 23rd, part of the 23rd Indian Division stood alone looking out over the jungle to the east and the unknown.

That day General Savory issued an order and it read:

"1. The Burma Army has passed through.

"2. The 23rd Indian Division is now charged with the defence of this part of the frontier of India.

---

[2] Liaison Officer.
[3] Anti-Aircraft.

"3. The following will be borne in mind by every man
of the Division:

(*a*) The safety of India depends on you.

(*b*) The enemy will be constantly watched by day
and night.

(*c*) He will be outflanked and surrounded whenever
possible and destroyed.

(*d*) There will be no withdrawal."

"There will be no withdrawal." That was the stark
prospect that faced those who stood in the breach. It is clear
that had the Japanese been able to muster their strength for
an immediate sally in force across the Chindwin, however
gallantly the Shenam defences had been held, they must
have been overwhelmed. There were no anti-tank mines, no
sandbags, no wire to strengthen these defences, and there
was no artillery support. These filled the breach—the
officers and men of 1 Seaforth, 7/14 Punjab, 1 Assam, 1
Patiala.

CHAPTER 4

The Breach fills Slowly

THE first of the refugees had come in with the head of the Burma Army, the forerunners of a second army retreating before the Japanese. But these knew not discipline nor had they officers to turn to for orders; theirs was no controlled withdrawal. They came past Shenam at first in their hundreds each day, then in their thousands, with only one thought in their minds—they longed for safety; and many were past caring even for this.

They were in ghastly plight. Hardly knowing from what they fled, they had left their homes, taking with them the few possessions they could carry, without thought for the morrow. Many would have fared better had they stayed behind to face the Japanese occupation, but they were caught by the frenzy of the moment. Some had heard the sounds of war, some had heard rumours of brutality; they saw men, women and children on the move and they rushed out to join the throng. They came from all parts of Burma—from Meiktila in the centre, from Bhamo on the Upper Irrawaddy, from Yennanyung hundreds of miles to the south—and all had been on the road for days, just walking on and on in search of safety, hoping that they would find somewhere the means to stave off starvation.

The ordeal was too great for many who staggered on until their strength could endure no longer, when they lay where their last step took them beside the roads and tracks. Some, too, fell an easy prey to dacoits who hovered like beasts of prey around the columns, ready to swoop in for the kill and plunder. As our patrols began to move out in June they found the tracks littered with the decayed corpses of these wretches. Many others died when they had grasped safety. They came through our lines, emaciated with hunger, clad in rags, without covering for their feet, their bodies a mass of sores, riddled with all the common diseases of the East.

Weakened by the ravages of cholera, dysentery, smallpox and malaria, their strength overtaxed, they were the wrecks of human beings.

By May 15th the stream had become a flood; a week later the civilian resources for relief had been overwhelmed and it fell upon the Army to render such help as was within their power. When five thousand refugees arrived at Shenam on May 24th, there was no food to be had except from Army stocks, which had not been prepared to help starving refugees. The three tons of rice sacrificed for their use sufficed to provide two days' food for the host, but these people needed more than daily sustenance. They were worn out and needed rest; they were sick in body and mind and needed medical attention and careful feeding. We were in no position to give any of these for, with the danger of a Japanese advance always to be borne in mind, the Army had to have the forward areas clear with all possible speed. Utterly exhausted though they were, the refugees had to move on, and as there was not enough transport many had to continue their trek. On the 25th there were two dozen lorries, each with a capacity of twenty, available to shift five thousand. It was pathetic that these wretches should have again to stumble out on to the road, but there was no help for it and those who watched could only echo the words at the end of the General's signal, "Wish I could do more to help." It fell to the Seaforths to find the parties needed to bury the corpses which lay by the road back to Imphal.

As the month of June advanced, the parties became smaller and arrived at wider intervals, but they were, if possible, in an even more miserable condition than those who had gone before and they seemed to have suffered more on the way. Out of a band of sixteen hundred who had set out from Katha, the survivors numbered a bare four hundred, and a party of coolies, who had been made to work for the Japanese at Bhamo, had lost a third of their strength. These later arrivals brought with them stories of Jap atrocities; one had seen a man beaten to death for refusing to work, others described how the Japs swooped down on to villages like locusts and pillaged all that was worth the taking. There is nothing but pitiless tragedy in the tale of the retreat of this "second army" from Burma. For us, it was almost over by the end of June and we were left with the jungle to ourselves.

The country east of the Imphal plain which we were to hold and patrol and through which the refugees had struggled to safety is tremendous in its grandeur. It is as though Nature had fashioned there a vast fastness over which she was to rule in undisputed might, defying man to penetrate her domain. For her stronghold she has chosen a great chain of mountain ridges, running roughly from north to south, thrusting their strength into the sky in a series of gigantic folds which rise and fall sheer to the valleys between. They were a mass of crags and precipices—and they were covered with dense jungle. That was part of Nature's cunning in this country of drenching rain and humid atmosphere, where her fruits flourish abundantly. The trunks of trees, packed close together, rise far above the heads of man, driving upwards to the light, vying with each other for the rays of the sun. These towering trees provide the hold for creepers of every kind, which twine their tendrils round the boles, crawl up them, snatch at support among the branches and trail their spidery arms down again to the earth from which they sprung. Often those who stray off the few tracks that thread this tangled maze can progress only by hacking their way through with the knife. Down in the valleys run the rivers or chaungs—pleasant streams, sparkling in the midday sun during the dry season but torrents of wrath when the monsoon bursts. From the beginning of June, the rains hurtle out of the skies, sheets of rain the like of which a western eye never beholds, and the wind roars among the forests. The nights are cold then at the top of those four-thousand-foot peaks and the body is never dry; and though the air is drier, they are cold at the turn of the year when the valleys are filled with mist like a carpet of snow until late in the morning. For all its grandeur, this is an inhospitable country far from the ways of men where Nature, untamed, is mistress and civilization seems thousands of miles away. London, Manchester and Glasgow are but dreams! Somehow the Nagas find a living there, small folk, wonderfully cheerful, with a smile always playing about their lips. Not long ago he was accounted the greatest among them who could point to the most numerous collection of heads adorning the mantelpiece of his hovel. But they have given up this unfriendly interchange of heads and now dwell in peace and squalor in their small villages, always set for safety on the mountain tops. By day they come down from the peaks to fish in the valleys and till their fields; as the sun goes down they wander back up thousands of feet to their villages. For a short while they resented our intrusion into their privacy and there was between us an early dispute over a mule which ended in the death of two of their number; but they soon came to know us and became our friends, providing labour for our road-making and guides for our patrols. We owed much to their unswerving loyalty and to the Kukis, a warrior race whose lands fringe Shenam.

A glance at the map will show the vital importance of preventing the Japanese from debouching into the Imphal plain. Into this oasis in the midst of the Manipur hills the main routes from the Chindwin lead and from it the routes out to the north and west begin; and it provides the only half-way house where a force advancing from the east could build up a firm base and reorganize before making the next bound forward. A brief description has been given of the eastern ranges of that vast expanse of mountain and jungle which surrounds and protects the plain on all sides, and it has been related how 1 Bde. came to Shenam to be astride the main route from Tamu.

Besides this earth road from Tamu, a few other recogniz-able tracks find their way through the barrier, and their western exits dictated the position of the other brigades as they arrived at the front. These exits are at Ukhrul, away to the north-east of Imphal, where a series of paths meet and provide an approach through Litan: at Wangjing, eighteen miles south-east of the town; at Shuganu in the hills at the south-east extremity of the plain; and at Bishenpur, where the Tiddim road, after descending from the heights, is sandwiched between the hills and the Logtak lake. In the absence of any other troops, 23 Ind. Div. had to cover all these approaches, their responsibility for the defence of the plain extending southwards from a line drawn through Kanglatongbi, fourteen miles out of Imphal on the main road to the north, and Ukhrul.

When 49 Bde., composed of 5/6 Rajputana Rifles and 2/19 Hyderabad Regiment, began to arrive from May 11th, they were at once ordered to block the minor approaches to the north and south; and to assist them in carrying out an order which necessitated the units being widely dispersed, the Kali Bahadur and Shere Regiments were put under command. With the Brigade H.Q. and two battalions established at Palel, these found detachments to cover the southern approaches at Shuganu and Bishenpur, and the nearer of the northern approaches at Wangjing. 5/6 Rajrif were sent on arrival to hold the route through Litan.

Thus the framework of the defence was established by the time the L. of C. began to disgorge the remaining units of the Division. It may have been only a skeleton defence in places, and where a brigade was to be later, perhaps there was nothing more than a company, but the shape of the future began to appear in the early days of June. When the battle for the plain began two years later, some of the toughest fighting was to rage around Ukhrul, Shenam and Bishenpur, and there we were now established. But the bones of the skeleton urgently needed filling with flesh.

The concentration of the Division was further impeded when on June 19th the main road from Manipur Road to Imphal collapsed at the forty-second milestone. There was to be a time when the skill of the sappers and the labour of countless coolies were to turn the track into a metalled highway that would defy the elements. Its early dangers have been described; it was a temperamental, fickle beast as well. The cliff side, loosened by the rains and shaken by the passage of heavy lorries, would come sliding down on to the road and hundreds of tons of earth would block the way; or, if the worst occurred, cliff and road would go tumbling down into the valley below. When the road collapsed, we could not turn to bulldozers and other mechanical contrivances for assistance as these were among the non-arrivals. The repairs had to be done with the sweat of men's brows and the paltry aid of picks and shovels. For week after week men toiled away at the beast, and all the time Imphal was cut off from the outside world with the scanty forces assembled for its defence awaiting the Japanese. Even after two years of improvement and organization, the Assam L. of C. was unreliable, and in June, 1942, it must have been about the worst in the world.

NAGAS REPAIRING THE BREAK AT MILESTONE 42
ON THE ROAD FROM IMPHAL TO MANIPUR ROAD

ROAD-MAKING, BURMESE PATTERN

Facing page 24]

When the road broke, 37 Bde., the H.Q. and one battery of 158 Fd. Regt. and 82 A. Tk. Regt. were the right side of the break; that is if the right side was the Imphal side where the troops were wanted, though an administrative staff officer faced with the need for maintaining extra mouths and vehicles might be pardoned for holding an opposite view. The maintenance of the force now assembling on the eastern and southern sides of the Imphal plain was not easy when all supplies, petrol and ammunition had to be manhandled across the hundred-yard gap at M.S.[1] 42. Deliveries fell short and half-rations were ordered on June 22nd, not the kind of reception one likes to give to newly arrived troops. On the same day there were eight hundred gallons of petrol forward of the break, with replenishment unlikely for ten days.

Mud and rain, masters of the front, involved all ranks in a hard, thankless battle with the elements. Never a day passed without torrents of rain. The rain washed away the bridges —three collapsed between Imphal and Shenam—and the rain and the wheels of vehicles churned the roads into mud. Real mud! None of that squelchy stuff where the ooze may come over the tops of the soles, but a thick, cloying substance feet deep into which vehicles sank up to their axles, with the engines groaning in protest as they struggled to be free. It took one troop of 158 Fd. Regt., ordered up to the Shenam defences the day after their arrival at Imphal on the 15th, seven days to complete the forty miles, and they hauled their guns into position only by winching them every yard of the last ten miles. The defences were further stiffened by the arrival of two batteries of 28 Mountain Regiment, hastily formed from artillery units of the Burma Army and destined to serve with us until our return to India, a battery of Bofors and a troop of anti-tank guns.

The deployment of 37 Bde. was as laborious for those involved as the strengthening of Shenam and they did not have the luxury of an imitation road leading to the positions they were to hold. Brigadier H. V. Collingridge, who had thought his chances of survival on the road from Manipur Road would be greater if he took over the wheel from an untrained Indian driver, met the General on the evening of

---

[1] Milestone.

June 2nd. General Savory took up a map and pointed to Ukhrul, the last of the exits that remained to be covered. In the dearth of fighting bodies, the best that could be done previously was to establish 5/6 Rajrif at Litan.

The next day the Brigadier set out for Litan in an old jeep which had been acquired for the occasion. The fight with the mud ended in favour of the Brigadier, but the issue hung in the balance for most of the twenty-odd miles and four hours required to cover the distance. Not that it was normal to arrive in a motor vehicle at Litan. The ordinary traveller motored the first seven miles to Sawombung, used mules for the next stage to Litan if there was baggage to be carried, and discarded mules in favour of porters if he was unfortunate enough to have to make the final stage to Ukhrul.

The tenuous character of this L. of C. prevented more than a small force being pushed out to Ukhrul. At the start, the Rajrif, who had been eating their last rations when the Brigadier reached Litan and were vaguely hoping more would arrive, sent out one company until they could be relieved by a similar force of the 3/10 G.R., who had their H.Q. at Litan. The rest of the Brigade was held back at Yaingangpopki, fourteen miles out from Imphal, where it was possible to keep them maintained.

The monsoon finally decided the composition of the Division. 49 Bde. had in the first place been loaned to us only as a stop-gap in the emergency and it was not the intention they should remain; but the break in the road caught some of our units on the northern side and among them the whole of 123 Bde. Though it was possible for men on foot to make their way across the gap, it was not the way to send one brigade up to relieve another which was urgently required elsewhere. In the event 123 Bde. less 4 Mahratta went to join 14 Ind. Div., 49 Bde. remained with us, the exchange being confirmed on June 30th. The Mahrattas, who had an officer killed when their mules stampeded near Manipur Road, struggled across the landslide in the last week of the month and became the third battalion of 49 Bde.

Thus by the end of June the Division was at last an entity. Out at Shenam, 1 Ind. Inf. Bde. held the "Saddle," with 1 Seaforth, 1 Patiala, 7/14 Punjab and artillery support on the ridge and 1 Assam forming an outpost screen; at

Palel 49 Ind. Inf. Bde. watched the southern approaches with 2/19 Hybad and part of the Kali Bahadur and Shere Regiments; while 4 Mahratta, less one company out in the hills at Shuganu, and 5/6 Rajrif provided the General with a small reserve at Imphal; from Yaingangpopki, 37 Ind. Inf. Bde., with 3/3 Gurkha Rifles and 3/5 Royal Gurkha Rifles close to the village and 3/10 G.R. split between Litan and Ukhrul, watched the northern tracks.

Come wind, come rain, come Jap, the Division was ready and the breach had filled slowly, though it would be wrong to give the impression that our strength was adequate for the defence of the Imphal plain. About 20,000 men stood on the frontiers of Burma and Assam, almost all of them without battle experience and many of them only partially trained; they had come to some of the fiercest country in the world at the height of the monsoon; they were maintained along a disorganized L. of C. that could not have provided for the needs of battle had one developed; and their supplies came ultimately from a land that seemed likely every day to be convulsed by political disturbances.

CHAPTER 5

The 1942 Monsoon

THE weather was dirty during that 1942 monsoon. The rain raced out of the sky for days on end, the mountain tops were shrouded in a continuous mist and the heavens were blotted out except when jagged streaks of lightning tore the clouds apart. It was as though Nature was determined to show that she resented our intrusion into her kingdom. For the first thirteen days of July it rained without ceasing, and during a violent August thunderstorm the 1 Bde. communications were dislocated when the signal office was struck by lightning.

Those who have experienced the fury of the monsoon know that it is beyond the mind's devising to keep dry unless you have a stout roof overhead and strong walls around you. In Assam officers and men alike were wet all day and all night. Out at Shenam even bamboo bashas were little protection against the elements as the wind thrust through the countless crevices and swirled round inside the huts, driving in the inescapable dampness to moisten the lives of those who could secure the pleasure of dryness only when they were relieved at their forward posts and sent down to Palel for a few days.

The shortage of essential equipment increased the strain of a life exposed to the elements. There were serious deficiencies of blankets, greatcoats and waterproofs and, perhaps worst of all, nearly everyone had only one pair of boots. It is little wonder that under these conditions the health of the Division began seriously to suffer. Owing to the ravages the climate and of malaria, many units were by early September reduced to half their normal strength and some were much lower than this, 2/19 Hybad at one point having only a hundred and twenty men fit for duty. One battalion commander has expressed the opinion that some units never fully recovered from the wastage during this first monsoon, when the medical resources were overwhelmed by an incidence of disease such as none had foreseen. With the road back to India washed away and air evacuation far away in the future, there was nothing for it but to hold casualties forward. Our medical units were small and few, so that at times battalions were holding as many as two hundred cases in their own lines. Among the diseases to be treated there was one which, if not dangerous, ranked very high for the utter discomfort it caused. Sufferers from "foot rot" will not readily forget the agony of each step and the sensation of complete helplessness when the skin cracked between the toes and the fungus began to spread until, in the worst cases, there occurred a process of internal combustion which brought up filthy blisters on the feet, as though they had been plunged in boiling water.

Mud, wet, cold and disease—these, the inescapable companions of our everyday life, worked insidiously upon the mind and spirit; there was no relief from, no easement of, the unending discomfort which sapped at morale. None could at times escape the feeling that life was not worth the living when, after a day's work in the rain and mud, which made each step a physical effort, men returned drenched to the skin to a sparsely furnished hut if duty did not demand that they continue to face the elements during the night. Even under cover the nights brought little relief to those who lay in wet clothes under insufficient blankets, trying to forget the cold which made a mockery of the desire for sleep. Gradually the mind became numbed and drove on the body to function as an automaton, and men went stolidly about their business because they were disciplined soldiers for whom there was no quitting. They could live only in the present: to glance backward was dangerous for the contrast the past presented; to look forward was futile, for there was nothing to support hopeful expectations.

Life was as dull as it was unpleasant. A letter from the U.K. rarely took less than a month to arrive and might take longer. There seemed no accounting for the vagaries of the delays and, welcome as letters always are at the front, there was little of the pleasure of true correspondence which demands a speedier exchange of news between home and the front. As newspapers, which came by sea round the

Cape, took at least three times as long as letters and wireless sets were few and far between, those committed to an existence in this wild region were living in a void from which there was no relief. These were too early days for the appearance of mobile cinema vans to bring an occasional glimmer of entertainment—and civilization.

Though the elements were hostile and life offered few attractions, there was an abundance of work to be done. As the enemy had not followed up the retreat of the Burma Army across the Chindwin at the end of May, it became immediately necessary to re-establish contact. By mid-June 1 Assam were in position forming a protective screen in front of Shenam, with their H.Q. just west of the Kabaw valley at Sibong and posts of varying strength pushed forward of Tamu to watch the approaches from the south and east. Sometimes their patrols would discard uniform and equipment and move disguised as locals, for they were close to some of the Kuki tribes, from which many of the men came.

All units, including the gunners, were called on to undertake patrols, and if the risk of an encounter with the Jap was slight, there was hazard enough, at the height of the monsoon, in battling over unknown ground with no better guide than quarter-inch maps, for none of larger scale existed. The Lance-naik of 1 Assam who fell into the flooded waters of the Lokchao river and was rescued by the gallantry of his Subedar and a naik, who plunged in to the rescue fully equipped, was more fortunate than some.

It was on June 23rd that a fighting patrol of 1 Seaforth set out from Shenam, a hundred and forty strong, under their C.O.,[1] Lieut.-Colonel Macfarlane. There were vague reports that the Japs were returning to the east bank of the Chindwin in the Homalin area, and the object of the patrol was to reach the west bank at Tonhe, about thirty-five miles lower down the river. The route lay across the northern end of the Kabaw valley, known to those with experience of Burma as an intensely malarial area, but we had not heard of its menace. The cost of ignorance in this case was that either during or at the end of a fifteen-day patrol, 71 per cent. of the force was stricken with malaria. One private died on the operation, an officer fell sick *en route* and had to be left

---

[1] Commanding Officer.

with a small party at Thanan, and an N.C.O. and private of the main body were given up for lost as they were swept away down one of the many swirling chaungs that had to be crossed. The patrol had been cut off from the outside world since the third day out as their wireless set failed to withstand the climate, and news of its progress only reached higher H.Q. intermittently through L.Os. who had to make their way back through the mud and floods at least thirty-five miles. One of these swam three of the chaungs to bring news of their officer casualty and of a shortage of rations, a message which resulted in an unsuccessful attempt to assist by air supply. In the end, the officer was extricated, reserves were sent from Div. H.Q., and the main body, who had reached Tonhe and found it clear of the enemy, returned on July 7th and 8th. It is pleasing to record that the N.C.O. and private managed to struggle to shore and to safety.

A Patiala patrol, which set out on September 8th, had an equally tough battle with Nature, and if they had in the end to admit defeat, it was not for want of striving. They were lead, as so often, by their C.O., Colonel Balwant Singh, a veteran of the last war and a great-hearted warrior. Their objective, Mawlaik on the Chindwin, was over a hundred miles by steamer below Tonhe, which will give some idea of the huge front that had to be covered. Ironically, though the rain never ceased, the patrol, which was moving on the 11th and 12th over the mountainous ridges west of the southern Kabaw valley, found no drinking water on either day; and the march on the 11th had ended with a 2,000 ft. rise in one mile. On the lower slopes and in the valley, the numerous chaungs were in full spate and had swollen to a width of twenty yards or more. The Patialas devised a method of crossing the lesser torrents by forming a chain of rifle slings and tying a log to the farther end; they floated the chain downstream at bends and waited until the log caught in the rocks on the far side and so formed a fairly secure guiding line. This device proved of no avail when they reached the main stream in the area of Yedok on the 16th, where they were faced by a swirling mass of water and stones twenty-five yards wide. Soaked by forty-eight hours' continuous rain and by an unending series of fording operations, they paused in the jungle on the next day to build bashas where they could dispel a little of the wetness that clung to them like a cloak. Failing to find possible crossing places farther south and with their emergency rations, which had been the only fare since the 11th, ruined by the rain, Colonel Balwant Singh gave the order to return on the 19th. They had ahead a week's march through the rains and were forced to live on the land, but when they reached home on the 26th, after completing three hundred and thirty-one miles, and eighty-eight of those straight through the jungle, they reported their sickness casualties at four, of which only one had to be carried back.

The incessant, deep patrolling, designed to search for the enemy and, on the return journey when the need for concealment had gone, to give heart to the local inhabitants by a display of strength, was a grim, relentless business with no apparent reward. There was first the administrative effort, involving the dumping forward of stocks of rations when the mules slipped and slithered over scarcely recognizable tracks or, if the ground was too difficult, men became the load carriers. Then the trek—mile after mile, day after day of discomfort. Through toil and hardship, the men came to understand the whims of the jungle and, by their experiences, to evolve a technique for adapting their lives to its many moods. Experience taught that during the rains nothing was more useless than a box of matches, for, however carefully protected, damp invariably affected the striker which disintegrated piecemeal under the friction of successive match heads; a cigarette lighter proved more reliable. We learnt that when living off the country, salt was difficult to procure and needed to be carried on the man; learnt how inadequate at this stage were the pack rations for both British and Indian troops; learnt drills for concealing the size of patrols from strangers; learnt how to keep direction when the eye could not see more than a yard ahead for miles on end; learnt that the jungle could befriend the small patrol. Above all, the Division learnt to know the country and the units to know themselves; the reward was that these were welded together in learning the elements of the soldier's job in the jungle.

A word must be said about the work of "V" Force, who were under command and operating continuously in advance of the long-distance patrols. These small parties of Burmans, each under a British officer who had known the country before the war, might be likened to an underground movement except that their role was essentially defensive in that they were to observe and report. Forward battalions were usually only conscious of their presence when these parties ran short of rations and complicated the difficulties of supply by making sudden and unexpected demands on units who never had much in hand. It would be wrong to suggest that these "raids" caused more than momentary disturbance. The officers of "V" Force remained out for months at a time in a hostile land, alone and out of contact with their fellows, with nothing on which to rely in a crisis save their own resourcefulness. Their task was as arduous as any in the war.

There were others who were wet during the monsoon, among them the sappers. In the War Diaries there is a moan by one of their number who found himself plastered with clay and quite unable to remove the unwelcome mud from his clothes and boots. It is a quiet moan and the victim had reason to mutter in that suppressed way which means that a British soldier is going to see an unpleasant job through to the end. June 5th was one of the joy days in the sapper history! That was the occasion when the Thoubal river rose fifteen feet in a night, making the diversion impassable and washing away in its career one pier of a new high-level bridge. The stream at Palel followed suit and took with it the bridge there, and that ugly child, the road from Palel to Shenam, not to be outdone, produced five landslides, for that stretch of road was as temperamental under the pressure of rain and Army transport as the main road northwards from Imphal. As the Division had moved to Burma without its Field Park Company, bulldozers were conspicuous by their absence and the work of repair had to be done with pick, shovel and explosive. Infantry units provided some of the labour, but we relied greatly on the help of the Nagas and other natives, who found a new source of income on the roads.

The difficulty of producing a road that would withstand the climate was increased by the shortage of transport and petrol. The elephant proved a useful ally, as he did later in

D

the Kabaw valley, and of necessity recourse was had to the creaking, lumbering bullock-cart and its somnolent driver; but when deliveries of road metal had to be made over distances of twenty miles, the tempo at which work progressed could not be fast; nor was it always easy to find carts as the locals had stowed them away in the most unlikely places. Some months after this, one of the sappers was surprised when a native asked leave to drive his bullocks into a pond opposite the R.E. office. After a deal of thrashing about in the water, the team began struggling up the bank and there emerged from the depths—one cart, bullock, Mark 1500, part worn.

Thus a motley throng of troops and coolies, elephants and bullock-carts was deployed on the roads to Shenam and to 37 Bde. at Yaingangpopki throughout the monsoon. A few British officers, who coped with a strange variety of languages and with the problems of tribal mistrust, were the overseers of the road-making and the countless other tasks that fell to the engineers in a moist and uninhabited country. There were camp sites to be surveyed, bamboo huts to be constructed, water to be purified, drains to be dug. Usually timber could be found only by searching, and when one dump had been discovered in the yard of a house, an anxious owner appeared, though, as transpired, he was not concerned about the loss of the timber. He started to dig feverishly under a bed and extracted six one-pound bottles, each full of wads of paper money and lumps of gold.

In addition, the lack of workshop facilities and of many items of ordnance stores resulted in the engineers of the Field Companies being called on to exercise their ingenuity in improvising equipment of all kinds. 91 Field Company, who were at Imphal, were best situated for this work and, with the aid of Manipuri tradesmen, they proved a fertile source of supply. One of their lines was the building of boats, and after a little practise they achieved one twelve-footer a day.

There was one engineering enterprise undertaken by "amateurs." The amateurs in this case were Lieut.-Colonel G. P. Chapman and some of the officers and men of 82 A. Tk. Regt.—about a hundred and fifty of them in all—supported by all the Nagas which they could attract to the "cause." The cause was the construction of a hundred and nine miles of road from Bishenpur due west along the trace of a bridle path to Lakhipur, and the object to provide a route out of the Imphal plain alternative to the unreliable northerly road, for beyond Lakhipur lay Silchar and the railway. Of this hectic race against time, of the hairbreadth escapes from destruction that befell some members of the gang, including the C.O., who disappeared in his jeep over the roadside into the jungle, of the eventual triumph of determination—of these one can read in the C.O.s' book, "The Lampi." Beginning with an assurance that the route, lying across a barrier of mountain and jungle as wild as that to the east of Imphal, had recently been reconnoitred and discarded as useless, Chapforce between July 19th and September 21st fulfilled the promise they had made to the General. They would be first to agree that the engineers were generous in meeting demands for explosives, but they had no other assistance. It was all the work of the "Force" who, not without a touch of irony, recorded on the stone set up at the end of the road that it was built "because everybody who knew said that it was impossible."

Last in this tale of the 1942 monsoon, the administrative units. It is literally true that the mules were at times worked to death. They were at work in all weathers carrying supplies to the forward posts inaccessible to M.T. over steep and slippery tracks where one false step sent them hurtling to death. Many of the animals suffered from disease, but they could not be rested if the troops were to be fed, and as grain was non-existent for days at a time, they lived on a ration inadequate to sustain their strength in less arduous circumstances. Vehicles and drivers were equally overworked, having to maintain the Division in everything excepting supplies over the hundred-and-fifty-mile L. of C. from Manipur Road. It may seem a short-sighted policy to have to forego vehicle maintenance, as so often happened, but that is the way in war—when a country goes into it unprepared.

Everything was short—food, equipment, men. Though the Division was through sickness 60 per cent. under strength, reinforcements were not coming forward, and when a party did arrive at the end of July they came, in the crisp words of a signal of remonstrance, "all unarmed, unannounced, unfed.   Result confusion." In the prevailing dearth, it became the regrettable but understandable practice for individual officers to go on the scrounge to the Ordnance depot at Manipur Road, a most unmilitary procedure frowned on and stopped once order began to appear out of near chaos.

The first glimmer of light came about the beginning of September after the tricks of the road back to Manipur Road had at last been mastered. On September 1st the Division went back on to full rations, though a reduction a week later to half-scale was a little damping. Fortunately, the lapse was temporary and by the end of the month the Indian troops were sometimes tasting the luxury of fresh goat meat and sampling the novelty of tinned mutton. The reopening of leave on September 9th gave a further boost to the morale of men who had patiently endured a very wet introduction into the rigours of warfare.

CHAPTER 6

Brief Sitrep (September, 1942)

THE continuous patrolling during the monsoon served to allay many of the inevitable rumours about Jap movements. It was clear by the time the weather began to improve in mid-September that there were no enemy in the Kabaw valley, and none had been met west of the Chindwin by patrols which had reached the river. On the farther bank there were no signs of any imminent build-up and it was considered that such forces as had been reported at Homalin were nothing more than local levies commanded by a few Jap officers. The one possible threat was from the area of Kalewa, forty miles below Mawlaik, where there were said to be several thousand Japanese with M.T. Some confirmation of these reports came from a Havildar-Major of 1/11 Sikhs. He had been cut off in the earlier fighting far away to the south, made his way up the Irrawaddy through Yennanyung, where he had witnessed a hundred British and Indian prisoners burnt alive, and passed through Kalewa early in September.

On our own side, 23 Ind. Div. continued to hold the front very much alone after H.Q. 4 Corps moved in mid-July from Imphal to Jorhat, where Lieut.-General G. A. P. Scoones took over command of the Corps. The only other troops that might be considered in the area were almost "off the map" for us. The under-strength 109 Ind. Inf. Bde. was split between Silchar and Aijal in the hills south-west of the Imphal plain, co-ordinating the activities of various guerrilla bands and local levies operating as far south as Tiddim, and a brigade of 17 Ind. Div. at Kohima was responsible for the protection of the L. of C. and for watching the tracks leading through the Naga hills on their flank.

Within the Division, there were a few changes in composition during and at the end of the monsoon. 7/14 Punjab were withdrawn at the end of June, and the two Nepalese battalions, who had done a variety of jobs, followed in September. Additions to the strength were the second battery of 158 Fd. Regt. released from a sojourn in Calcutta whither they had hastened in the May scare, and 305 Field Park Company, who, in their early days before they joined us at Ranchi, had twice put to sea to join 17 Div. in south Burma and twice been recalled. In October orders came for the addition of a third battery to the Field Regiment, the cadre being found from the existing batteries.

The position of the brigades remained unchanged—37 Bde. watched the north-eastern approaches, the most forward troops being the detachment of 3/10 G.R. at Ukhrul until they pulled back on September 11th to Sangshak to shorten the supply line; 1 Bde. held Shenam with 1 Patiala holding the outpost screen after their relief of 1 Assam on August 1st; 49 Bde., based on Palel, held the road back to Imphal against an advance from the south.

CHAPTER 7

The Wait in the Wilds Begins

MEN are singularly poor hands at the art of waiting, and they are not at their best if it comes to facing day after day of unvarying routine when the purpose in life is hard to discern. Millions had enough practice at the art during the war to last ten lifetimes, and 23 Ind. Div. was but one formation, among many all over the world, which endured a long vigil and was able to prove at the end, when the test came, that its mettle was unimpaired. We might accurately say that the vigil began in June, 1942; it ended nearly two years later when the Japanese assault began in March, 1944. Throughout that period, the only time when most troops experienced something approaching the excitement of battle to alleviate the monotony of waiting was early in 1943 when the Division was called on to undertake a series of minor operations in support of the first Wingate expedition. Certainly others had longer to wait, but few had so lonely a vigil or one which in a peculiar way demanded more of that inner spirit in a man which enables him to rise above the depressing effect of his environment. There were no periods of leave every few months in which to enjoy a taste of home comfort, there was no small town near by with a cinema. The green of the jungle surrounded us and the climate sapped at the vitality of those used to colder regions. But one of the remarkable points in war is that hundreds, thousands and millions of men—and, it should be added, women—snatched from an easy-going life and called to face tasks the like of which they have never contemplated, and those in the most taxing surroundings, throw off the lethargy of peace and prove equal to the call.

The Army always has one way of dispelling the danger that a time of waiting may impair fighting efficiency; it can, it must train. The Division, flung together on the borders of Assam and Burma, knew only the barest elements of soldiering on its arrival, and staffs and men had to master their respective parts and to learn to work as a whole; further, they were fighting in a new terrain. Though much had been gained from the monsoon patrolling, the lessons learnt had to be absorbed; nor did the patrolling afford the chance to practise handling weapons new to many of the men. Hence, as soon as the weather cleared in September, individual training began and all the brigades took part in field firing exercises. There had been a telephone battle to train staffs a month and a half before this at the end of July. The framework of the exercise was an accurate forecast of the Jap thrust in 1944—an advance through the Naga hills by way of Ukhrul and the cutting of the main road between Imphal and Kohima.

Training continued to the end of the year for all arms and units who were not employed on essential tasks. 37 Bde. less 3/3 G.R., who relieved the 3/10 G.R., were withdrawn first to Imphal and later to Wangjing; 1 Bde. sent a battalion at a time down from the heights, and the gunners experimented with new techniques suited to the country. One of their problems was that few of the roads and none of the bridges were strong enough to carry modern artillery, so they became expert builders of bamboo and tarpaulin rafts. In a country where formidable water obstacles abounded, it was necessary for all ranks to be able to swim and for a knowledge of the rudiments of boating to be disseminated among units. To this end courses in watermanship were run on the Waithou lake under sapper guidance.

The time of waiting was not squandered. The troops became hardened and through their training acquired the self-reliance, skill, spirit and sense of discipline which mark the first-class formation. Besides the firm founding of our future steadfastness in battle, there was that autumn another event destined to be of importance in the future history of the Division. 1 Bde. "thought it the last word in improbability at that time that Shenam would ever be defended against the Japanese" as they began to fell trees, dig section and gun positions out of solid rock and lay wire, but the future was to prove the wisdom of those who ordered the execution of a task which 37 Bde. continued in the first months of 1943.

The "operation" during the autumn of 1942 was the

"advance" of 49 Bde. down the main road to Tamu. This was preceded in the first days of October by wild reports from "V" Force that a thousand Japs were moving up the Chindwin to Sittaung, while another force double the size coming up the Kabaw valley was said to have reached Htinzin on September 26th. Extra patrols from 1 Patiala and 1 Assam proved the reports groundless—they had probably been disseminated by Jap agents in some of the villages and so had reached the ears of "V" Force scouts. In an endeavour to prevent similar alarmist reports arising in the future, four permanent patrols, each under a British officer, were established on the Chindwin and a fifth at Minthami in the centre of the Kabaw valley.

The object of the 49 Bde. "advance," which was an essential preliminary to cover road-making for the Wingate expedition, could not be revealed to those who took part in it. Two companies of 5/6 Rajrif took over the forward positions at Moreh on October 6th, with a company of 4/5 Mahratta guarding the left flank in the hills, while the main body, which had moved to Tengnoupal, waited while the sappers cleared the pile of debris blocking the way and turned a shambles into a road fit for heavy vehicles. Like all the roads in this part of Burma, the section from Shenam to Tamu had never had much to boast about at the best of times—in fact it became a "road" only when bulldozers drove over the track during the retreat; now, at the close of the rains, it sported fifteen major landslides. When these refused to yield to treatment, as they sometimes did, defying bulldozers and explosives, there was a further delay while the road was realigned and the jungle cleared. When it came to replacing the Inglis bridge over the Lokchao river, the sappers indulged in a fair imitation of hunt the slipper over the Imphal plain. Dismantled in haste at a time of crisis, its future use had not been given much thought and the bits and pieces were everywhere. Eventually the parts that mattered were found, but their return home was not easy as the transoms were seventeen feet long with weights and sockets at each end. Not so the biggest lorries available— they could carry with ease no more than a nine-foot load. 71 Field Company assembled the bridge at the gap and meditated how they were to hoist the finished article into position. Their very effective answer was to use one bull-dozer as a cantilever while a second provided the propulsive power behind.

As the road-makers neared the Kabaw valley, our patrol activity up to the Chindwin increased. Once again all infantry and artillery units took part, and there was a notable ten-day patrol by a civilian, Mr. G. D. I. Thomas, the Deputy Commissioner, Upper Chindwin, who went out in search of a notoriously pro-Japanese monk, U Nandiya. He failed to find the monk, but met no enemy in a tour which took him through Hlezeik to the west bank of the Chindwin, down the river to Sittaung and thence to Tamu. The Jap was still taking little interest in our part of the front, the one change being the post which was established at Mawlaik about November 20th, very shortly after a patrol of 3/5 R.G.R. had entered the place.

The only disturbance of the prevailing calm came from an "air-raid" on November 10th in the Imphal area. The morale of the Division was proof against the small, buff-coloured leaves which fell out of the skies from an estimated height of 20,000 feet. There were two encouraging messages, printed in English on one side and a makeshift Urdu on the other, and the text of the first is reproduced on the opposite page.

"The Japanese Army" did not repeat this attack on our nerves, nor did the "raid" cause an alarm to be sent to the anti-paratroop forces in the plain. Among these were 82 A. Tk. Regt., who passed to the command of 17 Ind. Div. on November 12th; 3/3 G.R. had a similar role before they relieved 3/10 G.R. in the hills at Litan, where they were joined by the Kali Bahadur Regiment on December 1st. This Nepalese battalion came to us again to enable the Gurkhas to push their H.Q. forward to Sangshak as the sappers of 91 Field Company had eased the supply difficulties by constructing yet another road. We were beginning to leave our mark on the borders of India and Burma! We hope the inhabitants of Ukhrul were duly grateful to the sappers who had made possible the grand spectacle of that day early in December when they saw their first motor vehicle, a jeep with an important passenger aboard. General Savory was not a man who forgot isolated troops.

N. 1010

LOOK ! WHAT A TREMENDOUS DEFEAT THE ANGLO-AMERICANS HAVE SUFFERED AT THE HANDS OF MIGHTY JAPAN.

1. TERRITORIES emancipated by Japan from the Allied Nations:—

> Malaya, Singapore, Burma, Hongkong, The Philippines, Guam, Wake, Java, Sumatra, Borneo, Celebes, New Guinea and Alleutian Islands.

2. ALLIED VESSELS sunk and destroyed by the Japanese

Navy	..	..	..	..	**370**
Sunk:	Battleships	..	..	..	9
	Aircraft Carriers		..	..	13
	Cruisers	..	..	..	38 etc.
Destroyed:	Battleships	..	..	..	9
	Aircraft Carriers		..	..	4
	Cruisers	..	..	..	20 etc.
Allied Merchantmen sunk and destroyed				..	**394**
Allied ships captured		..	..	..	**503**

3. CAPTURED Enemy prisoners **330,000**

4. ALLIED AIRCRAFT destroyed by the Japanese Forces **5,431**

THE occupied territories are now joyously co-operating with Japan in the glorious task of re-constructing **"Asia for the Asiatics."** Now is the time for India to get her Independence. **This is the golden opportunity to drive the British out of India.** The Imperial Japanese Forces have full power and are very sincere in their desire to assist you in your fight against Britain.

THE JAPANESE ARMY.

By the end of November, 49 Bde. and the road-makers were in the area of Sibong, ten miles from Tamu, and on December 20th the road Palel–Tamu was officially declared open to three-ton lorries. The Brigade moved in to Tamu over Christmas, but there was little or none of the customary fare to reward them or the rest of the Division for their labours in 1942. Not a drop of liquor or beer had percolated through from India during November to wet the whistle, and the Highland Lament from Shenam on New Year's Day, 1943, ran "No New Year's dinners or celebrations." They were an ungrateful crowd, those Seaforths! After all, furious signals from Division during November did conjure out of the hat the battalion vehicles which had been lingering in India since the Regiment started on its travels and were restored to their owners on December 14th. But even a Sassenach must in the end agree that a few gearboxes are poor compensation for an equal number of tots on Hogmanay. Still, a little was being done to provide some entertainment for the troops; the mobile cinema that came in the latter part of November and the December concert party were indeed welcome. It was unfortunate that the cinema arrived without British films, an omission rectified with satisfactory speed.

One or two oddments and a rumble end this chapter. On October 11th the Commander-in-Chief and the Corps Commander visited us, though the appearance of two such distinguished officers should not, perhaps, be described as an oddment. Later in the month there was a change of command in 49 Bde., Brigadier W. B. Thomas taking over from Brigadier Whitehouse, and on November 1st there was a change of units within the Brigade, 6/5 Mahratta relieving the malaria-riddled 2/19 Hybad, who were in urgent need of rest in a healthier climate and of reinforcement. December brought to the Division a tall figure who was to become well known and well loved in the person of Brigadier Andrews, who became our C.R.A. in succession to Brigadier Goulder, translated to 4 Corps.

The rumble came from the Chin hills away to the south and outside our area, though events there concerned us greatly as an advance up the Tiddim road would bring the Jap into the Imphal plain behind the Division. The refresh-

DECEMBER, 1942

OCTOBER, 1944

THE PAGODA, TAMU

ment, re-equipping and reinforcement of 17 Ind. Div. had begun as soon as it had assembled at Kohima after the trek out from Burma. Part of it was by the end of 1942 ready for a further tussle with the Jap, and a small force left for Tiddim in December, followed by a commando group from 48 Bde. on January 8th. The future was beginning to take shape.

CHAPTER 8

In Support of Wingate

THE need to push the roadheads for the first Wingate expedition close to the Chindwin settled the activities of the Division at the start of 1943. Wingate's forces were to cross at Tonhe and Auktaung, forty miles lower down the river, and besides covering these crossings we were to stage a feint attack to the south straight down the Kabaw valley. This plan required the repair of the nothern road up the valley between Moreh and Mintha and its extension beyond the latter village, the making of a road towards Sittaung, where there was nothing more than a track, and the restoration of the tolerable southern route to Kalewa. Engineer recce parties had a lonely time as they pushed ahead down these routes in jeeps often far in advance of the forward troops.

There had been a small dispute between Corps and ourselves at the turn of the year over the speed with which we should start on these new commitments. Corps, with their eye fixed on coming events, wanted the engineer effort reduced on the main Shenam–Tamu road so that some of the array of pioneers and local labour working under C.R.E. 107[1] could be transferred to the forward tasks. We, as we looked at our life-line, now classed as "passable to all M.T.," saw that it was not yet a thing of beauty and we were reluctant to have a collection of unmilitary labour roaming about the valley without increased protection for which supplies were not in position.

The General, who was away on a few days' leave when the order came, in the main gained the day for the Division. Only 1 Seaforth were sent forward to Tamu to strengthen 49 Bde. and the labour remained working on the lifeline with the addition of the two battalions of 37 Bde. from Shenam. One day the officers of 3/10 G.R. sought to overcome the boredom of acting as the supervisors of temporary coolies by organizing a shikar drive. If they were relying on filling the

---

[1] The H.Q. of a non-divisional engineer unit.

46

pot that evening, they were to suffer grievous disappointment as, after extensive beating of the bush, they had to record "net result one procupine." The misprint is theirs!

With the need to move stocks forward for the coming increase of our own troops in the Kabaw valley and with the assistance rendered to Wingate, our transport was at full stretch all January. That road back to Imphal was a long and exhausting grind, and it was four days before a lorry was back at Moreh with its load of stores. Supplies and equipment had to be moved from Imphal to the roadheads and the troops fed while they were in the camps constructed by the Div. sappers at Thoubal, Palel, Tengnoupal and Lokchao—these and our own requirements made it one of those occasions when "Q," by a mixture of coaxing and threats of violence, extracts lorries from all and sundry. Every vehicle that could be found went into the pool, even properly equipped office lorries being surrendered for the task in hand. Even so the vehicles were incessantly on the road with engines screaming under the strain of long periods of running in low gear.

The forward concentration of 1 Bde., which began on January 23rd, took a week to complete; on their arrival, the Yu became the dividing line between the two brigades from the point where the river turns east. Within their respective boundaries, 1 Bde. had the Patialas on the right covering the line of the Chindwin from Tanga and Sittaung, 1 Assam on the left with a frontage extending from the outskirts of Sittaung to Tonhe, and the Seaforths in reserve at Moreh; 49 Bde. had the Rajrif at Minthami, 4 Mahratta, who early in January had their most distant companies eighty-eight miles apart, at Sunle, with Bde. H.Q. and 6 Mahratta moving down the road between Witok and Htinzin. Div. H.Q. less the services moved up to the Moreh area to control the coming operations.

Our patrols had begun to range farther afield down the Kabaw valley and across the Chindwin from the beginning of January and clashes with the Jap became more frequent. 4 Mahratta had a skirmish in the Atwin Yomas on the 2nd, there was another brush in the same area on the 7th, while east of the Chindwin there was a clash at Paukkon on the 8th. 6 Mahratta reported Paungbyin empty on the 12th;

theirs and the Rajrif carriers sallied down the valley to
Yazagyo on the 17th, and sweeps at the same period through
the principal riverine villages, Yuwa, Sittaung, Thaungdut
and Tonhe established that these were clear. As February
came, with our two brigades concentrated and the time for
the start of the Wingate expedition fast approaching, the
effort was intensified in fulfilment of our task of dominating
the country up to the Chindwin in the area of the planned
crossing-places, preventing the enemy reaching the west
bank and gaining any information we could from forays on the
farther side of the river. Nearly the whole of 1 Assam swept
across the river to Paungbyin; they and the Patialas were
continuously up and down the west bank; another Patiala
patrol crossed to Ontha; a Rajrif party ranged far into Jap
occupied ground and came to within a mile of Indaw;
4 Mahratta sent a Company to Mawku above Mawlaik.
A pounce by 1 Assam on Minya, incidental to the main
effort, produced the valuable scalp of San Doke, a "gentleman" of U Nandiya's kidney, who had thrown in his lot with
the Jap. Clashes were infrequent and the information
gleaned was favourable for the start of the expedition,
showing that there were no Jap posts on the east bank and
probably none nearer than Nanbon and Banmauk.

On February 11th came Wingate and his men—to nearly
all of the Division like a bolt from the blue—came and
vanished across the Chindwin. One spectator was not sure
that the force was adept at handling mules, but none could
mistake their confidence and fitness and some eyebrows were
raised at the excellence of their equipment, some of which
they jettisoned, to the delight of one or two fortunate units
in the Division. The Patialas, who are known to have fared
well, have been reticent about their gains, but 3/5 G.R. have
not concealed their satisfaction which reveals by contrast our
own deficiencies. "A Commando Brigade is now passing
through and are leaving masses of equipment on the roads—
maps, bombs, blankets, ropes, grenades, ammunition, picks
and shovels, etc. We have been lucky in getting the great
bulk of this stuff and it means extensive field firing for
everyone with all weapons and a great deal over for use in
action. All men are now being given one grenade each."
One of the great luxuries was a "complete set of $\frac{1}{2}$ in. maps

of the whole of Burma." When the two main columns reached their roadheads, they cast aside yet more of their equipment, which the Division salvaged.

The advance guard of the northern column crossed the Chindwin on the night of February 13/14, followed the next day by Wingate and the main body. It was on the 14th that a company patrol of the Patialas moved over to form a bridgehead for the decoy southern column and, as they crossed, witnessed the start of a new technique in supply when several Dakotas lumbered over from the west, circled Auktaung and began to fill the sky with parachutes. Taking a long view, the successful use of air supply in this expedition far outweighed any other results achieved, as we and others were to find out a year later. The column collected the "drop," crossed part of their force that night, took another "drop" the next day and completed the crossing on the night of the 15th/16th. The Patialas moved on with the column for the next two days, protecting the right flank; they returned early on the 19th without meeting the Jap.

Meanwhile, the feints to the south by units of the Division had started. The lesser of these were fighting patrol operations by the Patialas east and 4 Mahratta west of the river, designed to give the impression that an attack was coming on Mawlaik. They met no opposition, but the major feint by 4 Mahratta, less one company, towards Kalewa brought the first battle, albeit a small fracas, in which a unit of the Division was engaged.

On the afternoon of February 15th the battalion left Sunle for the firm base established by 6 Mahratta at Khampat. They were short of their Adjutant, who was on leave, and filled the gap by picking up *en route* the commander of "A" Company, who had just reached Htinzin after leading the patrol to Mawku. The column had the carriers of 6 Mahratta and a section of 71 Field Company under command and could have the support of the guns of 15 Mountain Battery so long as it was within range of Khampat. They set off in M.T. at 0620 hrs. on D Day, the 16th, with the carriers leading, debussed at 0825 hrs. a little north of Yazagyo where the Japs had recently blown a culvert, and left the soft transport there. They harboured that evening at Okkan, nineteen miles from Kalemyo, intending to

F

raid Kantha the next day after a night recce, as they had learnt that there were a hundred Japs in the place with other forces in the neighbourhood. Their intentions were frustrated.

Okkan is, like hundreds of other Burmese villages, a collection of wooden huts on piles with a road running through the middle. The Mahrattas held the perimeter of the village, which was surrounded by banks, and very useful these were to prove in the early hours as the battalion had reached Okkan as the sun went down and were in any case very short of digging tools.

The battalion sat up about 0200 hrs. on the 17th to listen to the distant firing which was being directed against their recce patrol to Kantha, but when the noise died down after half an hour, most turned over for more sleep. They were unlucky; about 0300 hrs. hell was let loose in their midst and the Japs laid on a "Brock's benefit" free of charge. The Japanese raiding party had escaped detection because they had come down the chaung from Kantha and, though they were heard when close to the right-hand section of 10 Platoon, this happened to be the exact spot where our patrol was due to return. Hence the sentry did not raise the alarm when the first charge came, amid shouts of "Banzai," with an officer and W.O.[2] in the lead brandishing swords; though the Bren gunner killed the officer, his left hand was severed with the first sweep of the W.O.'s sword and he was almost decapitated with the next and the whole platoon was near being overrun. The situation here was saved by the determination of the section commander, who fought the Japs single-handed with a tommy-gun until they withdrew. There was an equally hot attack on 12 Platoon, and Coy. H.Q. had to defend themselves stoutly. The 12 Platoon position was held by the gallantry of the Havildar who was in command and rallied a weakened section when the Japs were ten yards away and on the point of charging. This check gave the company commander time to readjust his defence.

Meanwhile the rest of the battalion watched the fireworks and waited for their turn which never came, except for a continuous bombardment of the centre of the village by

---

[2] Warrant Officer.

"OKKAN"

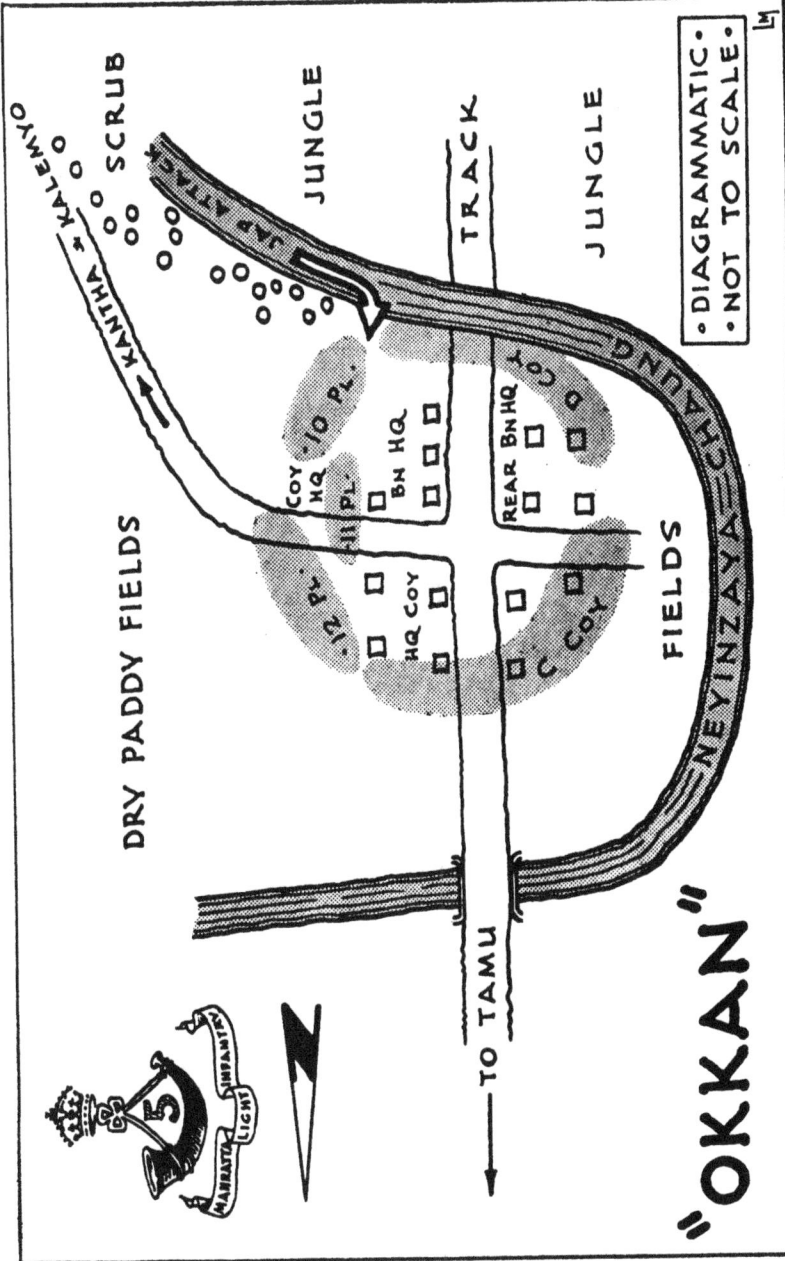

DIAGRAMMATIC • NOT TO SCALE •

JUNGLE

SCRUB

KANTHA + KALEWO

DRY PADDY FIELDS

JUNGLE

TRACK

JUNGLE

NEYINZAYA CHAUNG

FIELDS

Coy HQ

11 Pl.

10 Pl.

Bn HQ

Rear Bn HQ

12 Pl.

HQ Coy

C Coy

TO TAMU

MAHRATTA LIGHT INFANTRY

grenades and 2-inch mortar bombs, one of which went through the C.O.'s H.Q. without exploding. Lieut.-Colonel Knight had moved up his one reserve, the pioneer platoon, behind "B" Company early in the engagement, and when he had accurate information of the position and felt sure this was the main attack, he put the platoon under "B" Company's command. The company again reorganized and counter-attacked at dawn against an enemy already on the with-drawal; though the carriers at once took up the pursuit, the enemy were too far away for more than a long-range ex-change of shots. As the recce patrol had now rejoined through "C" Company after an exciting night out, during which they lost one man wounded and missing, the order to withdraw was given. Back at Yazagyo about 0900 hrs., the battalion had the pleasure of hearing the Japs shelling Okkan; they learnt later that a full-scale infantry attack had been launched on the deserted village.

The battalion had had a valuable inoculation in Jap methods, for the enemy, without regard for ammunition expenditure, had used every conceivable kind of fire effect from tracer to a particularly noisy though not very danger-ous kind of bomb; "Guy Fawkes, visitation last night" said the C.O.'s succinct and appropriate signal. The cost was two killed and seven wounded in addition to the man lost in the recce patrol. The two N.C.Os. previously mentioned for their gallantry gained I.D.S.Ms.,[3] and Sub.-Maj. Gunpatrol Salvi Bahadur, O.B.I.,[4] was presented by the General with the reward of one hundred rupees for the first Jap proved to have been killed by the Division.

After this affray, comparative calm settled over our front. Rumours of a Japanese attack against Thaungdut proved baseless and, apart from two haphazard artillery shoots from the west bank, we had no alarms unless we so class the affair of March 7th when a buffalo set off the booby traps round the 4 Mahratta position and caused the battalion to "stand to." We were waiting for the return of Wingate.

In the interval, it is convenient to pick up a few loose threads. There was a brief visit from the Commander-in-Chief on February 6th after he had said farewell to Wingate's

---

[3] Indian Distinguished Service Medal.
[4] Order of British India.

expedition at their final parade at Imphal. H.Q. 4 Corps returned to the town on the 8th. 1/16 Punjab joined us late in February to relieve 1 Assam, another battalion that had suffered heavily from malaria; from that moment, apart from the occasional demands of battle, the composition of the brigades remained unaltered for nearly three years. With the Punjabis came 2 Indian Anti-Tank Regiment to set a continual poser for their active employment in the absence of Jap armour. At the beginning of March, 37 Bde. had finished with their road-making activities and began to concentrate forward; they were still without 3/3 G.R., left alone to their vigil at Sangshak until relieved by the Kali Bahadur Regiment at the end of the month. To give 6 Mahratta a short interval for training, 4 Mahratta took over the forward positions in the Kabaw valley from mid-March; on the 27th Brigadier Esse assumed the command of 49 Bde.

Our existence continued to be one of toil with little relief. Nine days of the mobile cinema in the second half of January provided the only entertainment we were to have for seven months. Hopes had been aroused by the prospect of the belated arrival of a drink ration, but the ration, when it arrived in mid-March, belied the hopes. There was welcome news early in March of a fairly generous extension of the leave programme for officers—31 days' leave and 10 per cent. of the unit strength to be away at a time. Here was more disappointment; within a fortnight, the scheme was altered to a ten-day rest in leave stations and the quota was halved. Those affected shrugged their shoulders and put on the jungle green battle-dress which began to appear or, if they were interested, watched a travelling team explain to Indian troops how their religious scruples were satisfied in the preparation of tins of dehydrated goat meat. Meanwhile there was another job to be done.

The scheme for the reception of the Wingate force was for 1 and 49 Bdes. to have, near the west bank of the Chindwin, a series of forward reception posts from which the survivors were passed with all speed to Tamu. As part of this scheme, 49 Bde. increased the number of rowers available on our boat service between Yuwa and Kyaukchaw by giving some quick instruction to the Mahrattas, who achieved an adequate degree of skill in a short time. Once at Tamu the survivors were given the best taste of civilization that we could provide—hot baths, barbers for those who were willing to sacrifice their two months' growth, fresh clothing and boots and food, with a double issue of milk, tea and sugar. After a twenty-four-hour rest, transport was waiting for the last stage of the journey back to Imphal.

But we were far from passive spectators of the return of the exhausted survivors of a gallant expedition. Technical language would describe the Japs as "reacting vigorously" to the presence of a hostile force in their midst, and everyone knew that Wingate must have a very difficult task to extricate his troops when the order for withdrawal came at the end of March. The Jap, a slow animal in moving to meet the unexpected, at least had the sense to realize that the raiders must go back across the Chindwin in the area where our troops were known to be. Hence the task set us was to draw off the Japs who were watching particularly the area between Mawlaik and Thaungdut, and the result during April was that the ground between Tabaw and Sittaung on the east bank of the river became for about thirty miles inland a vast No Man's Land where there was a mêlée of Japs trying to intercept the Wingate force, ourselves trying to distract the Japs, and Wingate's men trying to reach safety.

The plan was that the Patialas should simulate 1 Bde. with a special wireless build-up and the Seaforths a subsidiary force advancing against Pinlebu and Pinbon respectively from bases at Kaungkasi and Wetkauk; main H.Qs. of the battalions were to remain on the west bank. The Seaforths crossed on March 31st with a company of 3/5 R.G.R. under command, the Patialas a day later, and a dangerous game of hide and seek began with neither side knowing when the other would appear out of the jungle. The Patialas were involved in two clashes in the first week and laid a successful ambush on April 7th, after which they observed the Japs removing seven laden stretchers. At this point, partly as the first stage in our coming withdrawal during the monsoon and partly to give 37 Bde. more experience after their road-making, 3/5 R.G.R. and 3/10 G.R. began to take over from Patialas and Seaforths, the command trans-Chindwin passing to 37 Bde. on the night of April 13th/14th.

From the middle of the month many parties of Wingate's

force reached the river. It was on the 15th that Flight Lieutenant Thompson and his band bumped into one of the last Patiala posts to be in position. Needless to say, Colonel Balwant Singh was still on the east bank and, after conducting them across the river, he had the pleasure of offering a sample of Patiala hospitality. When they reached the farther bank and safety, the Warrant Officer with the party had marched his men off as though they were on a drill parade! The spirit with which the force set out had not gone though the survivors came back half-starved, emaciated, utterly exhausted; but that is a tale which others have told.

The 3/5 continued where the Patialas had left off, and the Seaforths, who were not relieved until the 21st, had a hard last week. On the 16th one of their platoons encountered two companies of Japs, and in the stiff engagement that followed an officer and three other ranks were killed against enemy casualties estimated at forty; another officer and nine other ranks were reported missing after a further skirmish on the 18th; on the 20th a patrol from the west bank ran into a strong Japanese force as it landed; two men were killed and two posted as missing, but the rest of the patrol escaped to safety across the river, covered by the sergeant in command, who gained the Military Medal for his gallantry.

3/5 R.G.R., who were more fortunate over casualties, had five clashes between the 12th and 25th. After one, a wounded rifleman who became separated from his party paddled back across the Chindwin with his hands; on another occasion the interpreter with a patrol was lost after he had been wounded in the pelvis, despite which he swam the Chindwin and reported back to H.Q.; in a third encounter, the courage of the commander was rewarded with a Military Cross. Some indication of the intensity of effort called for is given by the statement that 3/5 R.G.R. undertook fifty patrols at this time. The fate of those unfortunate enough to be captured alive is unknown, but a rifleman of 3/10 G.R. had an experience that does not encourage the belief that the enemy was other than barbarous. He was on a two-man patrol which met a party of about a hundred Japs; his partner escaped, but he was taken prisoner, had his hands tied behind his back and endured the stabs of a bayonet in his face and blows on the head with the butt end of a rifle. By good fortune the Japs ran into another Gurkha patrol of similar strength, took alarm at the first volley and allowed their prisoner to escape.

On the evening of April 28th, a party of five spent, ill-kempt men staggered into the H.Q. of "B" Company 3/10 G.R. at Iepantha on the west bank. One of the five was wearing an old, battered pith helmet—Wingate had returned. The War Diary records that Major Anderson was of the party, but that is an error; this officer was still on the east bank with the bulk of those that Wingate had led out from the farther side of the Irrawaddy, and it was to organize the extrication of his men who were beset by Jap patrols that Wingate had swum the Chindwin. That evening Wingate and the Gurkhas went down to the agreed crossing-place, but no signal came from the east bank. During the 29th, messages came from Anderson fixing a new rendezvous and that night, with the Japs bringing a mortar into action, the Gurkhas rowed across the river and brought out the rest of the party. Their Brigadier was waiting to receive them.

Though small parties continued to straggle back until the middle of May and even later, the burden of our task had been discharged by the end of April and an uneasy quiet settled over the Chindwin front, with the air full of rumours.

CHAPTER 9

Monsoon Withdrawal

THE first plan for our withdrawal for the 1943 monsoon was issued on April 10th, and the first step in that plan, the relief of 1 Bde. by 37 Bde., was carried out on time as has already been described. But in war not much goes according to plan though far more does, fortunately, go according to outline, and the most usual cause for upsets is that war is a two-sided affair. Hence plan one—49 Bde. to the Pantha area, 1 Bde. back to the Imphal plain, 37 Bde. take over the line of the Yu from 49 Bde. and 49 Bde. back to the plain after a pause at Moreh—went no farther than step one.

There were round about the beginning of May many rumours that a Jap crossing of the Chindwin was imminent. The sort of reports that came in may be illustrated from the information given by San Paw, another of the pro-Japanese Burmans who was captured by 3/5 R.G.R. on one of their trans-Chindwin patrols. He gave the strength of the attacking force as likely to be 8,000. We could not say whether that was a deliberate lie or false information imparted by the Jap or approximately true, but the continuing reports could not be disregarded. To give every chance to the remaining survivors of Wingate's force, to enable the considerable forward supply dumps to be cleared and to protect the labour force still working on the road, the overriding concern was to hold the front intact until the monsoon. The backloading of second-line ammunition and heavy equipment began as soon as the withdrawal order was issued, but the clearance of the dumps could not proceed at the desirable speed so long as all the fighting troops were forward.

To meet the rumoured Jap advance, 1 Bde. were ordered to stand fast at Moreh on May 5th and to take up a defensive position for the protection of the roadhead. This led to plan two, which was current for a fortnight before 49 Bde., who were due to pull out through 1 Bde. to the second crossing of the Lokchao, were held in the Pantha area to give more assistance to stragglers who continued to reach the Chindwin. It should be recorded that Div. H.Q. did move to Lokchao on May 12th "according to plan."

Renewed anxiety about Jap movements in the Chin hills dictated the next move, when 5/6 Rajrif were sent hastily back to Wangjing and thence to Mombi to protect the entry into the Imphal plain through Shuganu. The battalion moved on May 30th and 31st, the former being the day on which the Japs occupied Fort White, from which they subsequently withdrew. This threat caused H.Q. 17 Ind. Div. to be sent to M.S. 109 on the Tiddim road to take over operational command of the area where they already had one brigade, and further postponed our withdrawal as we were called on to stage a farewell diversion down the Kabaw valley, though the monsoon had broken.

4 Mahratta were entrusted with the diversion, which took place between June 8th and 13th and took the form of a company sally against the Jap L. of C. south of Kantha and an advance down the valley by two more companies, each simulating a brigade; a false reconnaissance and dummy cipher traffic were part of the plan. Though the rivers were in spate, the solo company contrived to fulfil its task and made contact with the Jap; the other two withdrew as agreed after reaching Sunle.

So the rains came on June 2nd with the whole fighting strength of the Division forward except for one battalion, and the last forty-five miles of the main L. of C. to Moreh an earth road, as were nearly all the routes in front of roadhead. The withdrawal during the monsoon cannot be described as a difficult operation of war as the Division was not in contact with the enemy, but it was a conspicuously arduous and wearing battle against mud and rain which imposed a fresh strain on the morale and health of troops who had had their share of discomfort and fatigue. It was one of those not uncommon occasions where operational requirements had forced "Q" to accept a course of action which they knew would present difficulties.

The "battle" belonged to "Q," but the troops could not escape sharing the effects of this fresh struggle with the elements. The atmosphere was humid, the rain fell and the night was full of those myriads of insects which come to life at this season; but adverse weather could not put a stop to "stand to" night and morning, nor to patrols, nor to fatigues such as clearing the supply depots and working to keep the roads open. As in some cases units, which had been forced by changed plans to bivouac in unexpected places, had no protection other than hastily erected shelters of bamboo and tarpaulins, it is no surprise that sickness began rapidly to increase. Battalions might have as many as twenty fresh cases of malaria in a day, and surra, which had never been stamped out, spread as fast among the mules, so that in the end 1 Bde. had no more than twenty fit animals. Here science came to the rescue. May 9th, the day on which the Seaforths, Patialas, Mahrattas and Divisional Signals were put on to a suppressive treatment of attabrin, is as important a date in the history of the Burma campaign as the start of air supply. Once the treatment began to take effect, new cases dropped to two or three a day. It was about the same time that, in the technical jargon, gloves, anti-mosquito made their appearance.

Unfortunately, science could not grapple with the monsoon or ease the problem of withdrawal! The 49 Bde. commitments down the Kabaw valley in the first half of May necessitated the birth of plan three, which lived for a week before its successor saw the light of day. This was the final solution which came out in print on June 17th—37 Bde. to Shenam, less one battalion forward with the H.Q. at Sibong to form an outpost screen and to patrol the Kabaw valley; 49 Bde. followed by 1 Bde. to the Imphal plain for rest, except for the battalion of 49 Bde. watching the southern flank from Shuganu.

In the midst of this spate of plans the Division was deprived of its commander. On June 13th Major-General Savory said good-bye to the formation that he had created out of the rawest of materials that he might, from his new position as Inspector of Infantry at G.H.Q. (I), see that others were properly trained and equipped for warfare in the jungle. We were to see no more that strutting, perky walk which some said had inspired the designer of the "Fighting Cock," but the owner of the walk left behind a legacy. There are good divisions and there are poor ones. Those that are good have a "soul," a spirit that pulsates through them and causes the individual members to rise above themselves when faced with the perils of war. The 23rd Indian Division had a "soul" and it came, despite appalling difficulties, from the efforts of its first commander.

As no successor was nominated immediately, it fell to Brigadier Collingridge to officiate as G.O.C. during the final stages of the withdrawal from mid-June, when it was obvious that it was touch and go whether we should clear the dumps before the road disintegrated. Already one convoy had toiled for five days on the short stretch of road between the upper Lokchao crossing and Moreh, for the road had been made in haste with too little attention to drainage so that it soon became a monsoon victim. We were faced with a repetition of our experiences a year ago when we fought a stiff battle with General Mud. And how the stuff stank!

As the crisis approached about June 15th, Corps elected to move in M.T. part of the large labour force who had worked on the road. We surveyed the deepened ruts that could have been avoided had the men marched, muttered a curse and turned to C.R.E. 107 to repair the damage; but this officer had been transferred to another appointment so that there was a complete hiatus in organizing the work so urgently needed. As two-way traffic soon became impossible with the up and down traffic manœuvring for position, where the mud and ruts were worst, to gain the only tolerable piece of ground, one-way convoys had to be arranged right back to Palel, and the A.P.M. took control of the Lokchao crossing.

The A.Q. came down to Moreh on June 19th to supervise the final stages, assisted by the C.R.I.A.S.C.[1] There remained to be cleared a hundred second-line vehicles, feeble things all of them and incapable of moving in the mud unless towed by a four-wheeled-drive lorry, a hundred and fifty first-line vehicles, among them thirty carriers which could be relied on to destroy what remained of the road, some two hundred and fifty-five lorry loads of stores, the sick, both men and animals, and three brigades with a

---

[1] Commander Royal Indian Army Service Corps (Lieut.-Colonel); commands all transport and supply units in an Indian Division.

couple of pioneer battalions and a field company which Corps had thrown in as a makeweight. The rain came down, the mud thickened and twelve winch lorries, borrowed from the gunners, stood on guard where the mud was most clinging.

On the 30th the first-line vehicles moved, on July 1st the brigades began their march, on the 2nd two Hurricanes shot up the flying ferries over the Yu and lower Lokchao crossing. "They finished the boats and snapped the main wire cable by ·55 mm. cannon fire. The sappers almost cried." It so chanced that part of 91 Field Company were crossing the ferry when the R.A.F. began this target practice, for which they subsequently sent a suitable apology; when they were sure their lives were no longer in jeopardy, they set to work to repair the damage, which they made good within twenty-four hours.

This incident at crossings to the east of Moreh did not interrupt the race against time to clear the depots, where the problem was to find enough lorries to make use of the road until it finally gave up the ghost. 70 G.P.T. Coy., one of the Corps units, was rendering assistance, but its lorries disappeared in strange fashion until we browbeat Corps into putting it under command on the 7th. It was nearly too late; the road was blocked by a landslide between the 14th and 18th with a convoy on the far side. "Road ghastly" they reported on return, but back they went on the same day to Palel and struggled through again to Moreh by the 23rd. Determined effort had prevailed. On the 25th the last convoy left, 1/16 Punjab, who had covered the final stages, began their wearisome march through the mud, and the Kabaw valley became for most of us a horrid dream. There were left behind one emaciated armoured car and some 2,000 empty petrol cans.

If some be inclined to fancy this description of the monsoon withdrawal as too highly coloured, their doubts may be quietened by the story of a Madrasi signalman who set out from Div. H.Q. at Lokchao at the height of the rains for 1 Bde. at Moreh. As his jeep broke down early in the run, he completed his journey on foot, after he had pushed the vehicle into a roadside unit for safety. At Moreh he hoped for transport to take him on his next leg to Tamu, but there was none to be had so off the man went once more on foot. With Tamu equally barren of transport, the D.R.[2] decided to stay there for the night as he was faced with a forty-five mile run north to Thanan for his final leg.

Nothing daunted, he walked on and on the next day until he came to a flooded river, where some might have turned back—but not this man. He found a place upstream where he thought he could cross, entered the swirling waters fully clothed and reached the farther bank. Utterly exhausted, he managed to walk for five more miles to a camp of 1/16 Punjab, where he was properly cared for that night.

On the third day out he reached Thanan, delivered his despatches and set out for home; that night he was again with 1/16 Punjab, but his troubles were not over. On the fourth morning he came to a river where a bridge had been washed away and here his resourcefulness came to his aid. Noticing an elephant camp not far away, he persuaded a mahout to lend him a taxi which was propelled towards the river. Then he mounted, sat in triumph on the back of the creature and with the mahout ejaculating in the rear, forded the torrent; thence to Moreh, where there was a jeep waiting to reward the D.R. for his fine perseverance. The story is nearly at an end—but not quite; the road collapsed that evening and the last eleven miles had to be done on foot.

Few will have pleasant memories of the Kabaw valley in 1943 except for the excellent shooting it provided as relaxation to the jungle-weary and relief to the boredom of rations in which fresh meat was rare. The variety of game shot would satisfy the most fastidious connoisseur and it was easy to find. When green pigeon or snipe made a habit of settling on a company perimeter at the dawn "stand to," it was a matter of minutes to secure an appetizing addition to the breakfast menu. The end of patrols and recces provided many other suitable opportunities for the enthusiasts who went into action with weapons not always in their first youth. One, secured locally, disintegrated in its owner's hands at the first shot, though the battalion armourer made a fine job of repairing this museum piece; but any weapon would do at a pinch, though it is perhaps as well that there was no chance of studying a tiger's reactions

---

[2] Despatch Rider.

to a pistol shot which failed to find its billet from fifteen yards.

The fishing methods employed were more open to question. Some officers, in their idle moments, were ready to use rod and line, but this peculiar display of patience passed the comprehension of the Indian soldier, who was fully aware that a modicum of gelignite would provide quicker and more efficacious results. Alternatively a little atta was a useful bait to fish which rose to the lure and could then be stunned by a rifle bullet. This method had the virtue of preserving the scanty stocks of explosives, but who would query the method when a whole company had the enjoyment of fresh fish for dinner?

It would be serious to end the story of our stay in the valley without a passing glance at the nautical expedition undertaken by 1 Bde. shortly before they pulled back from the river. This combined operation, in which we did not, as later, have the assistance of the Royal Navy, took place without a hitch and must be accounted a signal success. It was the Patialas who acquired the fleet, as slow-moving a collection of variegated river craft as you could wish to see; and it was Brigadier Woodhouse who hoisted his flag in the choicest vessel to be found and gave the order to weigh anchor. On the east bank the native children ran fast and happily when they discovered that there were prizes to be gained for their prowess. Unfortunately, we could stay for only a few hours' holiday; the party re-embarked, lurched back across the Chindwin and turned to sterner tasks. None of our shipping was lost in this venture.

CHAPTER 10

Respite, Training and a Battle

It was a tired Division, with its strength and efficiency impaired by sickness, that concentrated in the Imphal plain by the end of July, 1943; for fifteen months we had been living hard in a taxing climate on rations that were often short. Being alone in the wilds, we had acquired a valuable self-sufficiency which we never lost, and in a sense, especially during the last six months, we had had a unique opportunity of training for war with a live enemy on which to practise. We had grown in jungle wisdom and from our encounters with the Jap we had evolved drills for combating his tactics and learnt that our foe was no superman. None who had heard a Jap squeal in terror could be in doubt on that score! Yet very few of our engagements had been more than patrol clashes involving small parties, so that our experience had been limited. We needed wider training, rest in a better climate and the tonic effect derived from the enjoyment of a few of the amenities of life.

In a large measure our stay in the Imphal plain met our needs, though not everything was perfect. 37 Bde. had to guard Shenam until October 12th, and it was a month later before 6 Mahratta could be released from its vigil at Shuganu; by then 1/16th Punjab had been suddenly snatched away and plunged into a hard battle in the Chin hills. Besides these unwelcome operational commitments, the leave arrangements and the rations were in no way all that could be wished. The flow of leave parties was so intermittent that the heavy fighting of 1944 arrived with a third of the Division waiting for their first leave since they arrived at the front, and the rations, if more plentiful, were unsatisfying.

This was the time when that unappetizing, unfriable pseudo-sausage, the soya link, appeared with monotonous regularity. Who devised this monstrosity we never knew.

Who imagined that the link, though most ingeniously cooked, could hide its true nature as the most unpalatable lump of nothing ever to see the light of day—of this also we remained in ignorance. The true estimate of its worth is that "soya link" was selected as the code word for "disaster" for the fly-in of Wingate's second expedition. The rations for the Indian troops were as unsatisfactory; among other troubles, the tinned milk, provided to give the right balance to the diet in the absence of fresh meat, itself became short. The Division was not hungry, but it fed on poor fare.

Thus operational commitments were some impediment to training and the menu had its defects, but the stay at Imphal was of inestimable value. In the pure winter air of the plain and with the aid of mepacrine, the men's health recovered remarkably as they took part in an intensive training programme, for this was a time of preparing mind and body for battle. When the test came, the toughness and resilience of the Division proved the preparation to have been as thorough as our new commander intended that it should be.

Major-General O. L. Roberts, who had previously been B.G.S.[1] 4 Corps, was not a man who believed in half measures. The Division soon felt that in this man of fine physique and strong character they had one who was worthy to succeed General Savory. Utterly intolerant of inefficiency as his predecessor had been, he was every inch a commander. Others have been that and have earned the respect of their men, but not many have been able to gain to the same extent the whole-hearted affection of those they led. General Roberts had a gift for talking to men—there is no other way to describe that delightful ease with which he could raise a smile from his troops, both British and Indian, under the grimmest conditions. He transparently enjoyed talking to them and the men were quick to sense they had over them a commander to be trusted and a friend with a kindly heart. Some few thought this man hard, but they misread his character because they were not masters of their own jobs.

General Roberts's qualities as general will appear as the story of the 1944 fighting unfolds, but those who worked

---

[1] Brigadier, General Staff—the senior staff officer in a Corps.

with him during the period of training had ample opportunity to judge the keenness and clarity of a mind that was always looking ahead into the future. We were to fight under a man who had earned the confidence of all as general and commander.

His training programme began at the beginning. While the 1943 rains continued and the ground was too wet for exercises, here was the moment to revise the handling of weapons and the other elements of the soldier's craft. So we went from the rudiments up the scale to brigade training, which none had previously had the chance to experience. The course was arduous, too arduous some muttered, but they had not the foresight to realize the stern days that lay ahead. This Division was to go into battle trained to the hilt and as fit as one man could make it.

There were T.E.W.Ts.,[2] weekly training discussions under the General, schemes with artillery support, and when 254 Tank Brigade arrived in January, 1944, schemes with tanks. In many cases the exercises took place over the ground on which we were, within a few months, to fight the Jap in pitched battles. Not least important here was the long-argued T.E.W.T. to settle the final layout of the defences at Shenam, which was turned into a fortress capable of resisting in isolation for a month. The infantry adjusted their positions and greatly increased the wire barrier, the sappers constructed a water system, the services moved up reserves of food and ammunition to this key feature which the Japs were to assail in vain.

All ranks underwent battle inoculation and particular emphasis was given to the training of individual officers, this culminating in an inter-brigade test of fifteen events. Courses in watermanship were resumed under sapper guidance and every opportunity was made of the vacancies available at the 4 Corps Jungle Warfare School at Shillong, for which we provided many of the instructors. The administrative staffs took part in the main schemes and exercises besides running their own courses, which included one where would-be cooks were taught to juggle with the rations. No one could complain that the training lacked drive, thoroughness or vision.

---

[2] Tactical Exercise Without Troops.

The General would be found here, there and everywhere and walked the course with the troops at many of the battle inoculations. One day, dissatisfied with the sight of shells bursting close in front of him, he decided it would be more exciting to have a flank view of the barrage. Off he set through the jungle with his A.D.C. until he reached a point very close to the objective, where he secured the battle inoculation he desired—but not from the guns. As the infantry reached the crest, they showed their worth by "blitzing" the "enemy positions" in the approved style. With the bullets falling thick and fast around him, the General disappeared out of view at a speed wholly fitting to a former international hockey player.

The fortunate might also find a little unexpected light relief on an infantry-tank exercise. Here the villain of the piece was the wily commander of 2 Ind. A. Tk. Regt., who, reverting to the days of Bannockburn, dug a series of brilliantly camouflaged tank traps in front of his guns. When one of the 3rd Dragoon Guards' tanks toppled very, very slowly into the abyss, some bystanders felt, not without a sense of eagerness, that they were to witness a stand-up fight between an irate C.O. of 3 D.G. and a triumphant gunner. The situation was saved when a head emerged from the turret of the ensnared tank and a very refined voice apologized to the bristling C.O. in the powerful Army vernacular. The incongruity of voice and language was too much for all and a loud burst of laughter banished anger.

The Field Park and the Workshop Companies may not have had such an arduous preparation physically as the combatant units; but, faced as they were with the overhaul of vehicles and equipment, much of it old and much more overstrained through long use and irregular maintenance, they had as hard a task as any. There is a limit to the number of hours that the skilled mechanic can work on some of the intricate jobs that fall to him in the repair of the machines of modern warfare. Many of ours we would gladly have discarded, but replacements were arriving in negligible quantities and such new vehicles as appeared often required attention because they had been tampered with *en route*. The bald statement that we were on November 5th deficient of 1,400 vehicles is enough to show that an army fighting in a theatre where equipment was short relied on its repair services to make even the worst crocks go.

As usual, a number of distinguished officers and visitors came to watch us at work. Among these were the new C.-in-C., His Excellency Sir Claude Auchinleck, the commander of the newly created Fourteenth Army, Lieut.-General W. J. Slim, and His Highness the Maharajah of Patiala, who had just reason to be proud of his State battalion.

If it was a time when all were hard at work, it was equally a time of healthy and pleasant recreation. By day, hockey, football and boxing reappeared in our lives, while the General joined the ranks of those who found odd moments to enjoy the excellent shooting. Of an evening there were canteens open where cheerful ladies served behind the counter, or officers and men could visit the cinema.

Mess parties were a popular form of entertainment among the officers of Div. and Bde. H.Qs., not least for the occasional appearance of the opposite sex. There is a ring of pleasure in the 49 Bde. entry of December 29th: "Officers' mess honoured by the presence of eight Q.A.I.M.N.S. to dinner and dance—most enjoyable evening." The Div. H.Q. dance was as successful, though the organizers had a moment of anxiety when they discovered that, despite living in the middle of nowhere, there were not enough partners for the thirty to forty members of the women's services who arrived from all parts of the plain. The deficiency was speedily remedied. Many, too, will recall with delight the "A" mess gala nights when the evenings were enlivened by a contest at "liar" dice with the General, an arch expert at the game, and by an original cabaret turn. Yes! A live cabaret provided by Manipuri dancing girls.

The training and the mess parties and the closeness of units to one another greatly enhanced the spirit of comradeship within the Division. With units scattered over a wide front in the Kabaw valley, each having their individual tasks, it had not been easy to come to know other folk; we lived compulsorily in our own orbits. In the Imphal plain we became splendidly aware of our identity with others who wore the sign of the "Fighting Cock," which was at last available for issue to all; acquaintance ripened into friendship, friendship into that mutual trust which means the world in enterprises of war. The Division went into battle in 1944 with its head held high and very conscious of its worth and unity.

There were a few additions to our strength during the period. 3rd Indian Field Regiment, I.A., with its Punjabi, Madras and Hyderabad batteries recruited from different parts of India, made a welcome increase to the Division's gun power. We were expecting as well a Div. H.Q. Defence Battalion, a reconnaissance unit and the Divisional Ordnance Sub Park. 2/19 Hybad arrived in February, 1944, restored in numbers and health, to fill the first of these gaps, but the other two units were not forthcoming. Brigadier R. C. M. King, who took over the command of 1 Bde., was another February arrival. The substitution of 3-inch mortars for 25-pounders in one battery of 158 Fd. Regt., R.A., should not be overlooked, and the gunners will recall the arguments between men and mules when one troop of this battery was given a taste of animal transport. Nor can the first appearance on January 10th of a daily paper called *S.E.A.C.* go without mention; this was an important fellow, because he came hot from the press in Calcutta and helped greatly to bring the jungle army into touch with the world outside. He met a long-felt need.

Before recounting the Division's part in the 1944 campaign, it is necessary to go back for a moment to 1943. Apart from one encounter at Thaungdut, when 3/10 G.R. were the forward 37 Bde. battalion, and two clashes which 6 Mahratta patrols had in the Atwin Yomas after they took over from 5/6 Rajrif at Shuganu in September, our front was quiet up to the time we handed over to the newly arrived 20th Indian Division. In the Chin hills, away to the south, 17 Div. had less peace of mind. The enemy began to build up his forces at the end of the monsoon and 17 Div., with only two brigades, had no reserve if the Jap threat developed.

When orders came on October 11th that we were to have a battalion and a battery of mountain artillery ready to move at short notice to assist in the Chin hills, the choice fell on 1/16 Punjab, as the freshest unit in the Division, and on 13 Mtn. Bty. At nine o'clock the following morning they were ordered to move down the long road to Tiddim and they came on arrival under the command of 63 Ind. Inf. Bde.

The battalion was given the task of sitting astride the main road high up in the hills a mile and a half north of Fort White, where all was quiet for nearly a month until the Japs began probing west towards the road in mid-November. A two-company attack by 1/16 Punjab on November 9th some distance from the main position had not been successful, and the C.O., Lieut.-Colonel S. D. Willcock, must have had some misgivings on the morning of the 13th when he was ordered to strengthen a guerilla post a mile and a quarter away to the north with a platoon and occupy another high point two miles to the east with a company. These moves were designed to heighten the morale of the Chins by a display of force. The danger of dispersing the battalion, which was out of reach of immediate assistance, was recognized, and it was arranged that "B" Company, 1/3 G.R., should be sent to reinforce the Punjabis, while the counter-attack task to assist the guerilla post was allotted in case of need to 1/10 G.R.

All day the battalion toiled at the readjustment of their position, "B" Company in isolation at Pt. 6531 and the rest of the battalion round M.S. 52. The northernmost locality given to the company of 1/3 G.R., where the jungle came up close, had to be left to chance as there were no hands to spare for the extra work. The Gurkha company did not arrive until after dark.

The early part of the night of the 13th was quiet. Suddenly at 2300 hrs. a message came through from the guerilla post to say that Japs were digging in there, and shortly after the peace of the night was disturbed by the sound of heavy mortars firing. Only the noise of the night-long battle at the post reached the main position, but the details related afterwards revealed a story of great gallantry. Though the attacking force was overwhelmingly superior (some put it between two and four hundred strong), the first attack delivered about midnight was beaten back. The tiny force stood waiting for the next assault which they knew must come, and when it came it met as stiff resistance as the first. There could only be one end to so unequal a contest, unless help came. At 0215 hrs. on the 14th 1/16 Punjab saw the

· 1/16 · PUNJAB · IN · THE · CHIN · HILLS ·

· LEGEND ·

CONTOURS	
ROADS	
TRACKS	
REGIMENTAL AID POST	R·A·P
3 INCH MORTARS	⊙ 3 M
L.M.G's.	
SHELL FIRE	
TREES	
POSITIONS	
MILESTONES	M.S. 32

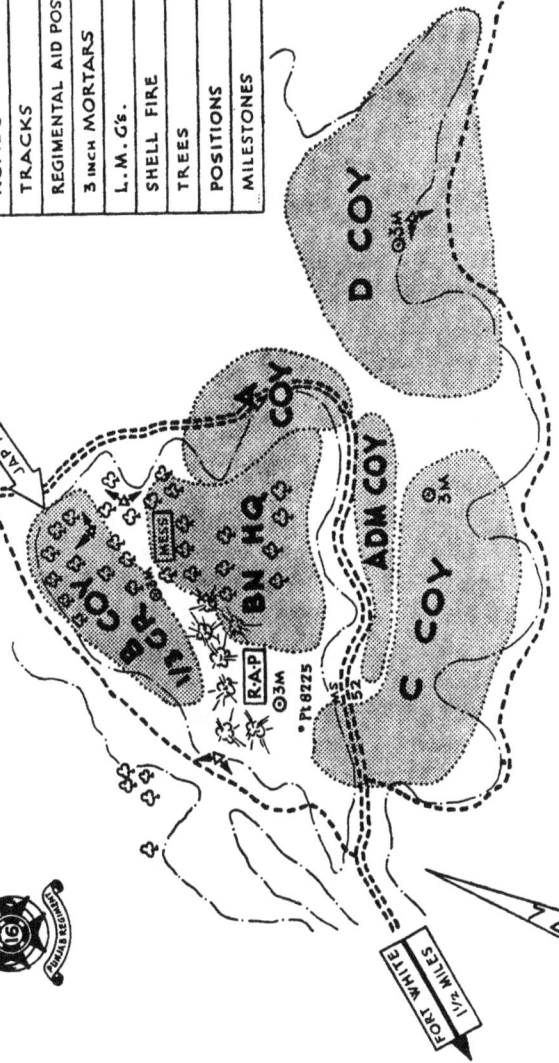

· SCALE OF YARDS ·

200   400   600   800   1000

B COY ON PT 6551 2 MILES FROM THE BOUNDARY OF D COY

D COY

8 PL A COY & GUERILLA SEC AT MS 54 (i.e. 1½ Miles)

TO TIDDIM & KENNEDY PEAK

JAP ATTACK

BR COY

MESS

BN HQ

A COY

ADM COY

R·A·P   ⊙3M   • Pt 8225

M.S. 52

C COY   ⊙ 3M

FORT WHITE 1½ MILES

signal calling for a counter-attack mount into the sky and they confirmed the request for help by phoning to the Gurkhas. The night wore on, no help came, the post hung on until the last round of ammunition had been fired before Lieut. Wynn Williams ordered his men to withdraw and covered their getaway by charging the Jap with the bayonet. His was the end of a brave man.

About the time the post fell, 0600 hrs. on the morning of the 14th, squat forms were seen moving through the jungle close to the 1/3 G.R. company position. In the half light they were taken at first for fellow-Gurkhas moving up to deliver the expected counter-attack. It was a mistake in identity. The hill-top was raked with intense fire from medium and light machine guns and 4-inch mortars, and the Jap charged shrieking and screaming out of and round the fringe of the jungle in close-packed waves. The attack had fallen, of deliberate design it seemed, on the one place where the defence was not co-ordinated. In the first rush the Gurkhas, who were forced to take up fire positions behind trees and bushes as they had not dug in, were swept back on top of Bn. H.Q.; two of the "A" Company posts had fallen in the same rush.

Within half an hour the position had been irrevocably breached and it was the more difficult to regain control because the Jap had penetrated through the gap he had torn in the defences into the mess and H.Q. area, where the presence of administrative personnel increased the confusion. At this crisis, while the C.O. was waiting for a counter-attack force from "C" Company, he heard that "B" Company were surrounded; he could only order them to fight their way back and hope that he might be able to help later. That was not to be. The two "C" Company platoons fought their way to the edge of the jungle, but had not the strength to hold on when the Japs thrust back in their turn; the C.O., the Adjutant and two other officers fell when a shell burst in their midst; bullets were flying through the dressing station, ammunition was short. It was an awkward moment to assume command, but Major Newall proved equal to the emergency; he gave orders to withdraw into the "D" Company area where "B" Company were beginning to arrive.

Slowly the tired battalion concentrated within this keep, with the Jap growling at them but not pressing too close, for he had not come off lightly. That evening 1/16 Punjab slipped away through the dark across country; encumbered by wounded and equipment, they moved up and down the steep ridges without pausing except for one halt of an hour and a quarter until at 0700 hrs. on the 15th they reached Kennedy Peak. There for the first time they could count their losses, which proved lower than anyone had dared to hope. Besides their four officers, twenty-one other ranks were known to have been killed and thirty-five in all were missing; they had brought with them eighteen wounded. The loss of equipment was serious; when the battalion set off in the dark, they tried to take mules and 3-inch mortars with them, but the lack of men for carrying and the difficulties of the route forced an abandonment of the attempt.

The full story of this engagement was not known to those who were training in the Imphal plain until December 21st on the return of the Punjabis and gunners who were engaged in hard fighting not far from the Punjabis and had, on orders, to abandon and destroy two of their guns before a difficult withdrawal. If the action enforced one lesson above others, it was the need to dig. That was something lacking in our previous experience in the jungle, but General Roberts had already set about repairing the omission when he organized his training programme.

When the Division started training, no one could be sure how short the time of preparation was going to be; all that could be foreseen was the urgent need for haste. It is probable that we were given longer in the end than the Jap intended that we should have had his plans gone as he wished. The warning order for operation "Dinah," the scheme that would in an emergency take us away from training and commit us once more to operations, went out on December 7th. The threat did not develop.

The respite made the difference between having the Division more or less fully restored and ready for battle and having to commit it when one brigade had been out of the line only eight weeks and one battalion was far away to the south. One of the 37 Bde. C.Os. remarked, "The battalion is at last having the chance to make itself truly ready for battle"; and the Brigadier, after discussing the value of the training, added, "I am confident that without this period at Shuganu, which put the men right as far as the physical side went (morale was always high throughout), the brigade could not have put up the magnificent show it did in February and March."

As it was, we were almost ready; almost—but not quite as the story of the Tiddim road will show. It was well the Jap could not concentrate in time for an attack early in December, 1943. The health of the Division had been seriously impaired during the 1942 and 1943 monsoons by the ravages of malaria, by the poorness and scarcity of food and by the exhausting struggle against the elements. Time alone can restore the sick and weary, and the delay in mounting the Japanese offensive allowed time to do its healing work.

CHAPTER 11

Background to 1944

ON the Assam and North Burma fronts, the Higher Command's directif for 1944 to Fourteenth Army was that all the frontiers of Bengal and Assam were to be held secure while North Burma was to be occupied to the line of Mogaung and Myitkyina on the Upper Irrawaddy. The force to be employed for the second of these tasks was a composite one of Chinese and American troops under General Stillwell, and could not achieve its object unless the attention of the main Japanese Army was distracted by operations elsewhere; hence the roles allotted to 17 and 20 Ind. Divs. and the fly-in of Wingate's second expedition early in March. Wingate was to cut the L. of C. supplying the Japanese opposing General Stillwell, while 17 and 20 Divs. continued to press hard in the Chin hills and southern Kabaw valley respectively to divert the Jap's gaze from North Burma—not that it needed much diverting for his eyes were fixed elsewhere.

Early in the year it was apparent that the enemy intended to launch a major offensive against the frontiers of Assam. The forecast of the plan of this attack was that there would be a thrust by one division in the Chin hills to cut off 17 Ind. Div., a second thrust by two divisions less one regiment up the main road from Tamu to Palel and across the Naga hills to Ukhrul, and a third but minor thrust towards Kohima. March 15th was the estimate of D Day.

General Slim decided to meet this offensive by pulling back his forward divisions for a close defence of the Imphal plain so that the Jap would have to fight at the end of lengthy supply lines which would disintegrate if the battle were not over before the monsoon broke at the end of May. The overall plan was for 20 Div. to hold Shenam, 23 Div. the Tiddim road a little south of the plain, with 17 Div. kept in reserve to provide the striking force against infiltration. In response to a request for reinforcements to free more of these divisions for mobile roles, 50 Indian Parachute Brigade, two battalions strong, was sent from India; they were initially to hold the wild country east of Kohima and take under command our old friends 1 Assam Regiment. None of these defensive measures was to interrupt the fly-in of the Wingate force.

To meet the threat of a Japanese advance across the Chindwin from the area of Homalin through the desolate Somra Tract, 49 Bde. was moved from the plain late in January to the ground 37 Bde. had held when they first arrived from India. The task of holding this area, where the tracks from the east converged on Ukhrul, was one of great difficulty, for the village is in the centre of some of the fiercest of the Assam country. The spine-like ridges rise and fall precipitously in rapid succession and their sides are densely covered with mixed jungle, including an unpleasant prickly bamboo which grips all that comes within its clutches. If one paused for a moment during the day, the mind felt the glory and loveliness of the place, for the majesty of the scene was enriched by the vivid colours of huge rhododendron bushes and later of a multitude of orchids. So much did one spot resemble the pictures of the jungle where the Australians were fighting the place was nicknamed "New Guinea."

Grand and beautiful—but the very devil to defend. The tracks meandered from crest to crest along the connecting ridges, but if the enemy lay astride one of the tracks and it was necessary to send reinforcements forward, it could only be done by descending thousands of feet into the valley and climbing as high again through the jungle on the further side. Immediate counter-attacks were impossible and a flank movement by a company across country became a matter of hours. The nature of the ground presented the further problem that water was almost non-existent on the hill tops.

It was on January 21st that H.Q. 49 Bde. moved to Litan, where the Kali Bahadur Regiment at Sangshak came once more under our command, with orders to have two battalions forward to block the main tracks. Accordingly 6 Mahratta took up their position four and a half miles north and 4 Mahratta about six miles south-east of Ukhrul; the

Kali Bahadur Regiment held Sangshak, while 5/6 Rajrif were kept back with Bde. H.Q. at mile 36 on the road from Imphal to form a striking force. The need to cover the tracks forced this dispersion of units and led to similar dispersion in some of the battalion localities. Thus the forward companies of 4 Mahratta were a mile or more apart on two peaks which provided strong defensive points, but they could not support one another. Once the brigade had settled in, they resumed training, covered by a screen of V Force outposts.

Early in February, when Lord Louis Mountbatten, the Supreme Allied Commander in the theatre, visited the Seaforths and 158 Fd. Regt. and met the officers of Div. H.Q., the clouds began to gather. February 3rd was the date when the Japanese offensive began in the Arakan and, as the month went on, intelligence reports indicated that the enemy might muster a larger force against the Ukhrul area than had first been thought likely. By mid-February the estimate was that up to a division might move on Ukhrul, with a further regiment available for deep penetration into the area of Kohima to cut the main road from Imphal which was the life-line of 4 Corps. 49 Bde., already faced with enough difficulties of their own, were warned that they must be prepared to take command of all troops up to the Chindwin on their front, which would be extended to include Kohima on the north.

That task they were not called on to fulfil. On March 10th 50 Ind. Para. Bde., recently arrived from India, were ordered to relieve 49 Bde.; the leading battalion reached Litan on the 12th and took over from 4 Mahratta on the 14th. The move of the Para. Bde. left only 1 Assam to guard the approaches to Kohima.

As soon as it had been foreseen that operations were probable in the wild country between Kohima on the north and the head of the Kabaw valley in the south, 4 Corps had undertaken the construction of a jeep track which ran east from Kohima to Jessami, where it turned south to Ukhrul and thence south-east to Humine at the northern end of the Kabaw valley. The General may be said to have performed the opening ceremony when he completed the grand round from Imphal by way of Kohima and the Kabaw valley. He reached Humine on the 7th and there he met Brigadier King of 1 Bde., which had been sent at the beginning of the month to ground they knew only too well. The Brigade had returned for a brief spell to the north of the Kabaw valley for the same purpose they had been there the year before; they were to provide a diversion for the new Wingate expedition. Along with them went 158 Fd. Regt. less their mortar battery, 16 Mtn. Bty., a squadron of tanks, and 3/3 G.R., who were to join a brigade of 20 Div. in the old Gurkha haunts near Sittaung.

The deception scheme, which bore the name "Amazon," was as complete as ingenuity could make it. To give the impression that considerable forces were about to cross between Thaungdut and Tonhe, patrols were to cross to the east bank, a local was to be caught and allowed to escape a few days later after he had been suitably impressed by the strength of our forces, a Brigadier or his double was to make a display of his red tabs, rafts were to be collected and an air photo carelessly left behind on the farther bank.

It fell to the Seaforths to carry out this programme, which was to culminate on the night of March 12th/13th, when the leading troops of the "advance" were to cross the Chindwin and make their presence felt, aided by a wireless build-up of bogus cipher traffic. 1/16 Punjab were in reserve protecting Bde. H.Q. on the road north of Moreh, and 1 Patiala with the artillery and tanks had been detached early in the month to fulfil the Brigade's secondary task of providing a mobile reserve for 20 Div., who were battling hard with the Jap in the Atwin Yomas.

Viewed in retrospect, the diversion must be accounted a failure for the simple reason that the Jap was long past the stage when he would pay the slightest attention to any of our activities; he was not even prepared for a considerable time to do more than sniff at Wingate's airborne force. His plans were made and nothing could divert him from his purpose. On the night of March 15th/16th he crossed the Chindwin in the Homalin area—the battle for India was joined and the issue was to be decided around the Imphal plain. A week before an excellent E.N.S.A. show was playing in Imphal, and one who was there remarked on the deep peace of the night as he sat watching with a full moon rising into the

sky. Even the drone of aircraft high overhead carrying
Wingate's men into the heart of Burma seemed but a slight
intrusion on the pleasure of the evening. The time for
pleasure and peacefulness was now past; we were a part of
one of the decisive battles of the Second Great War.

For us, the Jap had chosen a singularly awkward moment
to launch his offensive as the need to support Wingate had
caused wide dispersion of our troops. Though 1 Bde. was
already withdrawing, as Wingate had agreed with the
General should happen, it was still far away in the Kabaw
valley, its units were employed on two separate tasks, and
Seaforth patrols were on the east side of the Chindwin. Out
at Ukhrul 50 Para. Bde. were beginning to take over from
49 Bde. in an area where there was danger of an early battle
and only one of their two battalions had arrived, the other
being at Kohima. To the east of Kohima, 1 Assam were out
in the wilds on their own. The only troops at hand were 37
Bde., and even they were without 3/3 G.R., who were down
on the Chindwin; nor were they immediately ready for
action as they were, on the night of the 13th, engaged on
their final night exercise with 254 Tank Brigade nearly
thirty miles to the north of Imphal.

The Division, thus grievously dispersed, was by midnight
on the 13th well on the way to being yet more widely
scattered. The Jap thrust against 17 Div. in the Chin hills
had begun on March 7th, but the full seriousness of the
threat was not revealed until the 13th. With the road to
the north cut behind them in several places, 17 Div. were in
peril and there was very urgent need to draw off some of the
Japanese 33 Div. from their intention of forcing 17 Div. to
fight a hundred and sixty miles through a series of road
blocks held in strength. There was, at this most critical
moment, only one formation at call in the Imphal plain,
and this reserve was sent bundling down the Tiddim road.

At 2130 hrs. on the 13th the warning order to move reached
37 Bde.; the next evening they were eighty-two miles away
to the south of Imphal and on the 15th were engaged in a
tense battle at M.S. 100. Simultaneously with this move, the
Division had to withdraw 1 Bde. less the Patialas from the
Kabaw valley; and when it became apparent that 37 Bde.
had not enough troops to hold a firm base and act offensively

against the Jap, there was a third move on hand. 5/6 Rajrif were withdrawn from the Ukhrul area on the 15th and were ordered to M.S. 82 on the Tiddim road; they were followed the next day by H.Q. 49 Bde. and 6 Mahratta. To fill the gap at Ukhrul, orders went out to main H.Q. 50 Para. Bde. to move with the reserve battalion from Kohima with all speed.

These were hectic days when staffs, fighting troops and administrative services were at full stretch day and night. There were moves to plan and carry out, orders to issue, supplies of all kinds to provide. As each new move became necessary, the transport had to be found to move the troops, the convoys policed to their journey's end, recovery services organized. Drivers, provost, mechanics were ceaselessly on the road as the troops moved into position, knowing that they were going into battle. There was to be no more waiting.

By the evening of the 17th, the Division was in command of five brigades and its responsibilities stretched from M.S. 100 on the Tiddim road back to Imphal, where 1 Bde. had concentrated and 254 Tank Bde. had come under command, and thence to Ukhrul and Jessami, over forty miles farther north, where 1 Assam covered Kohima; in addition, it fell to us to protect the main L. of C. from Imphal to Kohima. The total length of the Division's front was not far short of two hundred miles, and fierce battles raged at both extremities and at Ukhrul. The mere statement is enough to show that the Division had its hands full, but it is worth remembering that all the troops had to be supplied over this far-flung front and that the battles were truly desperate affairs against an enemy who had staked all on his offensive and did not count the cost in lives spent.

The load was lightened a little on March 22nd when 1 Assam passed to the command of the Kohima garrison, but by then the leading brigade of 5 Ind. Div. had been flown in from the Arakan, making the sixth brigade under command of 23 Ind. Div. This was 123 Bde., which had in the very early days been part of the Division; they had come back at a perilous time. In the Sangshak area, 50 Para. Bde. and 4 Mahratta were surrounded; the defence did not flinch against great odds, but they were in a place very difficult to maintain by air and supplies dwindled until there was little left to fight the foe. On March 26th the General gave the order that the force was to fight its way out. This exposed the Imphal–Kohima road. 4 Corps had, at the General's suggestion, already cleared the many installations along the road, so when the Japs from Sangshak finally cut the L. of C., the depots were empty and the road to Imphal barred. 123 Bde., were in position at Kameng to block the approach down the Ukhrul road, and as the end drew near at Sangshak, 9 Bde. began to arrive and were ordered to hold the main road a few miles out of Imphal. Thus for a few days at the end of March, until the H.Q. of 5 Div. flew in, there were seven brigades under command.

There was little time to meditate on the value of the air superiority achieved during the preceding year, nor can it alone be decisive in battle, but without it the Burma campaign of 1944 would have been lost. The Dakotas of the R.A.F. and U.S.A.A.F.[1] were free to lumber from the Arakan to the Imphal plain with cargoes of troops, free to land on the airfields there with cargoes of supplies when the main L. of C. was cut, free to drop their loads down the Tiddim road when the Japs appeared behind 49 Bde. Food, ammunition, letters—everything could (and did) glide to earth at the end of parachutes when necessary. The troops in the forward areas sustained by air supply felt confident they would have their daily "drop"; they could fight without worrying if the road was cut behind them, and fight they did until 17 Div. linked up with 37 Bde. on March 29th.

After the link-up, 17 Div. made short work of the last road block at M.S. 72 and they and 37 Bde. passed out of the battle for a few days' rest while 49 Bde. held a covering position at Torbung. On the night of April 15th/16th 49 Bde. themselves withdrew through the Bishenpur position, only sixteen miles out, where 17 Div. held the line which the Japs were never to pass. The first round in the battle of the plain was over; the concentration of 4 Corps was complete with the front intact. 5 Div. held the northern approaches, 20 Shenam, 17 the Tiddim road and 23, concentrated at last, formed the mobile reserve. There were anxieties ahead,

---

[1] United States Army Air Force.

but, though the troops who were fighting could not realize it, the most critical phase was over. The battleground was to be the one General Slim had chosen, the fabric of the defence, at one moment in great danger, accorded with his design, the time was mid-April and the monsoon a month and a half away.

Such, in brief, is the story of the first month of the battle. It has seemed best to let the story flow on and so to provide a setting for the account of the bitter actions between M.Ss. 98 and 100 on the Tiddim road and at Sangshak. Some hint has been given of the fury of the fighting in these places, where ordinary men rose to those heights of courage and endurance which they display in war despite the fear inherent in human nature.

CHAPTER 12

The Tiddim Road

No formation going into its first big action would choose to be withdrawn from a training exercise in the middle of the night and hurled straight into battle. It was not the fault of the Division that this was 37 Bde.'s lot—the error that led to their unpreparedness belongs, as has been unhesitatingly admitted, to the higher command who did not order 17 Div.'s withdrawal in time and so precipitated the Tiddim road battle, which was unexpected and unwelcome.

The night of March 13th/14th will live in the memory of those swept into the race against time. When the warning order came, 37 Bde. H.Q. was split, 3/5 R.G.R. and 3 D.G. were in harbour waiting to put in a dawn attack, 3/10 G.R. had provided a company as "enemy" and numerous officers and N.C.Os. as umpires. While units were concentrating in the darkness, commanders and their staffs unrolled maps of the Tiddim road, the one part of the front which had not been studied in detail, and the men laboured to collect stores, ammunition, rations and equipment. The preparation for battle went on all through the night, but there was no chance to sort out more than essentials, for by the time daylight came the transport would have arrived and loading must begin. Little was known about the future except that the vehicles were due at 0630 hrs. and 0900 was zero hour for the move. That order was carried out—at 0900 hrs. on March 14th the column moved with 3/10 G.R. in the lead.

It would be wrong to say that 17 Div. would never have reached the Imphal plain had 37 Bde. been slower into action, but it might so easily have come in very different plight with its guns and equipment left behind on the road. The Japanese penetration was much deeper than expected and reached an area near M.S. 100, where there were few fighting troops. A few hours' delay would have enabled the enemy to close the trap and had the jaws shut tight, as they so nearly did, the withdrawal of 17 Div. would have been more costly and more difficult for them and for us.

At the hour the column started, Brigadier Collingridge was meeting the General, who could say nothing more definite than that a large number of administrative units and 9 Jat, a machine-gun battalion, were engaged in confused fighting between M.S. 102 and 109. The immediate task was to reach M.S. 82 and to push on from there to link up with 17 Div. Were the Japs at M.S. 82? There was no information to say that they were; equally there was nothing to say that small bands of desperadoes might not be met. Thus comforted, the Brigadier moved on with a small party ahead of his troops.

When he reached M.S. 82 he found that he was fortunate enough to have anticipated the Japs, but he took one look at the throng of administrative units scattered for two miles along the road and decided that, once his troops were entangled in the mob who rumoured immediate Jap attacks, they would not be extracted in a hurry. He selected a site for his base to the east of the road and there, as darkness approached, he awaited for the arrival of somewhat greater protection than his small advanced party could provide. As he waited, the lorries were struggling behind him against the road. The surface was loose and the gradients severe; wheels spun round furiously as they sought for a grip, and where they found none they sunk into the churned-up earth. The most important unit held up on the road was 6 Bty. 3 Ind. Fd., whose worn-out "quads"[1] were typical of other equipment in this starved theatre.

It was 2000 hrs. before 3/10 G.R. began to appear at M.S. 82 after an exhausting day, for there is not much more tiring than being jolted from side to side for 110 miles in a tight-packed lorry. 3/5 R.G.R. were halted for the night twenty miles farther back at M.S. 62. While the battalion was still on the road, the Brigadier had heard from the General that a company of the Jats was being hard pressed at M.S. 100 and was to be relieved "at all costs," so he stopped 3/5 R.G.R. to give them time for rest before they were sent straight through on the morrow. It had to be accepted that

---

[1] Gun-tractors.

they would be a light force short of a company which was acting as escort to "A" Squadron, 7 Cavalry, and unsupported by other arms except for one troop of tanks—the guns, or more accurately their tractors, were still struggling.

To assist their deployment, a platoon of 3/10 G.R. was sent off at dawn on the 15th to make a preliminary recce. of the battle area. The officer in command successfully completed his task, and when the C.O. of 3/5 R.G.R. arrived, he took him to a hill from which the struggle at M.S. 100 could be seen. Lieut.-Colonel J. F. Marindin, who was to gain the D.S.O. in the coming battle, wasted no time; he left his rear H.Q. and the three tanks at M.S. 98 and set off to the rescue of the Jats. He had barely started when the Japs came at him through the jungle, but this was no moment for a grapple with an enemy of unknown strength; leaving one platoon of "D" Company to hold off the attack, he slipped away through the fir trees to the east of the road. He reached the Jats when they were almost at their last gasp; they had been forced to relinquish the part of their perimeter that lay west of the road, ammunition was short and they must have been overwhelmed during the coming night. Even after the arrival of the Gurkhas, the position was dangerous unless the enemy could be thrust back, for he lay very close to the road.

It was 1730 hrs. and an hour of daylight remained to eject the Japs when "B" Company formed up for their first battle. A quarter of an hour later the leading platoon assaulted in a westerly direction across the road, covered by the Jat machine guns. The Japs met the attack with all the fire they could bring to bear. As the Gurkhas began to close upon the enemy, their losses from machine-gun fire and grenades mounted until over half the platoon were casualties and the survivors were pinned. Without hesitation, the company commander, who was conspicuous throughout the action for his example, ordered his second platoon into the attack. The determination of the Gurkhas carried the day. The Japs left fifteen of their number dead where they had fought, the "A" Company attack which followed was not strongly opposed and the perimeter was restored; the Japs had lost their first stiff encounter with the Gurkhas.

The C.O. had watched the engagement from an O.P. thirty yards away from the battle. It was, in his own words, "a most gallant affair" and "for troops doing it for the first time . . . a splendid effort." Gallant—and typical of so much of the fighting in the Imphal battle where the close country prevented the deployment of large bodies of troops and made many an action a company affair where the determination and courage of each individual turned the scale. On this occasion an apparently insignificant encounter was of decisive importance. Had the Gurkhas arrived a few hours later, the Jats would have been eliminated and the road cut beyond breaching except by a major operation. This happily did not occur, and it was due first to General Roberts, who insisted, against the inclinations of 4 Corps, that 37 Bde. should be withdrawn post-haste from their exercise, next to the drive and resolution with which 37 Bde. executed a rush order, and lastly to the courage and skill-at-arms of a hundred or so men.

Reasonably secure for the moment, Lieut.-Colonel Marindin ordered up the troop of tanks from rear H.Q. to assist a further attack next day. Those tanks never arrived. They had moved somewhat under a mile when the leading tank was halted by a road block; there was a burst of fire and all but one of the infantry escorting the tanks lay dead on the road. After the first tank failed to surmount the block, the troop commander sought to make his way back to rear H.Q. In the darkness he reversed into the ditch beside the road and despite all efforts the tank could not be shifted. He sent one back to tell of his plight and when he heard that rear H.Q. had a battle of their own on hand and had no escort to spare, he and his men stayed in the two tanks for the night. The next morning two platoons of "D" Company passed by on their way from M.S. 100 to rear H.Q., but their offers of help were refused, and when the third tank appeared it too was ordered away, not before the infantry escort had again suffered heavy losses. There had already been a mortar attack which immobilized the tanks by destroying their tracks, and the troop commander decided to destroy certain vital parts of his tank and fight it out in the one vehicle which was in a position to fire. Accordingly the two crews assembled in the front tank and from it for a long time they beat off all attacks. Then they heard a voice outside speaking in a language which they thought might be Gurkhali. After some discussion, they opened the turret. A grenade burst inside the tank which was rendered useless for fighting purposes, though the crews were not killed. There was nothing for it but to run for the cover of the woods. One by one they dropped out of the turret on to the road, and as they ran they were picked off—all but one who survived to tell the tale.

There had not been much sleep throughout the Brigade on the night of March 15th/16th. Both parts of 3/5 R.G.R. had to repel numerous attacks and there was a three-hour raid on Bde. H.Q. and 3/10 G.R. who, with a restraint worthy of a battle-hardened unit, fired a total of seventeen rounds while the assortment of units near by was shooting continuously at nothing.

The strength of the Brigade was now beginning to increase; the guns and the squadron of tanks had arrived on the evening of the 15th, and 5/6 Rajrif reached M.S. 82 at 0700 hrs. on the 16th. The Brigadier thus had the means to hold a firm base and to reinforce his forward troops, who were also short of supplies as they had set out from Imphal with nothing more than three days' rations. This need was met by sending up a small maintenance convoy, but at M.S. 96 they ran into a fresh Jap road block. There was no doubt about the next move—the enemy, who made these unwelcome appearances and behaved as though he was a quick-growing fungus, must be removed before he had time to establish a stronghold. The fourth company of 3/5 R.G.R. were sent forward immediately to destroy the block, and were assisted in their task by the appearance of the recce platoon from 3/10 G.R.; once the road was known to be clear, a second and larger maintenance convoy moved off, protected by a company of 3/10 G.R. and a troop of tanks. This convoy was not destined to reach harbour that night.

Heavy rain which fell unexpectedly the previous night had turned the loose earth into mud and the lorries, which had no chains, were in trouble on the hills from the moment they started; they were still well short of their journey's end when night came. Reviewing the situation, the Brigadier, for all his courage, must have felt some anxiety for the immediate future. He had every confidence in the fighting qualities of his men and he knew that he could expect up the next day the 17th, the 49 Bde. H.Q. and 6 Mahratta, followed the day after by his third battalion, 3/3 G.R., who had reached the Imphal plain after their accelerated withdrawal from the Kabaw valley. That would free him to strike at the enemy, but against this he had a vital convoy benighted on the road and liable to attack, and he had heard nothing for most of the day from M.S. 100, where he knew supplies must be almost exhausted. Air supply had been arranged and might enable his forward troops to hold their ground, but this relief could only come just in time and might be too late.

The untimely silence from M.S. 100 was due to the failure of their wireless as all the spare batteries had been left at rear H.Q., and it was not until about 1630 hrs. on the 17th that much was known of events forward on the preceding day. At this hour there arrived a Jemadar who had slipped past the Japanese and was able to give a first-hand account. As it turned out, the force at M.S. 100 did not have to repel a heavy attack on the 16th, and the Gurkhas stayed all day in the trenches they had scraped, waiting for the next move of an enemy who was licking his wounds; but supplies of all kinds were so low that withdrawal was inevitable unless the road could be cleared.

Withdrawal it had to be, for on the morning of the 17th, before the Jemadar's arrival, "C" Company's assault on the road block at M.S. 98.5 had failed. This block was established amid very close country which prevented any effort to feel round the flanks of the enemy, and lack of time debarred a wide recce as a prelude to an encircling move; hence the attack was more or less a frontal assault, which the Japs repulsed.

Meanwhile, after a night of jitter raids, Lieut.-Colonel Marindin and his force were being desperately hard pressed by an enemy resolved on their destruction. About 0900 hrs. on the 17th some infantry appeared moving southwards from the direction of M.S. 98. For a few seconds there was hesitation and in those few seconds, while men paused and wondered whether help had not come, the Japs hurled themselves on "B" Company. Surprise had been achieved and the initial impetus of the attack carried the Jap part of the way into the thinly held defences, for all the fury of the Gurkha resistance in a hand-to-hand struggle where the clash of steel on steel could be heard amid the crack of rifle fire and the cries and shouts of the battle.

The position was indeed precarious. The Japs were lodged in some dead ground, and unless they could be speedily ejected they would be able at their leisure to prepare for an assault which would finally overwhelm the defence. Despite mounting losses, "B" Company, with their commander again outstanding, thrust back at once in a counter-attack and turned the enemy out of the vital dead ground, but the Jap had the range with his heavy mortars. Unable to endure further casualties, the Gurkhas had to relinquish their hold.

"B" Company had no longer the strength for a further effort without assistance from "A" Company, and to use the latter meant that the perimeter defence would be weaker than ever; but the risk had to be taken, for the survival of what remained of the force depended on recapturing the dead ground. The action in the second counter-attack, which was delivered by an "A" Company platoon with the remnants of the "B" Company platoon, was, if possible, fiercer than any of the preceding engagements. Amid the confusion of this fight to the death, the issue was not immediately apparent; caught up in a ferocious struggle for survival, men fought to kill. In the end it was the Japs who quit, but the Gurkhas had sustained twenty more casualties which they could not afford; the only way to hold the restored perimeter was by bringing over another platoon from "A" Company. Among the casualties was the commander of "A" Company who had his hand shattered by a grenade when leading the attack.

As the day wore on, a day when time seemed to stand still, the C.O. realized that no help would come from the north, and at 1300 hrs. he decided he must withdraw when darkness fell. His force was exhausted and so depleted in numbers that he could not spare the men to collect the supplies which were dropped wide of his position in the late afternoon. In all, twenty-one had been killed, three were missing and seventy-five wounded. The survivors, amounting barely to a company, had not slept for three nights and their food and water was gone; forty stretcher cases had lain unattended in the middle of the battle for three days, and when the food was exhausted, they could not have such meagre comfort as their daily ration of two cups of tea and one biscuit had provided; there was ammunition enough to repel one more attack.

The march back began at 0230 hrs. on the 18th, when the force slipped away eastwards from the Japs, who took no notice save for throwing one grenade though they were no more than thirty yards away. The men stumbled along in that half-consciousness which overtakes those oppressed with fatigue over a rough track that dropped a thousand feet into the valley below. The strain fell heaviest on the Jats who, called on to act as stretcher-bearers, showed splendid patience as they waited in the forming-up place for the order to move and no less endurance as they carried their loads down the descent and up the two-thousand-foot climb on the farther side. The force tramped on and on through the night, unmolested by the Jap, until about 0745 hrs. all who survived had reached rear H.Q. at M.S. 98 where the supply convoy, which had been a second day on the road before it reached 3/5 R.G.R., was waiting to take back the wounded. The success of the withdrawal was in no small measure due to the guidance of the Jemadar who had found the route through the Jap lines. Once the withdrawal was known to be complete, the R.A.F. struck against the Japs down the road.

On the 18th the General came to H.Q. 37 Bde. at M.S. 82 and found them embarrassed by the appearance of several thousand administrative and other personnel who had been part of the 17 Div. rear base at M.S. 109 and had moved off across country when the Jap appeared. This additional commitment on the supply organization was one to be rid of quickly and was unwelcome when the eyes of all were fixed on clearing the road to 17 Div., who had reached M.S. 120. The General did not leave before he had issued clear orders about future operations. As those who fought under him in battle were to find, he was a man ready to listen to what others had to say and his keen mind was quick to sort out essentials. The conference might be held under a blazing sun or in the pouring rain and time might be short, but the end was always the same—a sound and clear order which left no one in doubt of their commander's determination and intention, but, once the order was given, there was no attempt to fetter the initiative of those under him. On this occasion 37 Bde. were ordered to exterminate the enemy between M.S. 100 and M.S. 102 and thereafter to feel forward to M.S. 109 while 49 Bde. from the firm base undertook a minor operation against Jap forces reported west of the road.

Even before the General had arrived, 37 Bde. had taken the first step towards putting this plan into effect, as 3/10 G.R. had moved up that morning to join one of their companies at M.S. 93, where it was protecting two guns covering 3/5 R.G.R.; and when 3/3 G.R. reached M.S. 82 later in the day, a company was at once sent forward to release the whole of 3/10 G.R. for the next stage.

It was not easy to prepare for battle in that arid region where the jungle found enough moisture to thrive though there was for miles no spring from which a man could slake his thirst. Besides building up the stores normally required for battle, "Q" had to move forward from M.S. 82 every drop of water that was needed to enable the troops to survive. This took time, and it took even longer to secure precise knowledge of the whereabouts of an enemy who had concealed his bunkers so carefully in the jungle that they were invisible more than a few yards away. As a message on the 19th said that 17 Div. hoped to reach M.S. 109 the next day, orders came from 23 Div. that the Gurkhas were to exert all the pressure they could from the north. Hence that evening 3/10 G.R. were warned to prepare for an attack on the 19th, but it was too soon; however anxious 37 Bde. might be to burst the road block and move to meet 17 Div., it was squandering lives to hazard an attack against an enemy who was only partially located and known to be dug in. There was still inadequate information early on the 20th, but the patrols probing the jungle on that day were more successful than previously and reported the existence of bunkers both to the east and to the west of the road. The R.A.F., who had been straffing the area, rendered further invaluable aid in the evening when they dropped air photographs. Earlier in the day "A" Company, 3/10 G.R., had left for a diversion planned to bring them out behind the Japs at M.S. 100; the main attack was to begin at dawn on the 22nd after the Brigadier had made a last recce in person on the 21st. 17 Div., who now had direct wireless contact with 37 Bde. and flashed a helio message through on the 21st, were still about fourteen miles away to the south.

3/10 G.R., under Lieut.-Colonel F. R. S. Cosens, moved out into the night from M.S. 93 at 0130 hrs. on the 22nd and three hours later had reached the point on the road five and a half miles to the south from which they were to turn off to their forming-up place. The plan of attack on the feature known as Fir Tree Hill, a few hundred yards south-west of the road, was simple—a "B" Company advance at zero hour against the right, followed, if this attack were successful, by a "C" Company advance on the left of the hill. Despite the closeness of the country, "B" Company were to have the support of a troop of tanks in addition to artillery and mortars.

At 0550 hrs. the artillery barrage opened, but by one of those mischances of war the range was wrong and the shells began to fall in the middle of our own troops; a British officer was wounded, a Gurkha officer and four other ranks killed, and instantly there was confusion. Owing to the atmospheric conditions, which prevented wireless communication between Bde. H.Q. and the forward troops all day, some minutes passed before the guns were directed on to the right target. Yet despite the difficulty of regaining control amid the noise of tank engines and bursting shells and mortar bombs, the Gurkhas swept into the attack at zero and within four minutes had overrun most of the right-hand hill. In this onset one bunker was reduced wellnigh single-handed by an N.C.O. who rushed up and hurled in grenades though his face was covered with blood from an ugly wound. There remained only the final objective where the enemy clung tenaciously to another bunker position. Though the tanks lumbered over ground that might have been thought impassable and brought their guns to bear, and our aircraft were dive-bombing the road close at hand, the Japs refused to budge. No means had so far been discovered for destroying their deep-dug and strongly

· SCALE OF MILES ·

0 1 2 3 4 5 6 7 8 9 10

M.S. 72. JAP BLOCK
ESTABLISHED 24 MAR

M.S. 82. 49 IND. INF. BDE
LESS 4 MAHRATTA

IMPHAL

· L E G E N D ·

DIRECTION OF 3/5 R.G.R.
ATTACKS ON M.S. 96·7
BLOCK 22-24 MAR.
INDICATED

M.S. INDICATED ╫ 98

93

HQ 37 IND. INF. BDE
AND 3/3 G.R.

JAP BLOCK
ESTABLISHED
TEMPORARILY 16 MAR

96

96·7

FIR TREE HILL. 3/10 G.R CAPTURE
22 MAR. GIVEN UP 24 MAR
REOCCUPIED 27 MAR

JAP BLOCK ESTABLISHED
22 MAR. CLEARED BY
3/5 R.G.R. 24-25 MAR.

98

98·5

REAR HQ 3/5 R.G.R. 15-17 MAR
HQ 3/5 R.G.R. 18 MAR
ONWARDS

JAP BLOCK ESTABLISHED
15 MAR. WITHDRAWN 27 MAR

100

3/3 G.R. LINK UP WITH
17 IND. DIV. 28 MAR.

102

3/5 R.G.R. LESS ONE COY
RELIEVE COY 9 JATS 15
MAR. WITHDRAWN TO
MS 98 ON 17-18 MAR.

17 IND. DIV.
NORTH FROM

WITHDRAWING
TIDDIM

BATTLE OF THE
ROAD BLOCKS

LY

built defences, so that the only practicable method was to overwhelm them by an infantry attack if enough infantry survived the approach.

At this moment, while the company was straining to complete the first task, the enemy put in a vicious counter-attack against its right flank. This was repelled after fierce fighting by Company H.Q. with the aid of the reserve platoon, and all the time the forward troops fought furiously to reduce the last bunker. Their task would have been eased had it been possible to communicate with the tanks and so bring their urgently needed fire to bear on the right place, but the troop commander's tank had been put out of action by a suicide squad who were all killed, and the two surviving tanks wandered about as though blindfolded. The battle raged in all for nearly two hours, and during this period a series of attacks was pressed home with the company commander, who earned a gallant M.C., always to the fore. The Gurkhas were not to be denied; by 0915 hrs. they had closed to within ten yards of the enemy; grenades burst in the bunker and there was silence from the Japs.

It was not long after this that "C" Company reported they were in control of the left side of Fir Tree Hill after an advance which met only light resistance, but the battle was far from over. When a demolition party tried to blow in that last hard-won bunker, they were driven off the top by snipers before they could lay their charges. Fir Tree Hill remained a very unhealthy spot; the enemy, not many yards away, were ready to shoot at any target, and the intermittent arrival of shells and mortar bombs made life continuously uncomfortable as the Gurkhas dug in.

Nightfall came without 3/10 G.R. having to repel a second counter-attack, but though they held their gains, the Brigade was as far off as ever from being able to exploit this success. Quite early in the battle, the morning road patrol of carriers had run into a fresh block at M.S. 96.7. The carriers had escaped partly through the quick wit and courage of a naik who stood up and blazed away at the Japs with his tommy-gun while he ordered the crews to drive out of the trap at top speed. Bde. H.Q., which moved up to M.S. 93 with 3/3 G.R. during the day, had sent a company of this battalion up to M.S. 96 as soon as they heard of the block. The company succeeded in overcoming the opposition there, but as they turned back the Japs swooped upon them from out of the jungle and a savage hand-to-hand struggle ensued in which there was no room for manœuvre and every man fought for himself. All the Gurkhas could do was to hack their way out to the north, leaving the road littered with their own and the enemy dead. "A" Company, 3/5 R.G.R., made two efforts late on the 22nd to remove the block from the south, and the battalion attempted a two-company assault on the 23rd; but the air support was late, and when it came the strike hit some of our troops so that the attack was stillborn. Thus 37 Bde., having staged a set-piece attack towards the south, were faced with the prospect of laying on a second in the opposite direction.

Had it not been for the advent of air supply, this battle of the road blocks, where the enemy was continually sand-wiched between our forward troops and their base, could hardly have continued. Troops coming on to air supply for the first time were reasonably nervous, but once they had seen the containers floating out of the sky they went into battle with full confidence that they need not be looking over their shoulders. It was on the 21st, when the mainten-ance convoy failed to arrive, that 37 Bde. sent in their first call, and they heard within a few hours that their demand for water and ammunition would be met on the next day. Their comment, "a most encouraging piece of co-operation," reveals appreciation and relief. Sure enough, on the 22nd the Dakotas came over, and when, that evening, two of the battalions were known to be cut off there was no hesitation in repeating the demand. They were to need their supplies as three more days were to pass before the road was again cleared, and during that time, quite apart from the exhaus-tion of ammunition stocks, many must have come near dying of thirst.

All through the night of March 22nd/23rd, the forward companies of 3/10 G.R. were engaged in repelling con-tinuous enemy attacks, and in the early morning light a heavy assault on a detachment holding a small knoll just east of the main road ended in the Gurkhas being thrust back. This success exposed the Fir Tree Hill position, but "C" Company scraped together a tiny counter-attack force of two sections

under a havildar. Dashing across the road, which was swept
by machine-gun fire, he led his men through the jungle until
he was behind the knoll; from there he carried out a fine
assault which drove off the Japs, and on the feature he
remained until a less hastily organized force of two "D"
Company platoons came up to complete the removal of the
enemy. It had been from the start and was still stern battling,
as the General appreciated when he sent a letter, dropped by
air on the 23rd, in which he wrote to the Brigadier: "Well
done all of you. I am very pleased with what you are all
achieving." He added that the object henceforth was not so
much speed as the extermination of every Jap there was
between 17 Div. and the Brigade.

It was not easy for 37 Bde. to be more than the anvil on
which the hammer of 17 Div. fell. Two of their battalions
had fought fierce battles which had cost considerable losses,
and one of these was at full stretch holding off the Jap, who
made renewed attempts to break through the 3/10 G.R.
defences on the night of March 23rd/24th; further, they
had the enemy in their vitals, and until he was removed
from M.S. 96 there was not a man to spare for any move
south. As it was, there were barely enough troops, as
appeared on the evening of the 24th when 3/10 G.R. were
withdrawn from Fir Tree Hill to strengthen the 3/5 R.G.R.
position at M.S. 98.

All day there had been more savage fighting, this time
for the ejection of the enemy at M.S. 96. While part of 3/3
G.R. with two troops of tanks made a recce in force from
the north, two companies of 3/5 R.G.R. and a troop of
tanks attacked from the south, and it was on these companies
that the brunt of the battle fell; they were supported by the
guns of 6 Fd. Bty., which fired five hundred rounds during
the day, and by the battalion 3-inch mortars. The ground
over which the 3/5 attack went was on the west of the road—
hilly jungle as usual, with the Jap holding two successive
ridges.

The advance began at 1000 hrs. when two platoons of
"D" Company moved off to assault the first ridge, while a
"C" Company platoon pushed out east of the road, where it
remained throughout the action protecting the right flank.
On the ridge a hot fire fight developed, the Japs on the more

northerly hill bringing to bear fierce and accurate fire which pinned the Gurkhas to the ground. The artillery F.O.O., while directing the guns, fell mortally wounded, the lines back to the mortars were frequently cut, and the Japs lashed out in a furious counter-attack at the left-hand platoon. This was driven back twenty yards, but without the subedar who had been in command; as the Japs charged, he stood his ground trying to rally his men. His body was found riddled with wounds when, a little later, the company commander brought up two sections for a counter-thrust. The lost ground was regained, but, with the impetus gone out of the attack, both the assaulting platoons were held as in a vice by 1145 hrs.

At this point it was decided to make the attempt to bring up the tanks on to the first ridge. The ascent was precipitous, the ground strewn with logs; according to the text-books, no tank should have come near the top, but two of the three did and on went the attack with another platoon deployed on each flank wide of those that were held. On the left the ground was swept by fire and the fresh platoon was held; on the right, where the tanks were giving support, there was slight progress. It would have been faster, but the tanks lost direction, and once more there was the difficulty of communicating with them; on this occasion they were only put on the right line of advance by the personal efforts of the infantry commander, who was to gain a bar to his M.C. for his fine leadership, and the tank squadron commander. Pursuing the tanks on foot, continually a target for the enemy, they diverted them back to the axis of the attack where they could again help the infantry. In the end, the right platoon fought their way round on to the crest and by this threat to the enemy flank enabled the rest of the force to gain the objective. During the consolidation a naik, directing the mortars like a veteran, broke up an enemy counter-attack while it was still at a distance; this N.C.O., one of several to gain the M.M., had instinctively taken the place of an F.O.O. wounded during the battle and was personally responsible for repairing cut lines besides directing fire. This is not the last story there will be of junior N.C.Os. rising to the responsibilities thrust upon them in the heat of an action.

H

It was 1630 hrs. on the 24th and another day of hard fighting was over. There seemed no end to this slogging match in grilling heat, especially when the news came through that the Jap had established another road block to the north of 49 Bde. at M.S. 72, which meant air supply for both brigades. The day brought one ray of comfort—letters and newspapers were dropped after a ten-day break, but there were many who were not alive to receive their mail as the end of this battle of the road blocks approached for, despite appearances to the contrary, the heavy fighting was over.

When 3/10 G.R. took over from the 3/5 R.G.R. companies on the 25th and resumed the advance against some bunkers that had not been reduced, the Japs had no stomach for a further combat and ran for safety. The final attack on the M.S. 96 block was due the next day, but the enemy preferred not to wait for a further taste of the Gurkhas' fighting qualities. To tie up final details for this attack, the tank commander, whose fearlessness throughout the Tiddim road battle gained him his first D.S.O., had decided that he would try to break through the block from south to north with an officer patrol from 3/10 G.R. during the night of the 25th/26th. His success made it clear that little resistance was to be expected; 3/3 G.R. moved early on the 26th and the Brigade was again united shortly after midday. By now the Japs were pulling out from the area of Fir Tree Hill, which was reoccupied by 3/10 G.R. on the 27th when 3/3 G.R. relieved 3/5 G.R. and began to push south. Though a patrol of 9 Borders from 17 Div. had already reached 37 Bde. by a route east of the road on the 25th, the link-up must be dated to 1700 hrs. on the 28th when 3/3 G.R. met the forward troops of 17 Div. at M.S. 102. As they passed through on the 29th, they signalled to the Gurkhas: "All black cats[2] congratulate you on busting road block. Good show. Keep it up and give him no rest." The next day there was for a short while a pleasant reunion by the roadside when 1/3 G.R. and 1/10 G.R. arrived and were greeted by their brother battalions; a few brief greetings and they were off again, followed later in the day by 3/10 G.R. For the time being we were turning our backs on the Tiddim road.

---

[2] The divisional sign of the 17th Indian Division.

The Brigade had fought for nearly a fortnight in a series of fierce engagements which tested the endurance of man to the utmost; none had wavered whatever the danger or the hardship. The wounded faced the prospect of enduring for several days with little medical aid; rations were often short, water was short; in the end men were short and they lacked sleep. The casualties in 3/5 R.G.R. alone totalled two hundred and sixty-eight, a third of the battalion's strength, and when the Jap began to pull out there was no force left to pursue and to hammer him. By then the task for which 37 Bde. had hastened down the Tiddim road was well-nigh complete; the Gurkhas had acquitted themselves in a manner worthy of the great traditions of their race.

The final stages of our withdrawal back to the Imphal plain began early on April 2nd after 17 Div., with both our brigades under its wing, had scattered the road block at M.S. 72. 37 Bde. formed the rearguard and by midnight on March 31st were concentrated near M.S. 82, with 3/3 G.R. at M.S. 89 ready to fence off the Jap follow-up. A quarter of an hour after midnight on the 2nd, the best part of an enemy battalion marched negligently down the road into this position and withdrew in some disorder after they had received treatment from the Gurkhas. More good work by 3/3 G.R. in a company ambush on the evening of the 2nd shortly before they withdrew so checked the Jap that the getaway from M.S. 82 on the 3rd was not as worrying as it might have been.

He had shelled the area for two hours on this and the previous morning and his guns, outranging ours, had caused losses, the commander of 71 Ind. Fd. Coy. being among the killed; he must also have seen 3/3 G.R. move back to join the Brigade, and he cannot have failed to see the smoke rising into the sky as dumps were burnt, but there was no hot pursuit. 3/3 G.R., with grand stamina, reached the main body at 1530 hrs. after an all-night march, part of it over appallingly rough country where demolitions compelled detours. An hour and a half later they were again trudging determinedly down the road, for the Brigadier, after waiting, as ordered, until the last stores' lorry left M.S. 82, chose to start the move back at 1700 hrs. when it was broad daylight; he relied on his recent experiences of a lack of inquisitiveness in our foe, and if he were proved wrong, he preferred to fight by day rather than take a chance in a mêlée by night. Had the Japs followed up, and found a way round 3/10 G.R. who formed the new rearguard, they would have come upon a force entangled in a large traffic jam which formed soon after the move started and caused the commander some last moments of anxiety.

On the 4th, a day of heavy rain which reduced the road to a mud trap and caused more weariness to tired men as they pushed lorries out of quagmires, the Brigade reached M.S. 41 to time; there they were met by the General and at last had a moment's rest before they fell back at 1845 hrs. on the 6th to hold positions between M.S. 37 and 32 while 49 Bde., with 2 Hybad under command, were completing temporary defences at M.S. 30. There was a great event on the night of April 7th/8th when a 3/3 G.R. patrol bagged the Division's first prisoner, a fitting end to the Gurkhas' fine work before they passed through 49 Bde. on the 8th after a few hours' delay caused by a final Jap attack. This left the Japs free to occupy the high ground overlooking M.S. 30, and from there they shelled 49 Bde. and caused further casualties, including serious losses to the survey party of 3 Ind. Fd. Regt., before the Brigade passed on the night of April 15th/16th within the Bishenpur defences. We had done with the Tiddim road; our future tasks lay on other parts of the front.

It is a truism to say that no large-scale battle can be fought unless the administrative services are working at full pressure behind the front line. The men who drive lorries and turn spanners rarely come into the limelight and they cannot point to a long list of honours and awards for gallantry. That is their misfortune, but they are none the less an integral part of the battle. As long as the road remained open, the vehicles of the transport companies were jolting along the Tiddim road to M.S. 82 and the provost were out manning control posts to keep the traffic moving over a route that was one-way for most of the last forty miles.

It was important to avoid breakdowns on such a road and E.M.E. provided two mobile repair trucks equipped with the more normal types of spares; these trucks were on continuous patrol, and if the breakdown was beyond their resources, a wireless message brought a recovery vehicle to the spot. There were other vehicles besides crocks on the convoys that needed recovery; between M.S. 82 and the Imphal plain there were about two hundred and seventy assorted army lorries with defects of varying seriousness. While the battle raged a few miles ahead, C.I.E.M.E.[3] set to work to move back and restore to order those that could be made to work. All the extra recovery vehicles that Corps could find were put under his command and the task of repair and recovery began, only to be interrupted when the Japs appeared at M.S. 72 at a time when every recovery vehicle was south of the block. A total of sixty-four vehicles was put back on the road, the remainder being destroyed before the withdrawal began. There was another call for skilled E.M.E. personnel when several of the 37 Bde. wireless sets proved unequal to the strain of warfare in the jungle. So bad were communications after the cut at M.S. 72 that Div. H.Q. misinterpreted the battle for a time until a mechanic was flown in by light plane to effect urgently needed repairs—incidentally, this construction of a small forward landing ground was our first experience of a technique that was developed later in the campaign into a principal method for evacuating wounded.

Drivers, mechanics, provost and medical staffs all discharged their appointed functions and, as was likely in a battle that flared up in unexpected places, some were called on to prove, and did prove, that they were good soldiers besides being efficient at their specialist tasks. One or two won decorations, among them an E.M.E. sergeant, awarded the M.M., and the medical officer of 3/5 R.G.R. who won the M.C. for his tireless devotion to duty while he tended the wounded for hour after hour in an improvised dressing station which was often under gunfire and sometimes a target for snipers from the jungle.

---

[3] Commander Indian Electrical and Mechanical Engineers (Lieut.-Colonel).

CHAPTER 13

Sangshak

THE story of Sangshak will live in the annals of 4 Mahratta, who had been left behind in the Ukhrul area, as 50 Para. Bde., under Brigadier Hope-Thomson, had only two battalions. They were a little disconsolate on the evening of March 16th, by which time the rest of 49 Bde. had left for the Tiddim road, because they felt they had been left out of the impending battle. Reports had come in from "V" Force on the 14th that their posts facing Homalin had been forced back, and their C.O. said on the 16th that he was sure that the Jap intended something more than a Wingate raid; but the impression persisted that the Mahrattas had been left to fight off a diversion while their comrades of 49 Bde. fought a pitched battle. The reverse occurred. For eight days in that wild hill country south of Ukhrul an action was fought against great odds, and the brunt fell on the C.O. and men of 4 Mahratta, the only experienced battalion. They carried the burden without faltering.

Early on the morning of March 19th, news came that the Japs were on the move four miles away from our forward troops. Unpleasant as it was for a brigade to have to face an attack so soon in a country strange to them, it was the worse because 50 Para. Bde.'s concentration was not complete. 152 Para. Bn. held the southerly position vacated by 4 Mahratta, with "B" Company right on the feature known as Gammon, "D" Company left on Pt. 7378, and the H.Q. and "A" Company on Pt. 7386, which was called Badger. 4 Mahratta lay half-way between this battalion and Sangshak at Kidney Camp with a mortar troop of 158 Fd. Regt., the Kali Bahadur Regt. were at Sangshak, and a skeleton Bde. H.Q. with 15 Bty. of 28 Mtn. Regt. at M.S. 36 on the Imphal road. The machine-gun company of 50 Para. Bde. was sent to Ukhrul as soon as it arrived on the 19th, but

The terrain is a mass of jungle covered mountains intersected by deep ravines

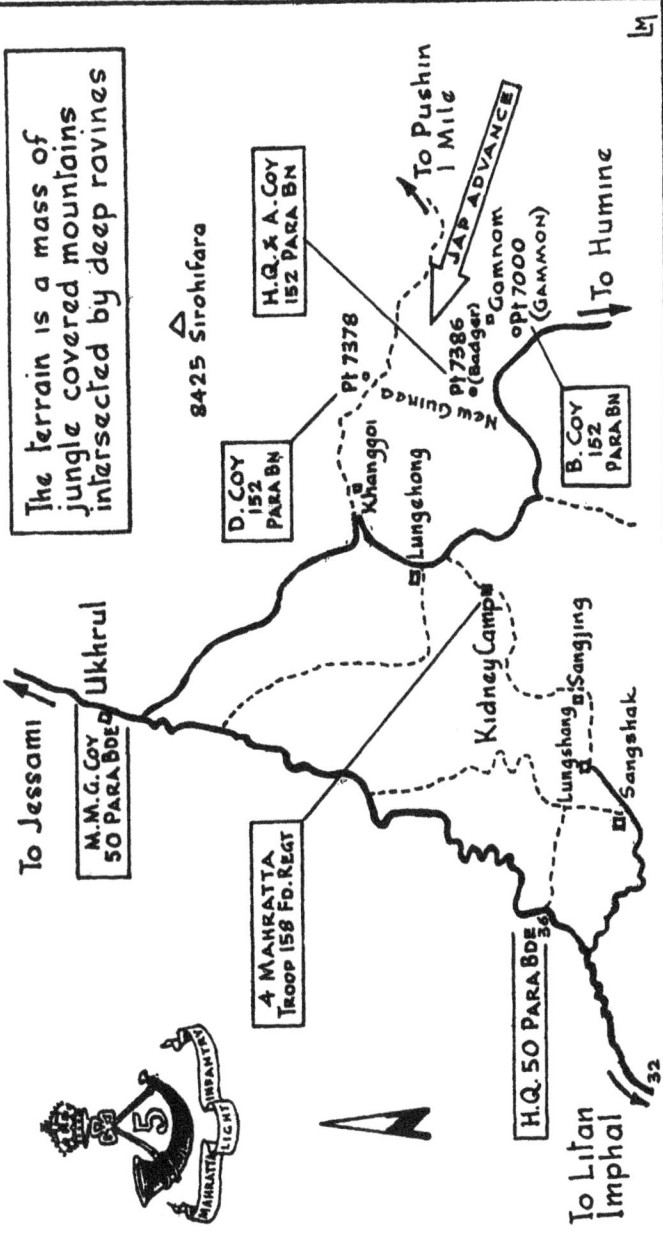

To Jessami

Ukhrul

M.M.G. Coy 50 PARA BDE

4 MAHRATTA Troop 158 Fd. Regt

H.Q. 50 PARA BDE

To Litan Imphal

8425 △ Sirohifara

D. COY 152 PARA BN

Khanggoi

Lungchong

Kidney Camp

Lungshang

Sangjing

Sangshak

H.Q. & A. COY 152 PARA BN

To Pushin 1 Mile

JAP ADVANCE

Pt 7386 (Badger)

New Guinea

Gamnom

Pt 7000 (GAMMON)

B. COY 152 PARA BN

To Humine

Pt 7378

· SANGSHAK · PHASE I ·

SCALE OF MILES

JEEP TRACKS ----- HILL TRACKS

MAHRATTA LIGHT INFANTRY

153 Bn. did not reach Litan until the afternoon of the 20th; by then the battle was raging.

When the message came on the 19th, the C.O. of 4 Mahratta, Lieut.-Colonel J. H. Trim, was sent up to "Badger." Before leaving his battalion, he ordered the removal of all but essential stores back to Litan and the destruction of such as could not be shifted, and he moved "D" Company to the Lungehong ridge to protect his northern flank and to threaten any of the enemy who slipped past Pt. 7378 and made for Ukhrul. When he reached "Badger," he could see away to the north a column of squat figures climbing up the winding track from Pushin. The Jap deployed immediately against Pt. 7378, and by the time the Brigadier came forward a hot attack was in progress. As it was still felt this was nothing more than a Jap raiding party, the reserve company of 152 Bn. was sent on a wide encircling move to take the enemy in the rear by coming up the Pushin track. "A" Company, 4 Mahratta, was ordered up to "Badger" to provide a fresh reserve, and "D" Company was moved north to Khanggoi with twelve hours' rations as no more were available. Darkness came, the Mahratta moves were complete, but "A" Company, 152 Bn., had vanished.

At 0300 hrs. on the morning of the 20th the telephone bell rang in the office of 4 Mahratta at Kidney Camp. The latest message from "Badger" was far from reassuring—this might be a Jap raiding party, but it had attacked Pt. 7378 in sufficient force to overrun part of the defences. The C.O. of 152 Bn. was proposing to send "A" Company, 4 Mahratta, to the relief of Pt. 7378 along the track that had been hacked through "New Guinea," and he called for yet another company to provide a fresh reserve. The Mahrattas watched "C" Company go off into the dark with misgiving, for their troops were disappearing in driblets, and as they heard the sounds of the night battle, they began to wonder whether they were not facing rather more than a raid.

The "A" Company attack was finely pressed home, but was from the start little more than a forlorn hope. The Company came upon the Japs astride the track after they had gone about half a mile, and as the commander looked at the position where the enemy held the higher ground and, though not dug in, had found considerable cover from fallen trees, he resolved that a "blitz" attack offered the only hope of success.

The attack went best on the left of the road, where the Jemadar platoon commander, faced with a hundred-yard advance, held his fire until within fifteen yards of the enemy and had a large part himself in silencing two L.M.Gs. After gaining this objective, he was ordered to turn across the track and attack a knoll, ten yards away, from which the Japs were holding up the right platoon. Three times he led his men at the steep-faced cutting on the farther side of the track, which was swept by fire; the third time he fell severely wounded, but he lay there giving orders until he lost consciousness. He was hauled away by his runner, a lance-naik, who, caring nothing for bullets, returned to drag back another wounded man and was himself wounded as he did so. Back he went again to the road to hurl grenades and fire his tommy-gun until his ammunition was exhausted, when he shouted abuse at the enemy and encouragement to his platoon before he was ordered out of the fray.

Well might the commander write: "The chaps were splendid. They went in just as if they were on a training scheme. They couldn't have been better." Yet gallantry of a high order which earned a M.C. for the Jemadar and a M.M. for his runner was of no avail. A third of a weak company had been hit, several by tree snipers, of which five were brought to earth with a tommy-gun by the eagle-eyed second-in-command, and more by grenades which the enemy lobbed down from above. The company was held, and as they reorganized and replenished ammunition, they saw that the Japs were already feeling round their flanks; there was nothing to be done save withdraw.

Lieut.-Colonel Trim and Colonel Abbott, the Brigade second-in-command, were on "Badger" at this time. They had left Kidney Camp together about 0915 hrs. shortly after the news had come in that most of Pt. 7378 had fallen, whereupon the Brigadier had ordered forward such of 4 Mahratta as had not yet been committed and the mortar battery. The situation was not encouraging when they reached "Badger," for the Japs were by now holding the whole of Pt. 7378, and the sounds of battle from "New Guinea" showed that "A" Company was hotly engaged;

but as they looked towards the north they saw troops toiling up the hill from Pushin. The unexpected appearance of the lost counter-attack company was indeed welcome and gave fresh hope that the Japs might be ejected from their gains. A plan to achieve this was made requiring co-ordinated attacks by "A" Company, 152 Bn., and "A" and "D" Companies, 4 Mahratta. The difficulty was to establish communication, for the low-powered 48 sets, which were all the companies had, were often useless amid the hills and jungle.

All hope of putting in this attack vanished a little after 1300 hrs. when "A" Company, 4 Mahratta, signalled "I am being forced to withdraw and am being followed up by an enemy battalion." The news could not have been more ill-timed, coming as it did at the moment when the rest of 4 Mahratta was filing up on to "Badger." Lieut.-Colonel Trim, who was at once put in command of all troops on "Badger" by Colonel Abbott, ordered "A" Company to hold on as long as possible, sent the mortars to their aid, and told all to dig as they had never dug before. There was only one entrenching tool to every third man and those that had none used bayonets or any implement that could scratch a hole. Officers and men dug for their lives, and in a remarkably short space of time the force began to disappear below ground while "A" Company withdrew through a series of "lay-back" positions at each of which they hammered the oncoming Japs. It was 1615 hrs. when the Company and the mortars fell back within the main position, and by the skill and determination of their withdrawal they had given the diggers just the time necessary to organize and prepare adequate defences. The Japs looked at the position, decided against an immediate attack and left "Badger" unmolested all night, preferring to test the strength of "Gammon," where "B" Company, 152 Bn., beat off the attack without difficulty. "A" Company, 152 Bn., had been ordered to stand firm for the night on the feature they were occupying a little to the north of Pt. 7378.

That evening the Brigadier, anxious about the maintenance of his forward troops, had asked for an air drop of water, ammunition and supplies on "Badger." The demand was accepted and the Brigadier also received general instructions that he must form a defensive box as the attack seemed much more formidable than expected. In pursuance of this policy, he decided to concentrate his whole force on a feature known as "Finch's Corner," some five or six miles south of Sangshak, and he sent a liaison officer to "Badger" early on the 21st, asking Lieut.-Colonel Trim to send his plan for a withdrawal on the night of March 21st/22nd. Lieut.-Colonel Trim decided on Kidney Camp as the rendezvous for the troops under his command; those on "Gammon" and "Badger" were to move along a recently made jungle track, and "A" Company, 152 Bn., through Khanggoi, where they were to pick up "D" Company, 4 Mahratta, who were still out of touch by wireless. This plan was accepted.

During the day the equipment and reserve ammunition was carefully distributed into man loads, orders were issued and such other preparations were made for the night as were possible without attracting the eye of the Jap. The enemy, whom a patrol found to be very active on Pt. 7378, did not show a similarly inquisitive spirit about "Badger." Maybe he was deceived when some Dakotas flew over the spot in the afternoon and dropped a complete first-line lift of ammunition —good if unintentional deception, but most disheartening for men who, in the absence of transport, were already carrying full loads and had the exhausting task of collecting and burying the drop. Whatever be the reason, he was certainly not about when the mortar troop, who could not have managed the route by night, slipped away at 1630 hrs.

No night withdrawal in such country could be easy; the route was narrow and ill-defined so that it was only too easy for men to lose touch, it was a pitch dark, moonless night and the track was often steep. As on the Tiddim road, the stretcher-bearers carrying the wounded had a particularly arduous time, but all were heavily ladened. The prospect was not inviting and when, at 2015 hrs., firing broke out around the perimeter, it seemed that there might be something much worse on hand than a night move over difficult country. The firing died down, but the night was disturbed by fresh sounds of fighting farther afield to the west. All eyes turned towards Sangshak, which was on the line of withdrawal—the western sky was aflame with the blaze of its burning buildings and the flash from tracer and the flicker from exploding mortar bombs lit up the night. There was no means of finding out what had happened, there was nothing to tell that the Jap would not reappear, perhaps in force. The minutes dragged by; midnight, 0100, 0200—the withdrawal began. Within half an hour the timed programme was complete and "Gammon" and "Badger" were left to the enemy.

The only alarm on the first stage of the withdrawal occurred as the leading troops, a party of 4 Mahratta somewhat dubiously termed the advanced guard, approached Kidney Camp on the morning of the 22nd. These saw a party coming out of the jungle from the south and could not distinguish from a distance whether they were friend or foe. All that mattered was to seize the high ground above the camp and for this the Mahrattas and the leading troops of 152 Bn. made at the double. As they gained the crest, they found that others were there before them, but there was to be no battle—"A" Company, 152 Bn., had arrived through Khanggoi and, as the party emerging from the jungle turned out to be the mortar troop, all was well.

Gradually the force collected, all except "D" Company, 4 Mahratta, of which there had been no trace at Khanggoi, and Lieut.-Colonel Trim sought to resume contact with Bde. H.Q. before moving farther, in view of the blaze seen in the night. This took a little time as it was discovered that the Adjutant's clerk, while burning secret papers, had also destroyed the cipher key, so that there was for a time a stream of meaningless messages in code until Bde. H.Q. realized the truth. In the end a message came "Join me here at all cost—way clear." "Here" was assumed to be "Finch's Corner," and at 1400 hrs. on March 22nd the force moved on, with 152 Bn. in the lead. As they started, an officer arrived from Brigade with a small party sent to cover the withdrawal from Kidney Camp, and they had come in transport. The transport was a great boon to tired men and was eagerly seized on for carrying wounded, mortars, and equipment; but more important than the relief thus afforded was the news that the site of the Brigade box had been changed to Sangshak. So to Sangshak marched 4 Mahratta and 152 Bn. less their company which had been destroyed on Pt. 7378; they arrived about 1630 hrs. to find the battle of Sangshak had begun.

It was as well that there had been no trace of "D" Company, 4 Mahratta, at Khanggoi. They had seen the overrunning of Pt. 7378 on the 20th, and as they could make no contact with Bn. H.Q., the commander decided to move back to Lungehong to try his wireless there. From Lungehong, the Company had an excellent though distant view of the 4 Mahratta Q.M. destroying surplus ammunition and stores, but as they knew nothing of his orders, they assumed a battle royal was in progress at Kidney Camp. Patrols which visited the place later reported that it was deserted and most dangerous as ammunition was continually exploding, so the commander, still unable to contact his unit, made for Bde. H.Q. on the Litan road. After hearing there of the move to "Badger," he filled in part of the 21st at his own suggestion by laying a successful ambush on the Ukhrul road down which the Japs were advancing on the heels of the retiring M.M.G. Company. The next day the Company rejoined Bde. H.Q., which had moved on the 21st with 153 Bn. to the area of Sangshak, where there had been a night skirmish—hence the blaze in the dark.

Shortly after the Company arrived, Colonel Abbott decided that it was necessary to hold the high ground south of the village until the box to the north-east had been organized, and he assigned the task to "D" Company, supported by two mortar detachments of 4 Mahratta. As the commander neared the crest of the ridge, he had a presentiment that trouble might be brewing, and he hastened forward with his leading platoon and the mortar officer. There, a few yards the other side of the crest, was a Jap section bent on the same task as himself. The Mahrattas were quicker on the draw, the Japs were sent bowling down the hill, and the mortars, admirably handled, dispensed with preliminary ranging and came into action just in time to break up an attack by the leading Jap platoon. "D" Company's quickness stunned the enemy and gave time to organize a defensive position which held firm until the Company was withdrawn at dusk, when it went into battalion reserve. Colonel Abbott said later that he had rarely seen a company better handled, and the award of the

M.C. to the commander was but just recognition of his courage and resource.

The force from "Badger" arrived as this action was in progress and found that the unexpected appearance of the enemy had created a degree of confusion in the box area. The guides who met the column were uncertain where the units were to go, there was no one about to ask, and only after Lieut.-Colonel Trim had searched for the Brigade Major did he learn that the Mahrattas were to occupy the southern part of the perimeter, where the Kali Bahadur Regt. had already dug a number of trenches. This reduced the digging needed except in the "B" Company position, but there was plenty of other work to be done and all sensed that time was short. Fields of fire were cut through the jungle, "panjis" prepared in place of wire, and booby traps placed in those of the Kali Bahadur trenches which lay outside the perimeter. There was no time to fill in these trenches, which presented an obvious danger.

When nightfall came, the Mahrattas were firmly ensconced though the other battalions had not made the same progress—an example of the value of training and battle experience which enabled the Mahrattas to dominate and hold the defence together. Fortunately, the Jap selected the Mahratta position for their first attacks, which went on incessantly throughout the night of March 22nd/23rd. They formed up in the disused trenches, where some of the booby traps failed to go off, and hammered away at "B" Company, switched to "C" Company and were again repulsed, met equally stern resistance from "A" Company, and made a final effort at the junction of this Company and the Kali Bahadur Regt. before pulling out as dawn crept into the sky. The mortar troop of 158 Fd. Regt. gave fine support all through the night. On the "C" Company front, where there had been no previous ranging, the company commander took on the task of F.O.O. himself, and when the first bomb fell beyond the Japs, he ordered "Down two hundred yards." The mortar officer at Mahratta H.Q. protested vigorously to the C.O.: "Damn it all, sir! I am firing at 300 yards now and my minimum range is 250 yards!" The company commander had his way, the range came down 100 yards and the attack was dispersed. During the battle, while the ground between the Mahrattas and Bde. H.Q. was continuously swept by fire, two of the "D" Company platoons went to and fro bringing up ammunition from the Brigade reserve—a vital, but inconspicuous and nerve-racking task. The casualties for the night were only five wounded: in battle it pays to dig.

Div. H.Q. had only occasional glimpses of these events, and the cause was always the same—the wireless sets were inadequate for a country where the hills formed barriers and atmospheric conditions caused fade-outs each night. There had been a fairly full report of the earlier events on the 20th, including an estimate that the enemy force amounted to two battalions, on which a troop of tanks had been sent to the rear base at Litan and 2/1 Punjab, the leading battalion of 123 Bde., were put at one hour's notice to move up to the same place. Communications were open the next day, when an order went through to stock up while the road was still clear, but there was complete silence from 0001 hrs. on March 22nd. It was not until 1800 hrs. that evening that the veil was partly lifted with the news that Bde. H.Q., 153 Bn. and the Kali Bahadur Regt., were at Sangshak, while the force from "Badger" was on its way. Meanwhile 2/1 Punjab had been ordered up earlier in the day to Litan, which had been raided by a jitter party the previous evening.

The site selected for the box in the jungle north-east of Sangshak was far from ideal as there was within the box no clearing to drop supplies and no source of water. There was a small spring to the north, but that was four hundred yards away, and there was water in Sangshak village, but that was very much in enemy territory. Hence, besides attention to the defences, a search for further springs was urgently undertaken on the morning of the 23rd. Two were found on the Kali Bahadur and one on the Mahratta front, but all were small and outside the perimeter; though the Mahrattas were thereby enabled to provide some sort of a cooked meal for the first time for three days, the outlook was unpromising, especially as rations were not plentiful. A dump which had been left on the road outside during the night and had survived the battle was added to the store, but its usefulness was limited because these rations were for cooking and needed water. The daring of the Mahratta mess havildar brought another small increase, including the priceless acquisition of a little gin. It so happened that the Mahratta mess truck had been caught in the battle the previous evening while on its away to Litan, and the havildar, unwilling to see precious stores fall to the Jap, sallied forth to Sangshak with the cooks, a sweeper and a Goanese wine-waiter and rescued the contents of the truck, despite Japanese bullets.

All day on the 23rd there was a snipers' war with intermittent straffing of the "box," and dusk had hardly set in when the enemy assailed the Mahrattas in full fury, once more without the least success. As dawn came on the 24th, the Japs again pulled out and left the box in its isolation, for there was not yet a close siege. The Brigadier spoke at his morning conference of taking the offensive towards Sangshak, but felt he must know more about the enemy first. All night long watchers from the higher points of the box had seen a stream of hurricane lamps moving up past "Gammon" and "Badger" and had heard the sound of vehicles. The garrison of Sangshak, without news of the outside world, did not know that many of these troops were bound for Kohima, and felt that it could not be long before they were subjected to an overwhelming onslaught. Patrols were therefore sent to Kidney Camp, Sangshak and "Finch's Corner."

There was that morning an air drop of ammunition, and a heart-breaking sight it was as many of the parachutes floated away outside the box. Sangshak lies on top of a ridge and some considerable number were wafted away into the valleys miles below, while others which landed near at hand became the occasion of skirmishes between the Japs and ourselves; in the end barely a quarter of the ammunition was collected. The awkwardness of the dropping zone and the high wind was one cause of this depressing inaccuracy, but air supply was still in its infancy and, though one pilot was successful, the rest were inexperienced and had to acquire the skill which later came to be accepted as commonplace.

Meanwhile, it became increasingly evident that the Japs were resolved on the destruction of the garrison. About 1230 hrs. a long column was seen moving up from the east,

SANGSHAK · PHASE 2

LUNGSHANG

JAP POSN & ARTY

PUSHIN

KALI BAHADUR REGT

HQ 50 PARA BDE
HQ 4 MAHRATTA
153 PARA BN

A.COY
C.COY
H.Q.COY.
4 MAHRATTA
D.COY
B.COY

STEEP 3000 FT. ESCAPE ROUTE OF NIGHT 26-27 MAR.

FD. AMB
MMG COY
74 Ind Fd Coy

15 BTY. 28 MTN.REGT
TP 581 FD. BTY R.A.
152 PARA BN

SANGSHAK

JAP POSN

LITAN
IMPHAL

and half an hour later a gun started to fire from somewhere south of the village. A request for an air strike was accepted and three hours later over came the Hurricanes, who caught the column near Kidney Camp. A second strike was made on the enemy who had begun to close in east and west of the box and on the gun, which the aircraft spotted and destroyed. It was all wonderfully heartening for the men, who sat on top of their trenches and cheered as the aircraft swooped low over the box, but they were sent scurrying for shelter as the last Hurricane came in on a slightly different course and attacked the trenches. Some of the defenders say that the Japs had spotted we were using "XVT" direction signs and had devised some of their own, but others feel such intelligence was so abnormal as to be inconceivable.

The key to the Sangshak box was the north-west corner, where a high plateau extended westwards towards a church; this lay outside the main position and formed an obvious danger-point unless it were denied to the Jap. Hence a platoon from "A" Company, 152 Bn., and a section of machine guns formed a small garrison which began to attract the enemy's gaze, and as evening came the weight of his attacks shifted to this area. Four times before midnight parties of Japs managed to penetrate the outpost at the church, but on each occasion the defence mustered enough strength to close the gap. As the night wore on, both the parachute Battalions were involved in the fighting and kept the enemy at arm's length; for the third night the defences had held except that a small party found a lodgement inside the Kali Bahadur position. There was anxiety when a force of fifty, sent to eject the Japs, did not obey their orders and dispersed to section positions, but Lieut.-Colonel Trim was able to restore confidence with the aid of the Assistant States Force Adviser.

By the morning of the 25th all ranks were feeling the strain of lack of water, food and sleep and there seemed to be no end of the ordeal in sight; ammunition was also running short as again only a fraction of the drop fell within the perimeter. The Brigadier was still anxious to put in his attack towards Sangshak and he ordered the Mahrattas to send a further patrol to Kidney Camp as the first had not returned, but the Jap began to tighten his hold and thoughts of defence were uppermost. He had established snipers in the jungle on the front of "A" Company, 4 Mahratta, and so prevented the use of the only springs still flowing, for the other had been exhausted, and he was massing at Sangjing. An attempt to clear the jungle failed and "A" Company had to endure persistent sniping for the rest of the day. As they kept up their watch, pinned in their trenches, there was a sudden outburst of firing and the only unwounded man in the first Mahratta patrol scrambled into the position. He told that the rest lay wounded near the springs, so "A" Company put in a sudden raid and rescued all; the patrol had reached Kidney Camp and found at least a battalion assembled there.

That evening all knew a fresh attack was imminent and they felt they were to undergo a test even sterner than those of previous nights. The Brigadier, in his message to Div. H.Q., expected that the Kali Bahadur would have to endure the onset, but it was not there that the blow fell. The enemy began shelling about 1845 hrs. and directed his fire especially on to the Mountain Battery and Mortar Troop which occupied part of the plateau close to the western edge of the perimeter; by accurate and determined shooting in a stiff artillery duel, the battery commander temporarily stopped the shelling, and it may have been at this time of stress that one of the gunners with the mortar troop saved his detachment when the bombs caught fire after a direct hit. Badly burnt, he fought the flames until they were out and then continued to fire his weapon—the incident remains undated, for when men looked back on the last days at Sangshak, their memories were sometimes vague. The bombardment was the prelude to an all-out onslaught on 152 Bn. and a furious battle raged for some hours while the rest of the box waited. About 0530 hrs. on March 26th the defences broke, the Japs surged in at the north-west corner; one of the guns was overrun and the rest were in the front line.

The Japs were not far from destroying the whole box there and then, and had it not been for the gallantry of the gunners and of two detachments of 4 Mahratta mortars behind the former 152 Bn. position there would have been a disaster in the half-light of the dawning day. It was not these few men's task to hold the perimeter and they could have fallen back as other flanking troops did, but they stayed to hold their ground against great odds when there was little else to bar the way. Here it was that a havildar remained propped up in his post after a bullet had drilled a hole in his chest, and by his encouragement inspired his men to resist until they were relieved. There were other deeds as gallant. Somewhere the gunner whose previous exploit has been mentioned was crawling about with a comrade bringing in wounded, and a Mahratta lance-naik was creeping towards a flag which the Japs had planted at the limit of their penetration to use as a ranging mark. By hugging the ground, he kept out of sight until he reached the flag, which came out with a jerk. The sudden effort exposed the man for a few seconds, but they were enough; he fell riddled with bullets. No less fine was the end of the two officers commanding the guns and mortars as they charged the Jap, firing Brens from the hip, in an effort to recapture the lost gun.

The full light of day revealed the desperate plight of the garrison. The Japs were firmly established on the highest ground in the box and there was chaos elsewhere. As the A.D.S. had to be evacuated, several hundred wounded were wandering about seeking shelter, many of them horribly torn and ghastly to look upon; most crowded into the Mahratta lines, where the R.A.P. was already overwhelmed by recent casualties, filled the H.Q. Company trenches, and when these were full huddled into any hole that could be found. The arrival of the mortar battery added to the confusion in the Mahratta area, where, besides the wounded, a hundred or more dazed and half-crazed men from 152 Bn. strayed helplessly about—and the Jap guns shelled the box persistently. The turmoil was increased when the Dakotas came over for the daily ammunition "drop."

Already the Brigadier had frittered away the two Mahratta reserve platoons in separate counter-attacks, and he was now about to launch part of 153 Bn. As the Mahrattas sought to grapple with the confusion in their midst and to form a box of their own in case the Japs burst through, there were some ugly moments when 153 Bn. began to waver and came streaming back past the gunners, but a hunting horn sounded a rallying call and the captain of the Fd. Regt.

mortars encouraged his men to sing. The rest of the box took up the tune and the danger of an immediate rout passed. When 153 Bn. delivered a second counter-attack, they drove the enemy by hard fighting from all but the western extremity of the plateau, and the Brigadier decided to adjust the perimeter without making a further attack on this hill; he asked the Mahrattas to provide one company as a Brigade reserve. This was used to man the northern part of the defences, where the removal of 153 Bn. to hold some of the 152 Bn. positions left a gap; the Mahrattas filled their own gap with men from H.Q. Company. These readjustments, which included the removal of the guns, were carried out under heavy shelling, but when the Jap artillery was spotted, back went one of the mountain guns into its emplacement. Seventy splendidly accurate rounds fell in the target area while the Japs sniped continuously at the gunners.

Sangshak was by now a shambles. The few buildings in the box were gutted, the trees were many of them blackened stumps; the wounded groaned and cried out for water, the dead lay unburied and the stench from these corpses fouled the air. Occasionally, to keep up morale, there were words of help being on the way, but within him each man felt that he was destined to fight amidst the carnage until his ammunition gave out.

Div. H.Q. was not ignorant that the garrison was in desperate plight. News of the failure of the early counter-attacks came in at 0900 hrs.; an hour later the report was that the Brigade could only hold out for the day with luck; at 1220 hrs. a message sent at 0900 hrs. gave the limit of endurance as two hours. A long silence followed. The next signal received at 1723 hrs. read "troops very tired. Doubt ability to resist further sustained attack. Send help. Very few officers." The G.O.C. had already acted—at 1705 hrs. Div. H.Q. signalled "Fight your way out. Go south then west. Air and transport on the look-out."

It was about 1830 hrs. that Lieut.-Colonel Trim was summoned to Bde. H.Q., where he was shown the message which had arrived in "clear" so that time was short. In the discussion that followed, the main concern was for the wounded. The senior M.O. of 50 Bde. volunteered to stay with them in the hope of persuading the Japs to show mercy, but the Brigadier was not prepared to chance Japanese clemency. In the end Lieut.-Colonel Trim's plan was accepted: the box should move south in its present formation, with the Mahrattas in the lead to clear a way through the Jap positions: units as they split up in the darkness should, if possible, remain a platoon strong: one friend to accompany each wounded man: the move to be south until dawn and then west to the Imphal–Litan road. Ten stretcher cases and one hundred and twenty walking wounded went with the escaping force; the rest, who were more grievously hurt and numbered a hundred, had to be left to their fate.

When Lieut.-Colonel Trim returned to the Mahrattas, he sent for the remains of the gin and, after his officers had assembled, said, amid tense silence, "Gentlemen, at half-past ten to night, at 2230 hours, the Brigade will 'Right turn' and will march out of the box." There was a gasp of incredulity. The enemy were hemming in the force on every side, they had attacked each night from dusk to dawn, they would certainly attack again tonight. Escape under the noses of the enemy? It could not be, and yet . . . slowly the realization came, as the details of the plan were disclosed, that this was not sheer madness. Before the conference ended, the gin was poured out and all drank to a safe journey and the next meeting.

About 2000 hrs. enemy jitter parties began their night's work on the northern part of the perimeter; 2100 . . . 2200— half an hour more of waiting. Still the noise of rifle fire persisted and then, on a sudden, spluttered away into silence. The leading company of the Mahrattas moved to the top of the embankment in front of the box, slithered down the sheer twelve-foot drop, crossed the road and were away into the night. The units waiting their turn to leave listened for the sound they knew must come, but unit after unit disappeared into the darkness without a shot being fired. It was uncanny, unbelievable—and yet it was true. The Japs had pulled back to prepare for a full-scale onslaught and chance directed that the box marched out in the interval. The Japs only realized what was afoot as the last troops were leaving, among them the Mahratta company lent to Brigade as a reserve; many of these were taken prisoner when the Japs charged in with the bayonet.

The escape was not the end of the story of Sangshak. Hundreds of half-starved, battle-weary men were faced with a march over the great jungle ridges, where the enemy were using the main tracks; sent off with only a tin of cheese and two packets of biscuits, few were fortunate enough to have maps or a compass. There were some astonishing feats of endurance. One party of three, all wounded and one very seriously so, staggered in to Manipur Road fifteen days later, having covered a hundred and eighty miles through country continually traversed by Jap columns. Not all could survive the strain, even if they escaped the enemy, and five of another party of eight died on the way to Manipur Road. In the smaller parties leadership told. The sergeant of the mortar battery, by his encouragement and personality, kept up the will-power of a number of severely hurt gunners and brought all to safety, while a young lance-naik in charge of a signal detachment, after hiding at the start, battled through the jungle with his men.

The more fortunate reached Imphal in three days and among these was a large number of 4 Mahratta. Lieut.-Colonel Trim's descent down the embankment had been hasty as a sepoy clutched at his neck at the top and sent him down the slope head first. At the bottom he collected the Bn. H.Q. party, already less the second-in-command, who lost contact while looking for his rifle which he had dropped in the scramble. With the sound of rifle fire from Sangshak behind them, the party pressed on through high elephant grass until 0230 hrs. on the 27th, when they halted for an hour, but so cold was it that they were glad to be moving again despite their weariness. Progress had been very slow during the night, and when dawn came they continued south for some time, thus avoiding the fate of those who turned west too soon and ran back into the Japs, as outbreaks of firing showed.

An hour after dawn they joined up with a H.Q. Company party, and an hour later, just before they turned west and started the exposed 4,000-foot climb to Phalong, the appearance of "D" Company commander with a platoon brought a welcome addition to their strength. Near the village they

learnt from two Nagas that the way was clear, and such was
the surprise when a Jap officer and a Jif appeared on the
summit that the Adjutant, who was with the leading troops,
momentarily stood still and gazed at the officer, who
stood with raised hands, shouting "Fire mat karo.[1]" His
inaction can only have lasted a second, though it seemed an
age in retrospect; he pulled out his pistol and fired, but the
weapon merely gave out a cloud of white powder and a dull
"phut." Other weapons spoke more effectively; the whole
party moved rapidly across the ridge and dived into the
shelter of the jungle on the far side, where the Adjutant
sought for the cause of the misfire. He had been carrying a
tube of toothpaste in his pouch and most of the contents were
down the revolver barrel. There followed a long descent
into a valley, where they harboured for the night after marching almost continuously for nineteen hours; they ate half
their scanty rations and, despite the intense cold, slept for
several hours.

On the move at 0600 hrs. on the 28th, they had marched
for four hours, when they met the "B" Company commander
and twenty of his men. This party had been with many of
the 50 Bde. men the previous night when the Japs discovered
the harbour and set fire to the surrounding jungle. The
Mahrattas had led the dash for safety and broke right
through the enemy cordon without loss, but the rest were not
so fortunate. This incident had upset the commander's
sense of direction and it took Lieut.-Colonel Trim some time
to prove the error before they set off together on the gruelling
climb to Yongphu and Hengyol. There was no shade to
ward off the fierceness of the sun, which dried up bodies
that craved for moisture, and all were near the end of their
strength, but they endured. At each of the villages, the
Nagas were friendly and gave urgently needed water and a
handful of rice to each man, but they told of Japs near by,
so the party pressed on in the wake of the advancing Japs,
as the marks on the track showed.

Beyond Hengyol they met the second-in-command, "A"
Company commander, and another small Mahratta party.
The second-in-command had been alone for some time on
the 27th until he joined up with the H.Q. Company com-

---

[1] Don't fire!

mander, who had also become separated from his party. They were with some of the Kali Bahadur Regiment for a time, but there were suddenly two shots and a cry from the front of "Dushman, dushman,[2]" and all melted into the jungle except the two officers. They decided that no sane enemy would want to be in the middle of nowhere and walked on, but as they rounded the corner there was a bang, followed by another. Both caught a glimpse of a Jap sentry as they dived into the jungle on opposite sides of the stream bed. As the second-in-command had no answer from his brother officer, he set off on his own, with the Japs following behind; when they were tired and halted, he halted, and so the chase went on to the top of a ridge, where the Japs fired a parting shot and gave up the hunt. In the valley beyond he was delighted to meet the "A" Company party and a few of the mortar battery, and with them he set off on a long detour to the south by which they avoided all contact with the Jap. Apart from normal ten-minute halts and an hour's rest at midday on the 27th, after leaving Sangshak they marched continuously for twenty-five hours until 2330 hrs. on the 27th.

Lieut.-Colonel Trim's force, now swollen to three hundred, of which a hundred and eight were Mahrattas, set off from Hengyol to climb to the top of the last mountain ridge before the drop to the Imphal plain. Many were very, very near breaking-point, but they reached the top that evening, harboured and had a little food. At dawn on the 29th they moved on again, were forced into a last detour by the sound of firing ahead, and came out on the road a few miles north of Yaingangpopki. There stood two tanks—and they were British. The ordeal was over—once the tanks, who were suspicious of this wild-looking, ill-kempt mob, had been assured of their identity.

Lieut.-Colonel Trim was quickly taken to Brigadier Evans, commanding 123 Bde. of 5 Div. They had last met at Keren when a very dirty Major Trim had to take a message to the Brigade Major. That Brigade Major, now a Brigadier, surveyed the scallywag in front of him for a while before he said, with a smile, "My dear chap, I see you haven't washed or shaved since I last saw you." Lieut.-Colonel Trim and his

---

[2] Enemy, enemy!

Adjutant were soon passed on to H.Q. 5 Div. and thence to our own H.Q., where they were given a right royal welcome before leaving for Waithou, where the rest of the survivors were gathering. There many could not resist partaking of a richer diet than was wise, and there they learnt for the first time that the rear base at Litan had beaten off heavy attacks on the nights of the 24th and 25th before being withdrawn on the 26th, when 2/1 Punjab fought off the Jap during the move out.

Parties of varying strength continued to arrive during the next few days, among them a considerable number from "C" Company, who had been cut off at the end of the withdrawal. Most of these men had been deprived of their clothing and boots and used as porters, but the Mahratta is fairly content to march without boots and many of the prisoners escaped as their chance came. Few had been savagely treated, though an I.N.A. interpreter with the Japs had stopped a whipping that some were made to undergo for refusing to slaughter and cut up cattle. One of the last to arrive was a subedar whom the Japs watched more closely than the others, but he too found his chance while pretending to help his captors by searching for cigarettes among the ruins of the ordnance depot at Kanglatongbi. He brought with him a little notebook which he had kept throughout and filled with information about the enemy; this formed the basis of several successful air "strikes" and artillery shoots.

Sangshak, like the Gurkha struggle down the Tiddim road, was one of the battles that turned the scales against the Jap, as the Mahrattas learnt when the General and the Corps Commander came on successive days to offer congratulations. In deploying such strength over the tortuous and very inadequate communications through the Naga hills, the Japs had achieved the one complete surprise of their assault on India, and our troops, intended to fight delaying actions at Jessami and Ukhrul, became engulfed in unexpected battles against overwhelming forces. It was 50 Para. Bde.'s misfortune that their first taste of battle should be in this bitter struggle at Sangshak, and it is not surprising that so much depended on 4 Mahratta and their C.O. The resistance at Sangshak was sustained by Lieut.-Colonel

Trim's personal example and leadership and by the courage and steadfastness of his men in an action which gained precious time for the concentration of 4 Corps and the fly-in of formations, and inflicted such losses on the Japanese as seriously to delay and weaken the attack on Kohima.

The Mahratta losses at Sangshak in killed, wounded and missing were about two hundred and sixty, a far lower total than anyone dared to forecast; after a short rest and the arrival of reinforcements, the General revisited the unit and asked when they would be ready for battle. Their reply was "Ready now, sir!" and was a fit rejoinder to a Japanese broadcast which presumably related to the affair at Sangshak. This ran: "The victorious Japanese Imperial Army is forging ahead on its march to Delhi. Few organized British troops are left in Assam. The 23rd Division, the crack division of the Indian Army, has been almost wiped out; its shattered remnants are endeavouring to make their way back through the jungle."

The margin of time to spare had been slight. 123 Bde. were flown in on March 19th and 9 Bde. arrived between March 23rd and 25th; the withdrawal from Sangshak began on the 26th. 123 Bde. were first used to hold the main road to Kohima and to keep it open with motorized patrols, 2 Suffolk fulfilling this task. As soon as the seriousness of the Jap thrust was appreciated, the Brigade was switched to block the Imphal–Litan road, and 9 Bde., on arrival, completed the close defence to the north of Imphal by holding the Kohima road. Both brigades came under their own formation when H.Q. 5 Ind. Div. flew in on the 27th, so the subsequent course of events on the northern approaches forms no part of this book.

CHAPTER 14

Attack At Last

AFTER two chapters ending in withdrawals, it may seem inappropriate to begin a third, headed "Attack at Last," on the same subject, but it is not quite time to turn to the offensive. Though for most of 1 Bde. the retirement from the Kabaw valley between March 14th and 16th went according to the plan—that is as fast as their legs, mules and the lorries of 121 G.T. Coy. could carry them—"B" Company, 1 Patiala, fulfilled with distinction a covering role on the right of the 20 Div. withdrawal at Chamol, and there is a tale to tell of the three patrols left east of the Chindwin.

One of these was never heard of again, but the adventures of another provides a story of resource and determination. After reaching the river and finding no boat sent in answer to signals, the officer in command swam across to contact his unit, which he was naturally unable to locate. As he did not return, the three privates moved off on their own, but only two survived the long swim and these set off westwards together; they were fully equipped as they had made a raft which the stronger swimmer pushed across with the kits aboard, they had their wits and the officer's compass for keeping direction, and they had a biscuit a day. On their way they fell in with a Jif, whom they took prisoner, deprived of his money and used as a guide, and the tale should end with two doughty Seaforth privates reporting back with their capture; but he had to be jettisoned, though the privates won through after a ten-day absence. Later the commander rejoined as well after swimming back to the east bank to search for his men, recrossing to the west, and spending a few days in custody of the Japs, who treated him reasonably well.

As for the company at Chamol, this found ample scope for their Patiala skill in setting ambushes. Twice they allowed enemy parties a platoon strong to come within ten yards, where they delivered a knock-out blow which caused the Japs to pause; and if it came to a close-quarter scrap, the Japs found their masters. The skill and courage of this company played a material part in slowing up the Jap advance for four days.

After its withdrawal, 1 Bde. remained at Wangjing as the only reserve in the Imphal plain during the first phase of the battle, but the concentration of 4 Corps for the close defence of the plain was only the first stage in the battle for India. Even before the final moves were complete, plans were being made for harassing the Jap, and it fell to 1 Bde. to take the leading part in the first of these offensive operations. At the beginning of April, 1 Patiala were sent off into the hills to the east to lay ambushes on an enemy L. of C. which ran up from the head of the Kabaw valley to Sangshak, but this was only the prelude to a more ambitious plan.

Reports said that H.Q. Jap 15 Div. were at Kasom on the road between Litan and Ukhrul, and 1 Bde. were to assault the place and prevent the Japs using the road. There was hope that a surprise flanking march through the hills would lead to the capture of the divisional commander himself, a gentleman who was nicknamed the "Rat" and was reputed to move about with two wives in his entourage. Some said the wives were monkeys, but the dispute could not be settled as in the end the "Rat" escaped, though he was remorselessly harried from place to place. Simultaneously with the 1 Bde. attack, 37 Bde., with 4 Mahratta under command, were to provide the left arm of the pincer by moving up the Imphal–Ukhrul road from Kameng, while 5 Ind. Div. thrust up the Kohima road. As it turned out, the 5 Div. offensive met stiff resistance and developed slowly, but our own operations were a great success.

This was the first time that we had the chance to try out the Jap technique of using jungle tracks for wide flanking movements. The route selected for 1 Bde. led up the Thoubal river to Tumukhong and thence east across the mighty frontier hills to Singkap and so north to Kasom. Some will recall the magnificence of the country—the Ukhrul massif rose into the sky to the north, far below in a valley where a stream glinted in the sun the Seaforths clambered over the rocks, to the west more hills where monkeys chattered persistently in the jungle. There was a tang of adventure to this march through the wilds, but it was very exhausting for men carrying four days' light-scale rations and ammunition. This was a full load, and as it involved leaving blankets behind there was nothing to keep out the cold when tired men halted for the night among the hill tops.

The march began on April 10th and the Brigade, with 16 Mtn. Bty. under command, reached Singkap two days later. From there on the approach had to be by night and the columns stumbled on through the darkness with the mules continually falling through the bridges on the tracks. As the units moved into position in the early hours of the 15th, they could hear the R.A.F. bombing Kasom, and at dawn the Seaforths swept along the spur that runs north-west into the village and scattered the few Japs that remained there. A few minutes later 1/16 Punjab occupied the ridge south of the village. The last two hours of their march had been a nightmare as their Naga guide had missed the route off the main track and the column had to double back and pass the mules of the Mountain Battery before it could regain the right route. In the confusion Bde. H.Q. became separated. Eventually 1/16 Punjab found themselves in a village, where their sudden appearance roused a host of dogs, pigs, chickens and ducks, failed to find the exit and clambered up a sheer hill face, hoping that the din below had not roused the enemy; in the climb one of the guides was shot in the leg. It was fortunate that the ridge was unoccupied. As a company of Patialas sent to form a road block north of Kasom reached their objective without opposition, the operation can be recorded as a complete success and was over within a very few minutes with little loss. We had proved we could play the Jap at his own game.

The Japs recovered quickly from this surprise assault and did all they could to eject the Seaforths from Kasom. During the day there were two attacks and the weight fell on "B" Company, who held a small hill above the village. The first effort came long before there had been time to dig in properly and one section in particular had to bear the brunt. The sergeant in command was wounded, but his courage dominated the battle, and when the Japs put in a

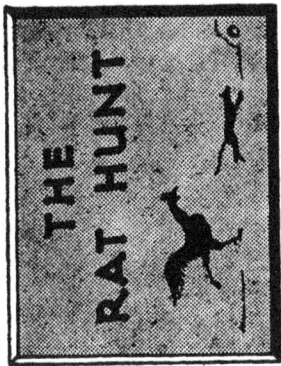

THE RAT HUNT

LEGEND.
JEEP TRACKS ——
HILL TRACKS ------

SCALE OF MILES

The terrain is a mass of jungle covered mountains intersected by deep ravines.

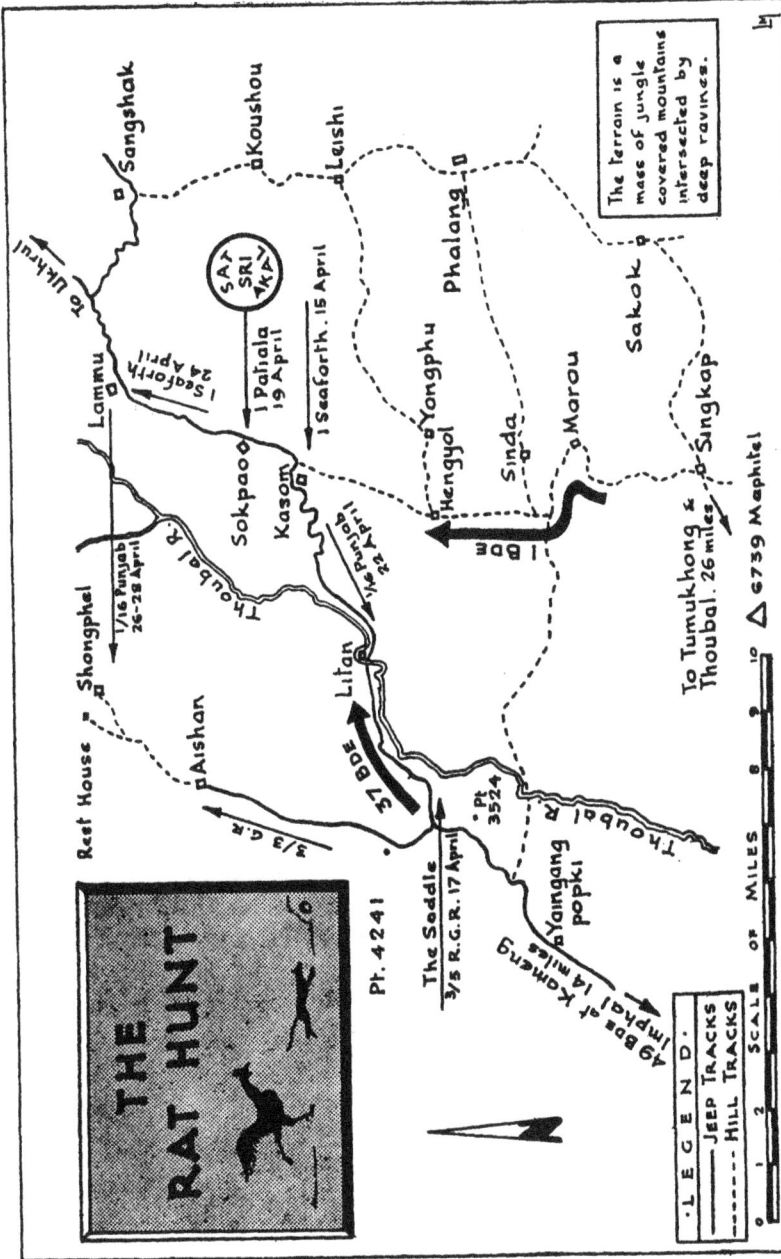

Sangshak
Koushou
Laushi
To Ukhrul
Lamu
Rest House ≈ Shongphel
Aishan
1/16 Punjab 26-28 April
Thoubal R.
Sokpaoo
Kasom
1 Seaforth. 24 April
1 Patiala 19 April
1 Seaforth. 15 April
Yongphu
Phalang
Hengyol
Sinda
Marou
Sakok
Singkap
1 BDE
1/16 Punjab 29 April
Litan
3/3 G.R.
37 BDE
Pt. 3524
The Saddle
3/5 R.G.R. 17 April
Yaingang popki
49 Bde of Kameng Imphal 14 miles
Thoubal R.
To Tumukhong & Thoubal. 26 miles
△ 6739 Maphlei
Pt. 4241
SA SRI KA

second assault immediately he was still there to hold his section together. Equally gallant was the conduct of the C.S.M., who moved fearlessly round the position, and of the C.Q.M.S., who was in command of a platoon; all three men were later awarded the D.C.M. for these and subsequent acts of gallantry, which included a lone venture by the C.S.M., who crawled outside the wire to bring in a wounded man under fire.

Night came but the enemy did not relax his efforts. At dusk he put in a third and fiercer assault and there were two others during the night, but the dourness of the Seaforths prevailed, with the fire from the Mountain Battery and 1/16 Punjab mortars in support. It was a wild night. While the Seaforths were hard pressed, Jap mortar bombs set fire to the jungle between Kasom and the ridge held by the Punjabis and Bde. H.Q., and the flames gradually crept up the hill. A jitter party who raided the ridge added to the uproar, but when dawn came and the smoke dispersed, there were the Seaforths still in Kasom and the 1/16th on the ridge. One of their naiks, summing up the night's activities, was heard to remark, "Bahut achcha tamasha, sahib, lekin dushman nai hai"[1]—an entertaining but not wholly accurate comment.

The defences were strengthened on the 16th, patrolling began in fulfilment of the order that the Brigade was to exploit north to Lammu, and the mule convoy came up with supplies on the long trek from Tumukhong. As the animals had to return at once on their twenty-mile march, many had sore backs when they reached road-head, and air supply was used on the 17th. Previous operations had shown that the need to encipher demands for air maintenance led to long delays and errors, so a simple code was devised for sending requirements and the dropping zone in "clear." Another improvement in the administrative technique for jungle warfare was the use of a mobile surgical unit, which was attached to 24 Indian Field Ambulance and ensured that major operations could be performed close to the battle without serious casualties having first to endure a slow and painful carry, when death might come before the surgeon could operate.

---

[1] "A very good display, sir, but there's no enemy!"

On the night of April 16th/17th the Japs had another tilt at the Seaforths, but made no headway; on the 17th the range of the patrolling increased; on the 18th "C" Company, 1/16th, put in a skilful raid down the road to the west to put out of action a 3-inch mortar which was troubling the Seaforths. Patrols located the gun after an approach through the jungle, and the raiding platoon, whose commander won the M.C., fell on the Japs while they were making tea. Twelve were killed on the spot and a concentration from the battalion 3-inch mortars killed or dispersed the rest; the gun was never fired again, though it was intact when captured a few days later.

It was clear to the Brigadier that before he carried out his instructions to move north he must first take the village of Sokpao, which overlooked Kasom, and he gave this task to 1 Patiala, who had concentrated at Singkap from the hills to the east on the 14th and had moved up in rear of the Brigade. The attack on Sokpao was no less a success than the assault on Kasom, though the cost was higher. By the evening of the 18th, "A" Company was established on a hill feature just west of the village, and there they remained unsupported for the rest of the action though for a long while they had a large enemy force between themselves and the rest of their battalion. The Jap reoccupied Sokpao during the night of April 18th/19th, and when "A" Company reported the fact they were told to give him no respite. Small patrols and snipers made sure that these orders were carried out, and the Japs who tried to dig in near by had a most uneasy time.

Very careful recces were made on the morning of the 19th for the main attack, which was to go in up a spur just west of the main road. At 1425 hrs. "D" Company rose up at the start line and rushed forward, shouting the Patiala battle cry, "Sat Sri Akal." The Japs, once again taken by surprise, were overwhelmed and in nine minutes the position had been captured. The fight had only begun. Six minutes later, when "D" Company was still hastily reorganizing, the Japs came from the east and hurled themselves on the rear of the company. There was no time to take up fire positions; the company commander charged with his reserve at the oncoming Japs; he fell in the hand-to-hand

K

grapple, but his action checked the enemy for the moment. Five minutes later the Jap came again a little farther down the ridge and was held by "B" Company, but he was not yet spent; a nine-minute interval and he came a third time between "B" Company and Bn. H.Q. Colonel Balwant Singh did not hesitate; as one of his officers had done a few minutes earlier, he charged magnificently into the fray at the head of his H.Q. The Japs were halted at last. The Patiala account of this tremendous affair runs: "Balance of the battle from 1425 to 1455 hours simply hanged round the gutts, it was anybody's battle during this time." The English is quaint, but there is no mistaking its meaning; fine courage gained the day. The Japs remained content with mortaring the position and with sniping, and they shot at a party which went forth to bring in the Patiala dead, but they were quietened when the R.A.F. arrived at 1700 hrs. within half an hour of a summons and delivered a very accurate attack on the village—a fine example of immediate support for an isolated battle where wireless was the only link. "A" Company had made a gallant attempt to reach their objective during the main attack, but they found the defences too strong and drew back to their isolated position. The day cost the Patialas sixty-six casualties, and among the awards gained were M.Cs. for the resourceful and determined commander of "A" Company and the Jemadar in command of the leading assault platoon.

Early in the evening the Japs made one small attack on the main position, which had been strengthened by bringing up "C" Company, but there was nothing to cause concern; the enemy was, in fact, busy withdrawing the bulk of his force. At 0630 hrs. on the 20th the R.A.F. came over again and the Patialas, full of confidence that the strike would be accurate, moved up within a hundred and fifty yards of the bomb line. When the attack ended at 0700 hrs., the Patialas advanced, and within three minutes Sokpao was theirs; "B" Company pushed on through the village to join hands with "A" Company.

With the flank secure, 1 Bde. were given as their immediate task the opening of the road back to Litan, which the Gurkhas reached from the west on the 21st. 1/16 Punjab moved off, found the way almost clear and linked up at

0800 hrs. on the 22nd; shortly after they winged a Jap signaller and presented the Brigade with its first prisoner. A 37 Bde. patrol from 3/5 R.G.R. had added a second to their bag on the night of the 19th/20th; they had advanced to within thirty yards of an enemy position and opened fire, to which the Japs replied; there followed a duel in shouting and shooting until the Japs quit, whereon the patrol leader followed up and swooped on a Jap who was tending his wounds. Japanese prisoners were rarities in a campaign where the enemy fought until he was killed, and these two were the objects of many a curious glance.

37 Bde. had left the Tiddim road on the 8th and were given three days' respite, which included a much appreciated cinema show, before they took over from 123 Bde. at Kameng on the 12th; they had under command 4/5 Mahratta, now refreshed and re-equipped, so far as was possible, with everything from bootlaces to 3-inch mortars. The Mahrattas formed the firm base at Kameng and will not forget taking over a position which had eighty unburied Jap corpses outside, the relics of a raid on a 123 Bde. unit the previous night. The 37 Bde. advance from Kameng was a picnic compared with the previous month's fighting, and one battle fought on the way up the road was described by a spectator as "an Aldershot Field Day." This was the attack on the ridge astride the road north-east of Yaingangpopki, no new battle for the Gurkhas as they had fought over the ground during training with the same tank units as were in support for the real battle. 3/10 G.R. captured the northern part of the feature in a raid on the night of April 16th/17th, and the main attack against the southern end was put in by 3/5 R.G.R. on the morning of the 17th. After an air strike which, though accurate, the C.O. thought "rather meagre," the guns of 158 Fd. Regt. and a Medium troop pounded the position for half an hour before the assault went in two companies up with a half squadron of Lee tanks divided between them. There was no hitch—the infantry advanced with the tanks neutralizing the enemy positions and the process was repeated until the feature had been captured. The whole operation took longer than expected, but it was over by 1500 hrs.; the small losses were evidence of the value of tank support and of the work of a sapper party from

91 Fd. Coy. who went ahead to clear mines and booby traps. Infantry, tanks and sappers had worked out this co-operation in training and here was the "drill" in action.

The opening of the road to Kasom on the 22nd greatly eased the maintenance of 1 Bde. A convoy drove through after the link-up and with it went General Roberts, who had set up an advanced H.Q. near Yaingangpopki to control these operations. After talking to Brigadier King about the pursuit of the "Rat" and kindred matters, he set off to visit his troops. At Sokpao he was walking round chatting to the Patialas when Colonel Balwant Singh appeared over the brow of a hill, propelled by that big stick he used to carry. The two shook hands, their faces lit by smiles which revealed the pride of brave men in acts of valour.

The General's orders to 1 Bde. were that the harassing of H.Q., Jap 15 Div., was to continue, and, as these were reported to be at Shongphel, the Brigade set off on another though less lengthy raid through the jungle; 1 Patiala, who were left to hold the road at Sokpao, disported themselves by sending "A" Company to harass the Jap L. of C. near Sangshak, where the Japs toppled into a series of brilliantly laid traps and lost upwards of thirty killed over a period of four days.

The Shongphel raid had an unfortunate start, as a rare lapse in patrolling involved the Seaforths in an unexpected all-day battle at Lammu, where the column was due to turn west. When the leading platoon was fired on, "D" Company commander, thinking the village was unoccupied except by snipers, pushed straight on down the track and was soon brought to a halt. "C" Company was deployed round the left flank through the jungle and crept up a valley towards the village; they reached the top, found they could only attack on a section front and, when the Japs held the first charge, were ordered back. Finally "B" Company were sent on a wide encircling move to enter from the north; their assault gained a footing in the village and the leading platoon was sweeping on when a Jap machine gun opened up from a flank. The young sergeant, who had distinguished himself at Kasom, was now the platoon commander, and he switched a section to deal with this gun while he pushed on to his objective; but the C.O., Lieut.-Colonel Macfarlane, realized that the cost of clearing the village would be heavy, called for air support, and withdrew his troops to a safe distance. The call went out at 1507 hrs.; at 1520 hrs. the R.A.F. were over the target and in a few minutes the village was in flames. This was poor recompense for the Nagas, who had cheerfully rendered unsought aid during the battle by evacuating casualties and taking water to the forward sections, but that is the way of war. After the bombing, the Seaforths occupied the ruins, but they had an uncomfortable night as anyone who walked unwarily was silhouetted against the flames and became a target for snipers.

After this delay, the Brigadier decided that 1/16 Punjab should push on alone on the evening of the 25th, but as they were loading the mules, the Japs put in a raid, stampeded the animals and set light to the grass inside the battalion perimeter. The mules fled from the flames and crashed about in the jungle, making it hard to locate the enemy and causing some indiscriminate shooting into the darkness. There could be no move that night and it was 1400 hrs. on the 26th before the battalion set off; they passed through Lammu, reached the Thoubal river, lay up until it was dark and then marched on through the night. They had as their chief guide Capt. Katin, a Naga schoolmaster from Ukhrul, who put on Naga dress and went out among the villages while the battalion slept on the 27th. He, and others like him, took their lives in their own hands, for they never knew when they might fall into Jap hands or be betrayed by a hostile villager. He brought back the news that there were two thousand Japs in Shongphel, a formidable force for a battalion to tackle.

The final night's march over country that was difficult even for Assam ended in a two-thousand-foot climb straight up a mountain side. There were countless obstacles on the track, which must have been lost but for the Naga guides, and there were repeated checks. It is excessively exhausting for marching infantry to halt for several minutes, move on a few yards and halt again; the Punjabis repeated the process over and over again, but none the less the leading company was on the ridge overlooking Shongphel at dawn and were quickly followed by the rest of the battalion. It was a fine feat by Lieut.-Colonel Newall and his men. After a short pause, "C" Company swept along the ridge and completely surprised a Jap post, whose occupants fled down the track to Shongphel.

The C.O.'s recce showed that the jungle on either side of the track was an impenetrable mass of great trees and lianas, and he resolved on a quick raid as offering the only hope of success; the Japs knew of his presence and he was out of touch with the section of mountain guns in support as the wireless sets had not withstood their battering during the night march. "A" Company put in the raid while "D" Company took up a covering position half-way down the track and the other two companies held the ridge. The raid went in fast and with zest and hit the administrative area of the divisional H.Q. Many of the enemy fled when the leading Punjabi section wrested their forward post from the Japs, but there was some skirmishing among the village huts during which the company commander was wounded; the Subedar took over and successfully withdrew the raiding force. Meanwhile there had been a sharp struggle on the ridge. Warfare in the jungle, which afforded cover for both sides impartially, was a cut-and-thrust business and, with an enemy as tough and resilient as the Jap, sudden attacks might come at any moment. "C" Company were at first distracted because some Jifs gave the P.M. war-cry, but they stood firm when the attack came in. During this action a lance-naik in command of a section which was hard pressed was seen to take over the Bren and completely stop the first charge with a withering burst; the Japs came at his post again and he kept his gun in action while he withdrew the pins from four grenades with his teeth and flung them one after another at the oncoming Japs. Coolness and determination of this sort were too much for the enemy. The N.C.O. and the leading section commander of the raid gained M.Ms.; "A" Company commander, who had previously been wounded in the Middle East by both the Germans and the Italians, won the M.C.

The 1/16th spent the night of the 28th/29th on the ridge, where they were joined at midday on the 29th by Bde. H.Q. and the Seaforths. Despite appalling weather—a reminder that the monsoon was not far away—the R.A.F. put in two strikes on Shongphel during the day and a patrol found the place empty. The "Rat" had escaped again. Hunting for the creature in such country was like looking for a needle in a haystack, but at least we made life as uncomfortable for him as for ourselves; there is evidence that we scored a near miss as he was later reported to have been at the Rest House a mile or two beyond Shongphel on the day of the 1/16th raid. We might, perhaps, have caught him had 3/3 G.R. been able to box the village from the west as was intended; they laid a successful ambush out in the hills, where a Jemadar held his fire until a large force of Japs was within five yards of the trap, but they could not complete their encircling move. A Seaforth company made a last effort on the 30th to bring the villain to book; they ensnared more Japs, but themselves suffered a few casualties when they ran into a Jap ambush. One of their officers showed fine resource in going alone through the jungle to bring information to Bn. H.Q., which was out of touch through a wireless breakdown.

During this chase through the wilds, 49 Bde. had been holding open the road back to Imphal as the Japs held on to the high ground to the west of the road. Two companies of 4/5 Mahratta had taken over Pt. 4057 from the Suffolks of 123 Bde. on April 19th, and when the rest of 49 Bde. moved to Kameng on the 22nd, five days after they had left the Tiddim road, the remainder of 4/5 Mahratta moved to their mountain peak two thousand feet above the plain. This point was known to us as "Sausage." The Mahrattas had an interesting time up on their lone height, which was linked to the mountains to the north by a narrow ridge. "B" Company held the foremost position and faced the Japs forty yards away in a bay along the ridge; it was an eerie experience to look out of a sandbagged loophole and see a Jap sentry peering back. At first sentries on both sides were shot until, by some form of telepathy, both sides agreed that sentries should be immune, though the truce did not extend to movement elsewhere in the position; not that the Japs took much notice of the Mahrattas even when they sent out hunting parties into the jungle to shoot pig and barking deer. These provided a welcome addition to the menu, for rations were not plentiful and it was not easy to maintain a battalion which had each of its companies on a separate peak. All supplies had to come on mules from the valley below and there was not a drop of water to be had, so that men had to descend to the plain to wash, while drinking water came up with the rations after being drawn from a water point in big drums and thence siphoned into two-gallon petrol tins. It was all very laborious for men and mules. On the hill-top the Mahratta posts were linked by tracks, one of them a home-made switchback eight hundred yards long and known after its perpetrator as "Scott's folly"; not all were out of sight of the Jap, who made no effort to interfere with the arrival of maintenance parties. He was an odd enemy, a foe of exceeding toughness who fought furiously yet lacked the enterprise to make full use of his fighting qualities.

There was farther up the road another hill, Pt. 4066, a bare, sharp-pointed peak christened the "Pinnacle," which the Japs occupied each night. As attempts by our patrols to seize the feature at dusk before the Japs arrived were not successful, "Pinnacle Hates" were devised. 4/5 Mahratta patrols went out and fired a green Very light if the Japs were in occupation, whereon the guns opened up. On April 23rd the signal failed to penetrate the ground mist, but the next night a green light burst in the sky and 5 Bty., 3 Ind. Fd. and 28 Mtn. Regt., who were in support of 49 Bde., let fly. The mixture was repeated on the following nights.

Preparations were made to clear the Japs from "Sausage" and "Pinnacle," and these included a recce in force by two companies of 5/6 Rajrif to "Pinnacle" on the 28th and a notable patrol by a Jemadar of 4/5 Mahratta to the enemy bunkers on "Sausage" the next night. There was also at work on "Sausage" a broadcasting unit which was endeavouring to secure surrender by the more peaceful method of peppering the Japs with propaganda. The great days for this unit were May 4th and 5th. On the 4th they brought to the microphone a Jap who had recently been captured at Shenam and made him deliver a speech. "B" Company, 4 Mahratta, waited eagerly, but not a Jap stirred opposite; apparently the broadcaster had made a thoroughly bad speech, so at least the interpreters with the unit said. The broadcaster protested that he had been hastened over his task, and that if he were given time to prepare a speech he

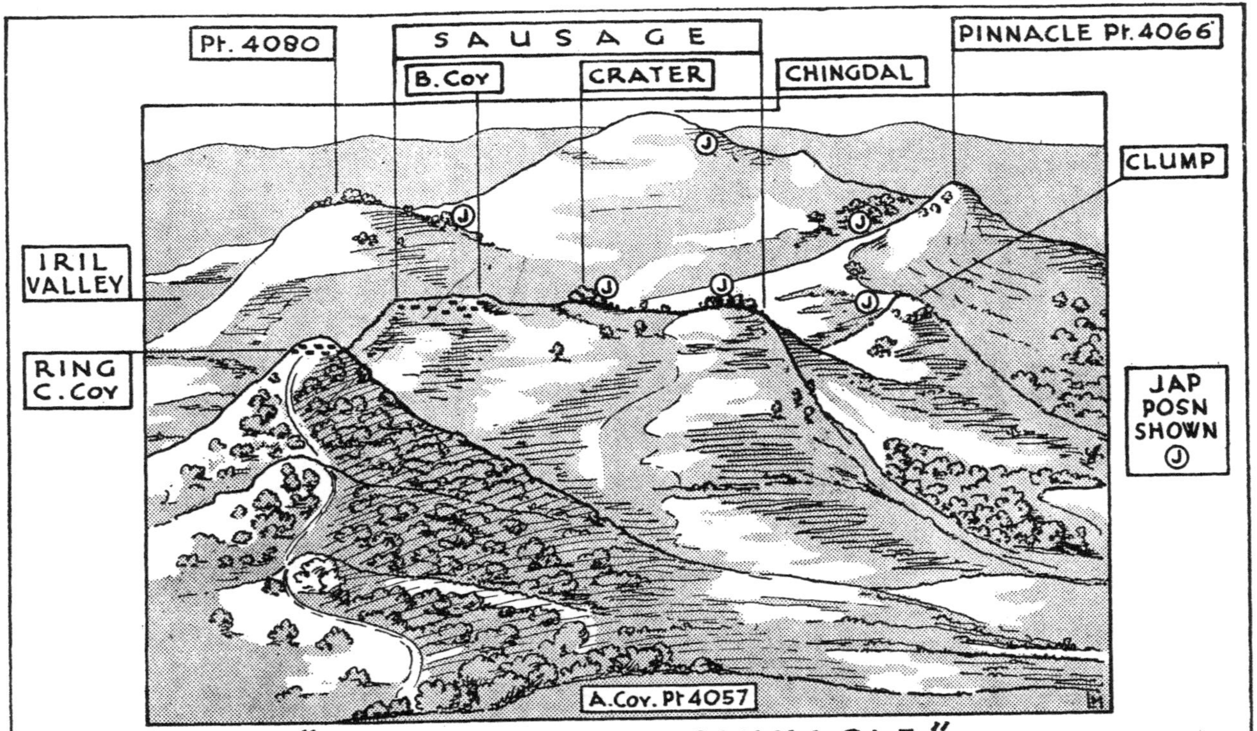
Pt. 4080
SAUSAGE
B. Coy
CRATER
CHINGDAL
PINNACLE Pt. 4066'
CLUMP
IRIL VALLEY
RING C. Coy
JAP POSN SHOWN (J)
A. Coy. Pt 4057

• "SAUSAGE & PINNACLE" •

would do better next day. On May 5th the prisoner was brought to the microphone again and, according to the interpreters, made a first-class speech. Among his remarks were these: "Here I am on the top of a hill 2,000 feet or more above the Imphal plain and what do I get?—peaches and cream. When have you last had peaches and cream?" Lurid and unprintable were the remarks of some British troops who were, as everyone else, on reduced and unappetizing rations, when they saw the Jap taking his fill; horrid, too, were the remarks of the Mahrattas when his impassioned oration produced a fusilade of grenade discharger shells which landed among "B" Company.

The propaganda unit withdrew and 49 Bde. reverted to more normal methods of warfare. The attacks were planned to go in on the 8th, but patrols out early on the 7th reported the enemy had flown. The Mahrattas took the rest of "Sausage," the Rajrif seized "Pinnacle," and 153 Bn., temporarily under command, gained Pt. 4080 away to the north of "Sausage." The Mahrattas found the Jap post they had taken in a filthy state. There were four shallow and inadequate graves close to the cooking-place which was strewn with the remnants of slaughtered cattle; the bunkers and sleeping-places stank. One useful acquisition for their pains was a quantity of paper which lasted for many months ahead; some, which was covered with Japanese characters, was handed over to Intelligence and revealed the travels of 3 Battalion, 151 Regiment, on their march to capture Imphal.

There was going on at this time another and bloodless struggle of which the fighting troops were hardly conscious, though as much depended on its outcome as on the successful defence of the plain. Once the Imphal road had been cut at the end of March, all supplies had to be brought in by air for the large force concentrated round the town. Though the size of the garrison was reduced by flying out "useless mouths," the tonnage of stores that had to be brought in each day was large. The Dakotas toiled to and fro from their bases in East Bengal, but the air lift was rarely equal to the Army's needs, especially after the monsoon broke at the end of May, when on some days few aircraft penetrated the cloud barrier over the mountains. The reserves in the Imphal plain began to drop and stringent measures had to be taken to effect economies. 4 Corps had a weekly conference with A.A.Q.M.Gs., who stated their requirements, but it was rarely possible to fly in more than essentials.

On April 12th the rations were reduced by a seventh and two days later petrol was rationed by the use of work tickets; the expenditure of ammunition was restricted to six rounds a day for 25-pounders except for specific operations which had Corps approval, other calibres being similarly limited. Men were hungry, particularly those on hard operations like the "Rat Hunt," and the diet was tedious; it was bully beef and tinned food day after day without fresh meat to provide variety and build up strength. On one occasion Div. H.Q. was startled to find that they had a succulent dish of real meat for their evening meal, and it is said that the General, when asked for his comments, described the meat as "tender." None had been more surprised by the meal than the A.A.Q.M.G., who knew nothing of a consignment of fresh meat; the next day he found the answer—a use had been found for some debilitated mules which were beyond repair. Mule did not recur on the menu. Despite the continuous feeling of hunger, most men were far more affected by the need to survive on thirty cigarettes a week—there were many like the Seaforth at Kasom who told the General that he liked to smoke forty a day. Such people would gladly have gone without a little more food for extra "fags," but these were not forthcoming, nor was there space to fly in the spirits and beer which did so much to bring a little comfort at the end of a hard day. The officers of Div. H.Q. and other relatively comfortable units earned deep gratitude by giving up the greater part of their rum ration to provide the evening tot for their friends in the battle a little longer. The lack of air lift for ordnance stores and the capture of the Kanglatongbi ordnance depot by the Japs increased the hardship of the siege, and the lack of spare boots, clothing and waterproof capes was felt increasingly as the monsoon became more severe. We had the means to ensure survival, but no more.

Those who were not fighting lived and worked throughout the three months' siege in defensive boxes. These were formed in the plain once it was clear that the Japs had launched an all-out attack; they were a result of experiences in the Arakan, where H.Qs. and administrative areas had been overrun because they were not organized for defence against enemy columns which penetrated far behind the front line. The boxes in our area were given the names of insects, and the Div. H.Q. fortress on the slopes of Palace Hill two miles south-east of Imphal had the salubrious title of "Bug" box. There was not overmuch room as space had to be found for 2/19 Hybad, the defence battalion, a battery of field artillery, a battery of Bofors from 28 L.A.A. Regt., 323 Fd. Pk. Coy. and their dump of engineer stores and other units. When the Fd. Pk. Coy. first surveyed their area they wellnigh despaired, for it consisted of a hundred and twenty yards of the sheer north face of the hill, forty yards of the north-west face where a man could just climb to the top by using the bushes as supports, and a stretch of paddy thirty yards in front of each face. They dug and dug until they had excavated a satisfactory home in a highly intricate series of inter-connected dug-outs which baffled visitors who had to thread their way through the maze on a dark night. One guest who had come to dinner reappeared by another entrance ten minutes after he had left, perspiring freely and somewhat earthy, and asked in a flowery speech how he made his way out.

It would be unfair to say that any one box was more attractive than others, but all admired the strength of "Ant," constructed by Lieut.-Colonel Kaye and his anti-tank gunners; there was a long waiting list for this fortification. "Bug" could boast of several attractions. There was a small artificial pond close to the perimeter where whistling teal settled each evening, and the Bofors crew on top of the hill, who were critical spectators of the shooting, could sometimes scarcely be restrained from trying the effect of their own weapon; they applauded loudly one evening when the G.S.O.1 hit three birds with a left and a right. Being next door to the Tulihal airfield, "Bug" was apt to receive the "overs" from the numerous Jap air raids at this time and afforded a vantage point for watching the Bofors in action when it was their turn to provide the spectacle. Fortunately only one stick of bombs caused casualties in the box during these raids, which severely tried the temper because they were often delivered about dawn and abruptly shortened the night's rest, for there was no more sleep when the quick repeated bark of the Bofors began. This crew certainly shot down one bomber in flames and they nearly scored a hit on the C.R.I.A.S.C.'s slit trench when their gun had a burst ten feet from the muzzle. A final attraction about "Bug" was that if you lived in Div. H.Q. mess, you would meet the officers of 254 Tk. Bde., who increased the manpower of the staff during a period of work at very high pressure and ran a devastating poker school in the few hours of leisure.

The boxes were each stocked with fifteen days' rations, a task which fell to the divisional transport in the middle of March when they were already fully occupied with vital operational moves; there was a further call on their services at the same time to collect the divisional baggage into a central dump. Each box had also to have its own water reserve, and the sappers called on to fill the highest of three tanks in "Bug" had to use all their ingenuity to pump the water up the last four hundred feet. In the end, by shifting the few available pumps, constructing two temporary staging tanks and mending innumerable leaks in the hoses, the 10,000-gallon tank on the summit was filled. One day all the water in this tank turned black and very malodorous and the process had to be repeated, but strict orders were given that the water, which came from a stream that meandered through the Imphal bazaar, was not to be drunk until it had been purified. The sapper in charge of the waterworks visited his tank some time after and found it dry —the defence battalion had changed and the relieving unit had drunk the nearest water they could find. No cases of dysentery were reported.

The technical arms and services were continually having to extemporize in a campaign where up-to-date equipment was always scarce and the circumstances of the siege prevented the replacement of ordinary stores as they were expended. Among other jobs 323 Fd. Pk. Coy. were called on to produce an explosive of sufficient power to blow in a Jap bunker and light enough for an assault party to carry. It was a very formidable task to destroy these bunkers, formed of two layers of logs with a six-foot mound of earth on top, and no shell or bomb in use up to this time had proved effective. The sappers felt that they had become "backroom boys" as they started to experiment. Their first successful charge was too heavy, after which they devised a method of splitting the charge into two halves, but this was considered unsatisfactory as the two halves might not marry up during an action. Finally they hit on a solution which satisfied all requirements and were told to go into production. The finished article was made up of sheet iron, old ghi tins and local stocks of plastic explosive which did not live up to its name and could only be made pliable when kneaded like dough. As the particular explosive used, like gelignite, gives a violent headache to men forced to handle it, the sappers had an unenviable time as they worked away like bakers day after day.

Equally numerous calls were made on E.M.E. and their tasks ranged from the inevitable attention to wireless sets —this was the more difficult because of lack of precision instruments—to the provision of cluster lights for a mobile surgical unit and the repair of such diverse equipment as typewriters and bulldozers. Time was always short and the lot of the men in the workshops was none the easier when part of the day went, perforce, to infantry training and work on the box defences. Our two bulldozers were particularly precious, so that the restoration of the machine which fell sick on April 19th was urgent and it could not be cured without oxygen. A bottle arrived next day, but was found to be empty; a fresh bottle came on the 21st and was hopefully uncorked. When E.M.E. discovered the contents were carbon dioxide, they ceased to use the normal methods of supply and made other arrangements; oxygen was acquired and the bulldozer was put back on the road. Bulldozer drivers do not often gain medals; there are few more exhausting or nerve-racking jobs than sitting at the wheel of one of these limb-shaking machines and working on a narrow track in the jungle on the brink of an abyss. Naturally, the correct ten-ton-load carriers for moving these 323 Fd. Pk. Coy. bulldozers from place to place were non-existent, and two-and-a-half-ton Studebakers, which had been taken over as non-runners, filled the gap, a tribute to American manufacture and the skill of E.M.E., whose key mechanics were British.

The heavy battles during the siege produced many calls for reinforcements. In our early days in Burma these had come from India and a more unsatisfactory system it would be hard to imagine, so much so that the camp at Gaya, west of Calcutta, became notorious as a cesspit which absorbed bodies and, if it disgorged them, only did so after months of delay. As the many defects of the administrative system were corrected, a satisfactory method of reinforcing battalions was introduced, and we had at the beginning of the siege a reinforcement camp in Imphal controlled by the proper unit. When the camp and the controlling unit were flown out as "useless mouths," the main 23 Div. reinforcements there were formed into a Division Reinforcement Battalion which ensured that men went to units properly equipped and when they were fit physically. Thus the strength of the fighting units was satisfactorily maintained and the case established for the existence of a Reinforcement Battalion for each division in war.

Life during the siege of Imphal was strenuous for all and devoid of comfort and it imposed a strain on the nerves. Certainly none of those who had to live in boxes would claim that they had to undergo the hazards or physical strain of the troops in the front line, but they had time to think and wonder what the issue would be. They saw 17 Div. and our two brigades come back down the Tiddim road, they saw the battered force stagger in from Sangshak; they knew they were cut off from the outside world, knew that the Jap stood at the gates, but they could not know the plan of the campaign. The future looked black during the early days of the siege and many were anxious. No one could have done more to bring courage in these dark days than General Roberts. Only those who have held high responsibility at a time of crisis can write justly of the strain of command when a man has to make vital decisions with little time to think and must mask the burden of responsibility by a heartening cheerfulness. The General never faltered. Those who saw him at H.Q. found the cigar between his lips and the vivacious sense of humour unchecked; they left feeling that there was no need to worry. The troops who met him on one of his many visits to forward units laughed with him after the battle and were strengthened by his words of encouragement and praise. General Roberts had the confidence of his Division and the Division was filled with confidence through their commander.

CHAPTER 15

Back to Shenam

ON May 1st, with 1 Bde. less the Patialas a little south of Shongphel and linked to 37 Bde. by a jeep track through Aishan which 3/10 G.R. had reached, we were well placed to continue our harrying role among the hills, and it must be assumed that, despite the grim difficulties of the terrain, this would have been to the liking of 3/5 R.G.R., who had grown restive under comparative inactivity as early as March 22nd when they wrote: "Another quiet night. It would not do us any harm to be shot up for a change to put us on our toes." They and the rest of the Brigade were soon to have fighting enough for any troops. The Jap was pressing hard on the southern front, where he was thrusting against 20 Div. at Shenam and 17 Div. at Bishenpur; he had moved round the north of Shenam and penetrated as far as Langgol, four miles as the crow flies from one of the main airfields near Palel, and there were signs that he was preparing for one more effort to exterminate 17 Div., who had been engaged in long and bloody fighting against the Jap 33 Div. The Jap's need to achieve a break-through was indeed urgent. It was the beginning of May and the monsoon was at most a month away, he was fighting at the end of long and fragile communications which would disintegrate under the rains, he had suffered very heavy losses and was as far off from penetrating the defences of the plain as he had been a month and a half ago. The doom of the Japanese forces attacking the frontiers of India was at hand, though there was bitter fighting ahead.

The signal that came from 4 Corps on May 1st began "Much regret necessity curtail operations your front for present owing necessity provide strong reserve for southern front," and we were ordered to have one brigade ready in the plain by May 5th, with a second at twenty-four hours' notice to move; we were at the same time not to relinquish

L

our grip on the base held by 49 Bde. from Kameng across to the hills north of the Litan road. In fulfilment of these orders, 1 Bde. moved to Wangjing as the Corps reserve, 37 Bde. were kept in readiness at the Yaingangpopki saddle, and 49 Bde. held their base and continued their operations to clear the hills. Further orders came on May 11th when we were ordered to take over "at the earliest possible date" the Shenam–Shuganu front from 20 Div., who were tired from their prolonged defence at Shenam. Hence 37 Bde., the builders and former tenants of the Shenam fortifications, returned to the battle-scarred heights with two extra battalions under command, while 49 Bde. protected the road up to Shenam and the Palel airfield. 49 Bde. had their H.Q. at Kakching, 6 Mahratta at Shuganu patrolling the hills to the south, and 4 Mahratta close to the airfield after a day's stay at Kakching, where they took hasty cover when in the line of fire of a Spitfire chasing a Zero at tree level, and two days at Yapo, in the hills south of the main road. 37 Bde. took over at Shenam on May 16th, H.Q. 23 Ind. Div. moved to "Bull" box next door to the airfield on the 18th, and 49 Bde. opened at Kakching the next day; meanwhile 1 Bde. were off on another footslogging expedition to clear the hills north of Shenam.

The relief of 20 Div. at Shenam, which took place unit by unit between the 13th and 16th, might have been a difficult operation had the Japs chosen to show any interest in our arrival. The forward posts on Scraggy were forty yards from the Jap front line and Malta and Gibraltar were always under his observation. Though he could see our advanced parties and relieving troops coming up, he showed that same lack of curiosity which we were beginning to take for granted; it was as though he would only fight when he could be sure of a tough battle. We were grateful for this weakness in the Japanese soldier; life was devilish unpleasant for the forward troops at Shenam, where the battalion holding Scraggy and Malta had to be relieved twice in a week, and it would have been much worse had the Jap interferred with these reliefs, which took place in broad daylight, or in the movement of supplies by M.T. which was driven daily to within a hundred yards of the front.

The original intention was that three battalions should

NOTE:— DURING DAYLIGHT ALL POSITIONS WERE UNDER OBSERVATION OF THE JAPS ON ADJACENT HILLS to the EAST

• LEGEND •
MAIN ROAD PALEL-TAMU
LESSER ROADS & TRACKS
BATTALION LOCALITIES

To PALEL OLD BRIDGE

Bn less two coys as mobile reserve with one coy on Assam Ridge and one coy reinforcing Scraggy-Malta Bn

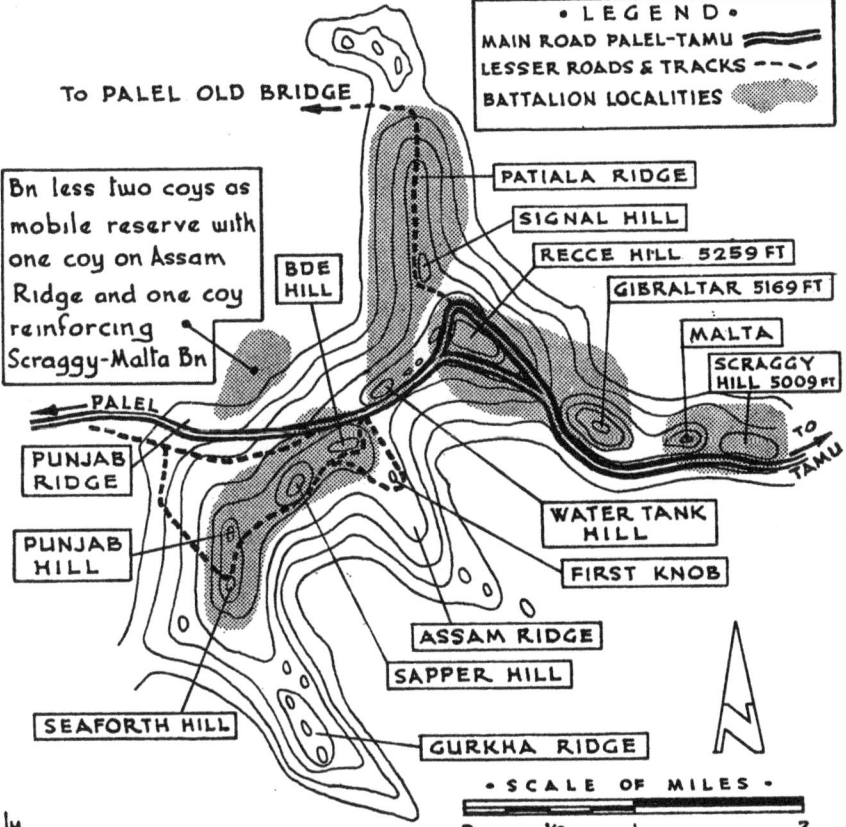

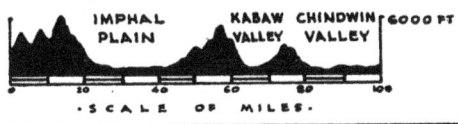

BDE HILL

PATIALA RIDGE
SIGNAL HILL
RECCE HILL 5259 FT
GIBRALTAR 5169 FT
MALTA
SCRAGGY HILL 5009 FT

PALEL
PUNJAB RIDGE
PUNJAB HILL
SEAFORTH HILL

TO TAMU

WATER TANK HILL
FIRST KNOB
ASSAM RIDGE
SAPPER HILL
GURKHA RIDGE

• SCALE OF MILES •
0   ½   1   2

IMPHAL PLAIN   KABAW VALLEY CHINDWIN VALLEY 6000 FT
· SCALE OF MILES ·
0   20   40   60   80   100

CROSS SECTION ON WEST-EAST LINE 20 MILES NORTH OF TAMU

SHENAM
NORMAL DEFENSIVE LAYOUT

suffice to garrison Shenam—such was the accepted answer to our T.E.W.T. in 1943—but the weight of the Japanese offensive had forced 20 Div. to stiffen the defence with two more battalions. 1 Seaforth and 5/6 Rajrif thus became part of the 37 Bde. garrison, which was supported by 158 Fd. Regt., 28 Mtn. Regt. less two batteries, a battery of L.A.A. guns, most of the 9 Jat M.M.G. battalion and a troop of tanks. Our task was that of the French at Verdun—"ils ne passeront pas"; lack of ammunition prevented us from being more than a buffer or from launching any considerable attack except for the flanking movement by 1 Bde. described later, which helped to relieve the pressure against Shenam. Against us the Japs could muster a composite group known as Yamamoto force, the ingredients being the Jif Gandhi Bde. south of the main road and a Japanese force which faced Shenam; there were some tanks and thirty-two guns in support, twenty-two of them mediums. As the Jif Bde. was unreliable and showed little aggressive spirit and the Japanese infantry, drawn from five different units, amounted to perhaps two and a half battalions—these were supplemented as usual by other arms used as infantry— we were containing a smaller force; but if the Jap lacked numbers, he did not lack ferocity, and he persisted in his attempts to drive through Shenam until by the middle of June he had whittled away his strength.

The defence of Shenam was a "dog fight," as it had been before, from the day 37 Bde. took over, and the troops occupying Scraggy, Malta and Gibraltar had no respite from shelling by day and jitter raids or assaults by night. These three peaks, standing one behind the other along the road, barred the way to the heart of the fortress at Recce Hill and were held against all assaults. Scraggy and Malta formed one keep, Gibraltar and Recce another, and in each a battalion lived in slit trenches for a few days until its turn came for relief and it withdrew, tired and battered, for rest on Patiala Ridge, Seaforth Hill or one of the other hills in the rear.

There was no chance of sleep forward. Nature had so shaped those cratered and shell-torn peaks that the sides dropped steeply away from a narrow ridge which formed the top and ran, like the spine of a fish, from west to east.

That was the wrong way for us as it forced us to site our defences on the northern and southern sides, which were exposed to the Jap's gaze, and every day he directed his guns upon our positions, where we had to endure the full weight of his mediums. On the 18th, two hundred and fifty rounds fell on Malta, on the 20th a hundred crashed on to Gibraltar in the space of an hour, and so it went on. All day there was that roar of shells driving through space and the crash as they burst, and the men who stood in the trenches wondered whether it was their turn to be in the wrong place. Casualties at first were heavy, for the trenches we had inherited were not of the best and nothing had been done to shore up the shale sides, which were continually slipping. Forty or more casualties would be carried out of the battle each day until the sappers of 68 and 71 Fd. Coys. had revetted the trenches and strengthened them against the continuous gun fire. Our own guns replied often enough in counter-battery shoots, and there was a gallant gunner officer who used to fly backwards and forwards in his tiny Air O.P. to keep the Japs quiet, but there was no complete answer except to capture the guns, and for that we had to wait. Periodically a shell scored a direct hit on a trench and the men, if not killed outright, would be buried under a pile of timber and debris. A naik of Div. Signals, who was manning a wireless set on Malta, was completely buried one day with all his men; he just had room to move, dug himself out and very soon had his set working again, after which he returned to his shattered trench and dug out his companions while the bombardment raged around him. Others were not so fortunate.

At night the guns continued to fire and the eastern sky was lit up by spurts of flame that had in them the threat of more destruction, and the air throbbed as the shells sped towards the peaks where men stood peering into the darkness and waiting for the attacks that would come when the firing ceased. Sometimes these were jitter parties, but no one could tell that the raids might not be the prelude to a fierce assault. Death lurked round the corner for the defenders of Scraggy, Malta and Gibraltar, and on top of this they had to endure the fury of the monsoon, which burst on May 27th. The storms raged among the hills and the lightning streaked down from the clouds to the earth—one flash detonated a third of our mines on the road below Scraggy and Malta. As ever, once the rains started there was no escape from the wet, and if the tempest ceased, a continual mist shrouded the hill-tops. "Mud, rats and, be it whispered, lice everywhere," wrote the Seaforths on June 15th, for, owing to the siege, men had only the clothes in which they stood, and if these were washed they could never be dried. The defence of Shenam offered nothing but danger, dirt and discomfort, and it called for that cold determination to resist which some call dourness but is more truly the height of courage.

The Japs made three major attempts to oust us from our positions, the first of which came shortly after dawn on May 21st after a night bombardment and two attacks on Gibraltar. The Rajrif were new to shelling as intense as they had to undergo on the evening of the 20th, but they held firm like veterans. One of their company commanders could be seen moving along the knife edges encouraging his men while the shells fell around him, and when the attacks came in, having no F.O.O., he moved to the battle area and directed our gun fire on to the Japs. Among his men was a young rifleman whose section commander had been killed by a shell. The rest of the section had been dazed and the Japs were assaulting their position, but the rifleman rallied his comrades and they beat off the threat; later, though a target for machine-gun fire, he hazarded his life and rushed over to a blown-in trench to haul another man to safety. Though the night was intensely dark, a platoon sent up as reinforcements managed to pick its way through the rocky jungle and reached the forward company during the battle—a fine effort.

By 0130 hrs. the Jap had had enough of his first real taste of our Rajputs, but he did not relax his furious assaults on Scraggy, where 3/10 G.R. were persistently assailed. Several times the battle was at very close range. At one point the Japs brought up a L.M.G. within fifteen yards of one of the Gurkha sections and poured bullets at it. The havildar in command slipped out of his trench and crept towards the enemy with a grenade in his hand; five yards from the gun he pulled out the pin and hurled his missile, which burst on the roof of the bunker and did no damage;

dissatisfied with his effort, the havildar worked round to the rear and dropped another grenade in the back door. This second grenade proved thoroughly effective, but the havildar had not ended his night's work. His section's blood was up and, when another party of Japs approached, a rifleman, taking orders from no one, leaped out of his trench and had done with four before the havildar, who rushed forward in support, could reach him and join in the fracas. The havildar was wounded in close-quarter fighting, but he was still with his men when the climax to the night's fighting came. Shortly after dawn the Japs came yelling and screaming over the summit of Scraggy in three waves, many of them armed only with grenades and gelignite bombs. Our Brens spoke and slaughtered the oncoming horde, but this did not content the Gurkhas. They were smitten with a "spontaneous loss of temper," leapt out of their trenches and charged with the bayonet on an enemy who "after a short while refused to continue the dispute."

The Japs left behind ninety-three dead; our casualties were twelve killed, forty-nine wounded. It was, as the Corps Commander said in his congratulatory signal, "a very high grade performance," and we had once more proved tougher than the Jap, who withdrew to meditate on his own side of Scraggy. Throughout the night the defensive fire of our guns was prompt and very accurate—158 Fd. Regt. and 28 Mtn. Regt. richly earned the Japanese swords which 3/10 G.R. were later to give them for their part in the defence of Shenam, and it was bare justice that one officer gained a Military Cross for his work as F.O.O. during this period; these gunner officers, spotting for the artillery which gave such fine support throughout, were ever to be found in the forefront of the battle. Less conspicuous, but equally important, was the work of the signallers. Under the heavy shelling, breaks in the telephone lines were frequent—one shell struck a tree outside Bde. H.Q. and severed all the lines attached to it—and the linesmen were continuously summoned to repair the damage; they went quickly and efficiently about their urgent work amid the battle.

The second Jap effort was a ferocious assault on the Rajrif holding Gibraltar, and it came on the night of May

23rd/24th. The jitter raids that continued to 2330 hrs. on the 23rd were normal and gave no sign of the intensity of the fighting to come when, after a very heavy artillery concentration, the Japs clambered up the northern slopes of the hill and gained the top. It was an astonishing effort of the Japanese. Gibraltar was garrisoned by two companies, "A" holding the eastern and "B" the western half of the hill; the "B" Company position included the highest point, which was linked to the rest of the feature to the west by a narrow, razor-backed ridge where at most two men could walk abreast; below the pinnacle, the cliff face fell almost sheer for over four hundred feet. The 10 Platoon position, which protected the pinnacle, looked unassailable, but the Japs proved otherwise. Under cover of their guns, they climbed up the cliff on an inky black night and overwhelmed such of the platoon as had survived the bombardment; several of the twenty-one defenders were dead and the survivors, dazed and stunned as they were, had not the strength to beat off the assault.

The battle for Gibraltar was on. The Japs had gained the crest and in the darkness and confusion were along the ridge and threatening the rest of "B" Company, who hurled the attackers back along the ridge to the crest. It was furious fighting with our guns, speedily directed on to the lost position, plastering the top, and down on the eastern slopes "A" Company was as fiercely engaged. The din was terrific and the night was made livid by the bursting shells and mortar bombs and the glint of tracer. "A" Company had been asked to counter-attack towards the crest, but they were fighting for their lives themselves and were barely in touch with the rest of the battle, for the aerial of their wireless set had half gone. They had lost one bunker, their counter-attack had been repulsed, and Company H.Q. was open had the Japs known it, but they were deceived by two determined men who fired their rifles from an exposed place throughout the night and were mistaken for a strongly held post. The Japs turned elsewhere, were firmly held, and just before dawn lost the bunker they had captured.

Dawn came and revealed to the eyes of all a Japanese flag fluttering from the top of Gibraltar. It was gone by the end of the day, but only after a heart-stirring display of

RECCE | MALTA | GIBRALTAR | CREST | PIMPLE

JAP BUNKER

MAIN ROAD

5/6 Rajrif and 3/10 G.R. counter attacks went up the ridge from Pimple to Crest. There 5/6 Rajrif came under fire from Jap bunker and were forced to withdraw. The leading platoon of 3/10 G.R. were also held on the Crest, but a second platoon came through and captured the bunker.

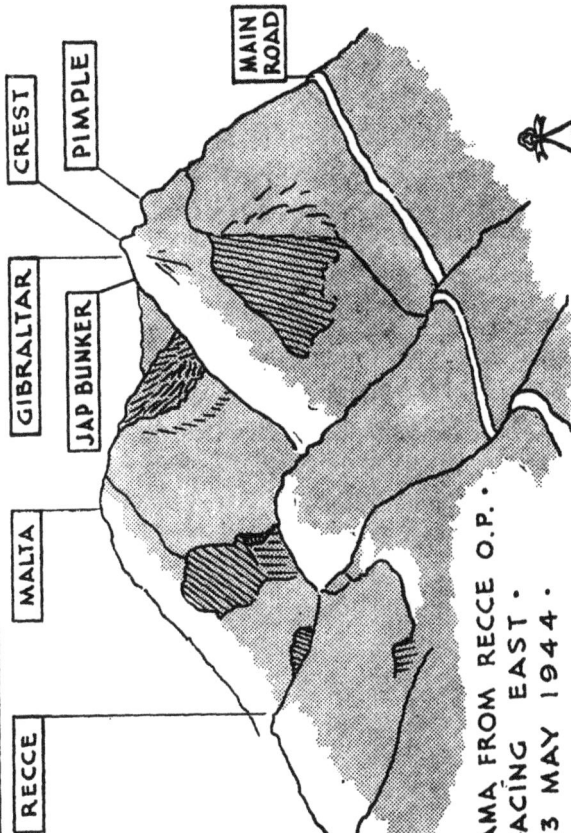

· PANORAMA FROM RECCE O.P. ·
· FACING EAST ·
· 23 MAY 1944 ·

RECAPTURE OF GIBRALTAR.

GURKHA RIFLES

courage by the Rajrif, assisted in the end by 3/10 G.R. The Japs were established west of the old 10 Platoon position, they had hauled a heavy machine gun up the cliff and the only way to eject them was to rush along the narrow ridge. At 0901 hrs. our guns pounded the crest while two platoons of "C" Company formed up for the attack; one shell scored a direct hit on a bunker and some Japs ran for their lives and started down the northern slopes, where they were picked off by 3/5 R.G.R. from Malta and sent tumbling to the bottom. For five minutes the shelling continued—and then the assault. It was tremendous to see. The lieutenant in command rushed, with the company havildar-major by his side, along and up the knife-edge which was swept by fire; the rest followed in pairs. Some fell at once, but enough survived to join in a tense, deadly grapple with the bayonet. The commander, though three times wounded, killed four; the havildar-major, a vast fellow, despite a gaping wound in his chest, bayoneted man after man and was seen to toss one over his shoulder down the cliff side like a bundle of hay. Two posts were cleared, but the enemy were many more than the two platoons they were thought to be; the Jap guns opened up, the gallant attackers had no strength for a further effort, and they went back along the ridge with only five of their number un-wounded. They had driven the Japs from all but one bunker to the left of the peak.

As the rest of "C" Company had been sent round the back of Gibraltar to reinforce "A" Company on the eastern slopes, "A" Company, 3/10 G.R., were brought up at 1100 hrs. to complete the Japs' destruction. Again there was that first rush along the ridge to be faced before the attack could fan out. Over went the Gurkhas, past the trenches the Rajputs had regained, until grenades and shells halted the leading platoon on the crest. A second was ordered through to top the crest and come to grips with the last of the enemy on the reverse slope. The Japs made one final effort to hold on—showers of grenades came over the crest and the Gurkhas replied with interest; then shells began to fall among them. The jemadar platoon commander steadied his men as the shells and grenades burst, rose at their head and swept over the crest. He was everywhere in the ensuing hand-to-hand combat, where the bayonet went home and the khukri came out when there was not room for the bayonet. After one khukri stroke, a naik was just in time to thwart a Jap officer who rushed in brandishing his sword; but the Gurkha proved the better with his native weapon and went on to deliver three more deadly cuts. Fifty Japs fled from death by steel, only for many to fall before the weapons on Malta. Gibraltar was ours again and the Japs left a hundred and forty-five dead on its slopes; our killed in the counter-attacks numbered eleven, the wounded a hundred and seven.

May 24th was a black day for the Japs as they were hurled off Gibraltar and lost the towering peak of Ben Nevis to 1 Bde. These two defeats brought some respite to the defenders of Shenam as the Jap guns were diverted towards Ben Nevis and he needed time to recover from his exhaustion. Not that all was quiet on Scraggy and Malta, as the Seaforths discovered when, on May 29th, they took over on the only occasion Gurkha units did not relieve each other in the forward locality. The Seaforths were out improving the wire round the position when they were speedily driven to their trenches by a fusilade of grenades and salvo after salvo of shells. A young platoon commander, scorning the danger and five wounds, moved among his men giving encouragement and handed off a falling grenade as he would an opponent on the rugger field. One trench was emptied of men three times within an hour, but there was no wavering by the Seaforths. The "hate" died down, no attack came, and the American Field Ambulance Troop came up to carry away the wounded. There were very brave men in this non-combatant medical unit which cared nought for bullets while on their errands of mercy, and many will cherish the memory of Neill Gillam, the bravest of them all, who was awarded the George Medal because, as an American, he was not eligible for the higher decoration his dauntless courage earned.

Sixteen days of comparative peace passed before the Japs came again in a final attempt to overwhelm the defences of Scraggy. The attack on the evening of June 9th against 3/3 G.R. opened, as the others had done, with an intense bombardment which virtually destroyed the forward platoon position and tore a gap in the defences through which the Japs rushed, carrying sandbags full of grenades. The enemy were nearly in, but not quite. They were thwarted by a lieutenant who saw the danger and charged into the breach with the one section not in action. The Japs halted and, as they paused, this officer gathered a dozen more men in the darkness and hurled the enemy back to his starting-point. He had not yet done with the Jap, for he collected another small force of two sections, not without some difficulty as the platoon commander had been temporarily deafened by the din of the shelling. A havildar standing by caught the urgency of the order which his commander seemed strangely unable to grasp, and he quietly fell in the men. The violence of the third charge pierced the enemy line, where a hail of grenades checked the Gurkha onrush; the officer was himself twice wounded, some of his men were hit and he was forced back, but his fine and courageous leadership had turned the scale. Reinforcements were on the way to seal the gap and with them came the company subedar, who was always to be found where the fight was thickest.

While 3/3 G.R. held the Jap at bay, preparations were made for a counter-attack to recover our lost positions near the top of Scraggy. In the early hours of June 10th "B" Company, 3/5 R.G.R., came to grips on the hill-top, but they made little headway and it was decided that only a carefully prepared assault offered hope of success. The guns shelled Scraggy, the tanks were brought up to shoot at the bunkers, and at 1500 hrs. the R.A.F. straffed the hill while the 3/5 R.G.R. Company and another from 3/3 G.R. moved up to the start line. Our attack was nearly stifled there and then. The Japs had the exact range, shell after shell screamed through the air, burst on the start line and left ugly gaps where they fell. Two British officers of 3/5 R.G.R. and one of 3/3 G.R. were killed, forty or so lay dead or wounded in all, including the platoon and the three section commanders of the leading platoon. It was a shattering experience even for battle-hardened and resolute troops, but the attack was pressed home. An officer who had been wounded saw that the front platoon was leaderless and lead it forward, with riflemen almost instinctively taking

THE SHENAM COUNTRY

These two pictures taken after the victory in July, 1944, illustrate
the steepness of the terrain

over the command of sections. Progress was slow. Despite our shelling, the Jap had held his ground and he met the attack with a grim resolution to hold on. The officer worked round a communication trench, was hit a second time, but, heedless of his wounds, killed four of the enemy. Near by one of his riflemen turned section commander rushed alone on a bunker, which he cleared single-handed. His men were worthy of his lead, but the fury of the fighting had taken its toll; there was not a man left unwounded and several were dead. He hung on with his small band, but the attack had spent its force; more Japs arrived with grenades and bunker-busting charges and the attackers were called off. In the rear of the withdrawal staggered a rifleman of 3/5 R.G.R., a lone figure and a target for the Jap grenades; he was carrying his own Bren and another's tommy-gun; that gun belonged to the Gurkha's platoon commander, whose foot had been blown off, and the Gurkha was half-dragging, half carrying him out of the battle.

Our casualties, twenty-three killed and a hundred and thirteen wounded, were serious, as the continuous fighting and the monsoon were beginning to leave their mark, but though the Japs were to hold the top of Scraggy for six more weeks, experienced eyes in 3/10 G.R., when they relieved 3/3 G.R. on the 12th, reported the "situation on Scraggy tactically sounder than ever before"; we had lost some ground, but there was now thirty yards of No Man's Land dominated by our Brens. We still barred the way and, grievous as our losses had been, the Japs had lost as heavily. He had nearly spent his strength, and when his last assault failed he never again made an all-out attack on the defences of Shenam; he had broken his head on a brick wall. There was to be one last effort to reach the plain on our part of the front, but that attack did not fall on Shenam.

Had Brigadier Collingridge been present when the counter-attack went in on the afternoon of June 10th, he must have admired another example of the steadfastness and courage of the men under his command, though perhaps it was fitting that his last memory of the Gurkhas in action should be of 3/10 G.R. storming up the highest peak of Gibraltar. When he left on June 5th to become Commandant of the Staff College at Quetta, he had commanded 37 Bde. for four years. His Gurkhas had come to him as young and raw recruits in 1940, and under his eye they had been trained and hardened until they were ready to prove in battle that they had a skill and toughness which the Japs could not master. Brigadier Collingridge was rightly proud of his all-Gurkha brigade, which owed so much to his leadership and care for their well-being. He understood and loved his Gurkhas and he understood the soldier's craft. Courageous and unflurried in action, he would not commit his troops to battle unless he was satisfied that the plan was sound and the administrative resources sufficient for the task. The proof of the man as a soldier is to be found in the record of 37 Bde., but that record cannot hint at a great quality, his deep loyalty to the two generals under whom he served. Brigadier Collingridge is one of those who counts most in the history of 23 Ind. Div., and his awards of the D.S.O. and O.B.E. are but just recompense for his fine record in Burma.

There were many awards for gallantry during the long drawn-out defence of Shenam and the deeds that earned some of the M.Cs., M.Ms. and I.D.S.Ms. have been recounted in the foregoing pages. There is little room to tell of more of these deeds, but they were not confined to the nights of the main Jap attacks. Three nights after 3/3 G.R. first came to Scraggy, shelling destroyed a forward section where the naik in command dug out his men and kept his post intact against four assaults; the next day twenty-three bodies were found on the fringe of the post, twelve of them five yards away. Another night two Japs stole into a trench ten yards from a 3/5 R.G.R. section, which they pestered with grenades; a lance-naik leapt unordered from his trench to give the Japs a taste of their own medicine; a few minutes later the Japs began again, the N.C.O. repeated his dash, and this time there was quiet for the rest of the night. Then there is the story of a 3/5 R.G.R. raid. The naik in command and another N.C.O. crept forward up a crawl trench to a Jap bunker thirty yards ahead and heard the sound of heavy breathing within; having searched in vain for the entrance, they climbed on top of the bunker and sat there scraping a hole until it was large enough to drop a grenade inside; the effect was instantaneous—

Japs appeared from all sides and a skirmish with grenades followed at six paces before the N.C.Os. decided the raid was a complete success and withdrew unscathed. So the tales could continue, but it is time to pass from Scraggy, Malta and Gibraltar, where men fought and died to hold three shell-torn peaks in the jungle, to the affairs of 1 Bde.

1 Bde., back at Wangjing in Corps reserve, started on their second hill trek on May 8th, two battalions strong as the Seaforths were engaged elsewhere and were destined for Shenam. On the 8th the Patialas moved up to Langgol, which had been captured the day before by 80 Bde. of 20 Div. with the support of 3 Ind. Fd. Regt. The Brigade's task was to clear the ridge running parallel to and north of the main Palel–Shenam road and so to remove the threat to Palel by way of the Phalbung ridge; a second task, the establishment of a base for attacks against the Shenam–Tamu road, followed on from the first. The whole operation was over in a fortnight, and for this the credit goes largely to 1/16 Punjab.

The Patialas found Maibi Khunou unoccupied on the 9th, but bumped into enemy astride the track going south to Khudei Khunou; after a day for reconnaissance, they moved on the 11th towards the village, but the leading company was held on the spur a little to the north of the place. The 1/16th were ordered to assault the next day, and a highly successful assault they delivered. When "C" Company were held a hundred yards from the objective, "A" Company were moved to the flank and stormed the key height. The Punjabis were a noble sight as, despite inevitable casualties, they held on uphill over the rocky ground with the company commander, who won the M.C., in the van. On the 14th, a day when the Staff Captain and Brigade Supply Officer surprised themselves by capturing a prisoner, patrols were approaching Phalbung; by the 17th the Punjabis had a company on the hill east of the village, and the crest of Ben Nevis loomed up ahead. This feature, with its twin peaks linked by a ridge and rising 4,500 feet, was strongly held by the enemy and demanded a set-piece attack. As a preliminary the 1/16th began intensive probing of the defences and, by such patrols as that of a naik who watched the Japs from twenty-five yards and pinned them to the ground while he withdrew his men, they built up a knowledge of the position.

As the main defences faced the north guarding the approach from Sita, our attack was planned to come in from the south; in outline the plan, as all good plans, was simple—"B" and "C" Companies to assault the right peak, "A" and "D" the left, with a Patiala company as reserve— but the simplicity of a plan is no guide to the difficulty of the task. Ben Nevis was a formidable feature to capture, as was recognized by giving 1/16 Punjab the support of our two field regiments, each less a battery, a troop of medium guns and three squadrons of aircraft. The attack, due to begin on the 23rd, was postponed for a day because of pre-monsoon storms, and the Punjabis concentrated in the assembly area on the night of May 23rd/24th.

On the 24th there was early mist and fog as the columns moved forward, and zero was put back an hour in the hope of the mist lifting enough for the air to strike. The weather cleared and the aircraft came over, but one of the Hurricanes mistook the target and attacked a similar feature to Ben Nevis five hundred yards to the south-west. It was an unhappy error; though soon corrected by the gunners firing smoke on to the right target, the damage had been done—the 1/16th tactical H.Q. had been hit and Lieut.-Colonel Newall seriously wounded. Major J. P. Lawford took over and won the M.C. for his cool and successful commanding during the operation.

The artillery concentration, which followed the air attack, ceased at 1055 hrs. and within thirty-five minutes "B" and "C" Companies had captured the right peak. It was harder going on the left, where the air and the guns had not reached some positions on reverse slopes; "D" Company struggled forward but were held two hundred yards from their objective and reported that it was waste of lives to send up "A" Company. The C.O. ordered them to halt, sent the Patiala company on to the right peak with orders to move along the connecting ridge to the left peak and then to link up with the assault. The first part of this move was completely successful, but such movements over steep hills take time and it was 1500 hrs. before the Patialas reached the left peak and were able to turn down the spur. For more than four hours the two companies had been out in the open trying to secure a glimpse of the carefully concealed Jap bunkers on the ridge above them; whenever they moved, the Japs shot down their fire lanes and men were hit, and the thick jungle prevented a flank approach. This was a taxing wait and the Patialas could do nothing to help; half-way down the spur they came under heavy fire, and when they sought a new line of advance, they became entangled in the jungle. So close were our troops to the enemy that it was dangerous for the guns to fire and it looked as though the Punjabis were checked for the day, but "A" Company made one last effort; at 1630 hrs. they charged up the hill. There was no subtlety about the assault; grit and determination were pitted against the toughness of the defenders, who stayed in their bunkers, protected by wire, and fired their weapons until they were killed. Casualties began to mount, but always someone stepped in to give the lead; in one section, when the two N.C.Os. were wounded, the Bren gunner took command and charged on in the lead firing his weapon from the hip; in another, where the Bren gunner fell, the section commander kept the gun in action and led his men on. They came to the wire, broke through and were up to the bunkers. By 1800 hrs. the whole of Ben Nevis was ours. It chanced that General Giffard visited the Division a week later, and when he looked at the defences on the western spur he remarked that it was miraculous any company had managed to break through single-handed.

The battle for Ben Nevis did not end with its capture. When the Jap guns began to register the hill early on the 25th, a counter-attack to remove the threat to the Jap right flank looked imminent, but it did not come for four days, a sure sign that Yamamoto force, with nothing to spare, needed a breathing space after the repulse at Gibraltar and was unable to launch out simultaneously in two directions. On the 28th the Jap thought he was ready and the 1/16th had to endure a furious bombardment such as the defenders of Shenam knew only too well. For three hours the Jap guns battered the position while the Punjabis stood stead-fastly in their bunkers, some of which were demolished by direct hits. One who stood there wrote afterwards these simple but expressive words: "It was not at all pleasant, in

M

fact it was awful." Amidst this inferno, the subedar of "A" Company moved from place to place bandaging the wounded and helping to evacuate the serious cases until he was ordered out by his company commander for attention to his own wounds. The casualties were heavy, the defences disorganized and it might have gone hard with the 1/16th had the assault come at the end of the bombardment, but the Japs bungled and in the two hours' interval the position was readjusted. The Jap stormed at Ben Nevis for three more days, the attacks usually coming at night, but from June 1st these attacks faded away into jitter raids apart from a minor effort on June 6th when one platoon position was smashed to pieces by shelling and the Company H.Q. in the area hit; with the Commander out of action, a jemadar stepped into the breach and repelled the ensuing assault.

The capture and defence of Ben Nevis brought the 1/16th numerous decorations, and if an estimate is to be made of the assistance 1 Bde. rendered to 37 Bde. at Shenam, it can be done in the form of two simple facts—the Japs did not attack at Shenam between May 24th and June 9th and the shells which landed on Ben Nevis would have gone elsewhere.

The Patialas had not been idle while 1/16 Punjab underwent their ordeal at Ben Nevis. On May 27th they had a company on another big feature to the north-west which we called Hambone, and when they were relieved there next day by our old acquaintances, the Kali Bahadur Regiment, who were once more under command, they pushed on down the track to Leitan, which they reached on June 2nd. There was an enemy position beyond the village and a havildar, sent out on patrol and dissatisfied with what he had seen, sent back all his men except one and crawled inside the post, where he remained for half an hour. The next morning he crawled back with a section and waited for the company attack to begin. At zero he rose from his hide and fell upon the enemy H.Q., shouting his battle cry; the enemy, utterly surprised, fled to the east and the attack was over in a very few minutes. The havildar's enterprise won him the M.M. One other Patiala venture at this time was less successful. On the night of June 1st "A" Company had been sent with a sapper detachment from 68 Fd. Coy. to blow the

Lokchao bridges, eight or so miles away on the road from Shenam to Tamu. It was a venture after the Patialas' heart, a deep raid into enemy territory calling for all their guile and skill in ambushes; if anybody could have reached the bridges, the Patialas would have found the way, but the bridges were strongly held and the Patialas had to rest content with causing a deal of confusion in a vehicle park.

Leitan was the limit of the 1 Bde. advance, for the moment had arrived to end the seige of Imphal. 4 Corps had been fighting hard, often desperately hard, for three months and as the moment for its relief approached there was not much to spare; certainly there were neither troops nor ammunition available for even a minor offensive on our part of the front. The 5 and 20 Div. operations up the Kohima and Ukhrul roads demanded their whole strength, and we were ordered on June 7th to provide two battalions as the Corps reserve. It was possible to send 4/5 Mahratta, less one company, without greatly weakening the 49 Bde. front, where the Gandhi Bde. remained mainly quiescent, but the call for a second battalion involved giving up Ben Nevis. The loss of 1/16 Punjab and the consequent readjustment of the 1 Bde. dispositions left a gap which the Japs were quick to exploit, but, though it brought more fighting later over ground we had once captured, this was of slight importance in the overall strategy.

On June 22nd, 2 (British) Div., driving down from the battlefield of Kohima, joined hands at M.S. 109 on the Imphal–Kohima road with the forward troops of 5 Ind. Div. —the three months' siege was over. That day the General wrote an order to the troops he commanded—it read: "British troops advancing south from Kohima have made contact with 4 Corps troops moving north from Imphal. This is a fitting time for me to express to all ranks my very high appreciation of their achievement in the battle for Imphal. You have had to wait nearly two years—two years of hardship and strain—for this opportunity to inflict defeat upon the Japs, but, now that the opportunity has come, you have made full use of it. I expected very great things from 23 Div., but your steadfastness, powers of endurance, will to victory and courage have surpassed all my expectations. I am more proud than words can express of the honour of having been in command of you. You can also be supremely proud of the success you have achieved. For over three months you have fought continuously, cut off for most of this time except by air. You have never wavered and have accepted cheerfully all hardships and privations, imbued solely with the determination to defeat the enemy. The Japs have been and are still being defeated on all fronts—in Burma and the Pacific. On this front they have suffered enormous casualties and are demoralized and exhausted. We must make sure we gain the full fruits of our victory. We must give them no respite, but attack them and drive back the scattered remnants from whence they came. I thank you all for what you have achieved in the past. Let us now go on to ever greater victories."

Yes, a great victory, but the 22nd was no Mafeking night for us, as the General's words came to a Division that had plenty on its hands. 37 Bde. looked out into the night at Shenam—the Rajrif were wrestling with the Japs who had come through the gap up the Sengmai Turel—the Hydera-bads and 4 Mahratta maintained lonely watches on the line of solitary peaks north of the Turel—and the wind tore at the jungle and the rain was part of men's lives. There was no respite for those called on to complete the rout of the shat-tered Japanese armies, and the end of the siege passed almost unnoticed except that we knew the enemy was beaten though he stood on the doorstep of Div. H.Q., and that our turn was coming to march to the east.

There had been little to relieve the strain of the last few months, but there were one or two moments when enter-tainment brought refreshment to tired minds and bodies. Those fortunate enough to be free were once able to enjoy a few hours' rest watching a cinema while the sounds of battle echoed in the distance, and we were more than grate-ful to Mr. Noel Coward who, coming to South-East Asia on the invitation of Lord Louis Mountbatten, brought his piano and his wit to Shenam on June 19th; as "payment" for "services rendered," we regaled him with lunch in "A" Mess before he sang and a view of a Jap bunker after the show. Finally we must pay a tribute to the gunners who had the ingenious idea of using H.A.A. guns as mortars. The day arrived to test their theories and a safety area was cleared.

The first shell soared into the heavens and enthusiastic gunners peered through their glasses at the target area. There was a pause, a very long pause, before the onlookers were disturbed by a loud explosion some way behind the gun. The gunners were not discouraged—a second shell was released on its journey and the eager peering began again. The telephone bell rang in Div. H.Q.—49 Bde. on the line to report bombing from an enormous height, but the mysterious point was the absence of an aircraft though the skies had been searched far and wide. The gunners heard the tale, they consulted together, they decided their shells became unstable over 40,000 feet; the gun went home in disgrace and the entertainment ceased.

CHAPTER 16

Out of the Main Stream

FROM the middle of May, the main tide of battle for 23 Div. surged round Shenam and the hills to the north, but there were on other parts of the front four actions which must form a part of this history.

Two of these actions arose from the need to chastise the Gandhi Bde. so that by periodic punishment they might learn the wisdom of obedience to our wishes, which required them to stay peacefully in the hills south of Shenam. A unit of 20 Div. was already on the job when 1 Bde. came back from the Ukhrul road on May 3rd, and they needed someone to act as backstops and catch the prey as they were flushed from their lairs; the Seaforths were billed for this role, with a troop of 5 Bty., 3 Ind. Fd., in support. They waited patiently for some days and, when the drive proved fruitless, asked leave to attack an enemy post they had found at Khongjol. The battle on May 18th, which was not much more than a skirmish, gave "B" Company and its commander a chance to show their skill in surmounting awkward country. The Jifs were perched on a very inaccessible hilltop which could only be assaulted on a one-man front, but the Seaforths, with carefully organized fire support, climbed to the top unnoticed and sent the Jifs packing.

The second of these "punitive" expeditions fell to 4 Mahratta, who moved out from their box south of the Palel airfield on June 2nd; they had with them a battery of 28 Mtn. Regt., who so cheerfully and successfully supported most of our operations in the wilds. The march was long and tiring, the route was steep, the tracks were slippery from the rains, but no one fell out though the men carried their rations on their backs and were weighed down by extra ammunition. That evening they rested at Mitlong, where they were met by the advanced guard who had found the enemy on a hill west of the next village, Mitlong Khunou.

There was a brisk fight next day, but the enemy did not show overmuch zest when he discovered our strength. The C.O. had decided on a night approach, though it meant a crossing in the dark over a boulder-strewn stream where the men scrambled through the water and rocks on hands and knees. The leading company surmounted the obstacle and were nearing the first bound when two Jifs came down the track to draw water. These ran back up the hill and gave the alarm to their comrades, who put in a quick counter-attack which was easily repelled. The guns then opened up on the line of the next bound, which "D" Company seized at the point of the bayonet; they too were counter-attacked, but a jemadar charged at the head of the men near him and some quick thrusts discouraged the Jifs for the moment. After 2-inch mortars had driven off a lukewarm attack put in as "A" Company formed up to assault the crest, the hill-top was captured and the enemy were seen flying to Mitlong Khunou. Patrols later found the village empty except for two wounded Jifs, who were made prisoner.

The Mahrattas had a cold and uncomfortable night and some were very thirsty as they had made tea out of rain water collected in ground sheets; the tea tasted strongly of rubber and produced a greater thirst than ever, so that some may have wondered whether it was worth saving the two-hour walk for purer water. They woke tired and wet on the 4th and resumed the chase. Patrols found the enemy on a formidable feature some miles on and plans were made to attack on the 5th, but the enemy gave up his fortress during the night. The Mahrattas, who had gone far enough, turned on their tracks and were back in their box on the 7th. This operation proved once more the value of the Mobile Surgical Unit. Even so, the casualties faced hideous discomfort—a four- or five-hour stretcher carry from R.A.P. to Mitlong, where the surgeon waited to operate, an eight-hour carry, when rested, from Mitlong to jeep-head, and a two-hour ride over a bumpy, rutted track. Fortunately casualties were light.

The Jifs hardly troubled us again, though we came up against the remnants when we broke out from Shenam. In the interval they were watched by a company patrol base at Liwa and by the battalion guarding the approach through

Shuganu. The only disturbances were a few encounters near Shuganu and an attack on Liwa; "C" Company, 1 Seaforth, were sent from Shenam to quieten the Jifs, who fled before a dawn attack and were then lured back on to ground where the Seaforths lay waiting to deal out punishment.

Jif hunting was exhausting, but the fighting lacked the fury of battles against the Japs who were the foe at M.S. 10 on the Tiddim road and on the Yaingangpopki saddle. "B" and "D" Companies, 6 Mahratta, were sent to assist in the defence of the 17 Div. H.Q. box on May 19th when the Jap offensive was at its height. The main battle raged round Bishenpur, but an enemy column had reached the village of Marbam, where it cut the main road near M.S. 10. Any attack to clear the village had first to cover three hundred yards over flat paddy fields which were swept by machine guns from a knoll east of the road. Two companies of 9/12 Frontier Force Rifles of 17 Div. first undertook this hazardous enterprise, with artillery and tank support, but the tanks could not leave the road and the small force which survived after the dash over the paddy came reeling back to the jungle whence the attack started. The need to clear the road, up which went all supplies to Bishenpur, was very urgent and a new plan was made to box in the west edge of the village for the night and so prevent the Japs moving from Marbam on to the road. "C" Company, 9/12 F.F.R., led the rush, followed by the Mahrattas' "B" Company. The rush succeeded, the Mahrattas escaping a single casualty thanks to the sound sense of their commander, who watched the pattern of the machine-gun bullets on the paddy and led his men clear, and to good fortune, for the smoke screen thinned as they were crossing but a mist descended at the crucial moment.

The Japs did all they could on the night of June 22nd/23rd to remove the box, and after heavy shelling and a series of attacks one Mahratta platoon had only six men left unwounded. Dawn came with the men tired, dazed and hungry, for no food came up with the ammunition during the night, but the position had been held. For most of the 23rd, "B" Company fought with such strength as they had left and with the help of a platoon of 9/12 F.F.R. to clear Marbam. The first attack at 0800 hrs. was brought to a halt after a hundred yards and there was a long pause before a fresh attempt was made in the late afternoon with the support of one tank. This destroyed two bunkers and the attack made progress, but the Mahrattas had not the strength to hold their gains or to deal with an automatic seventy yards away to the left. The attempt to destroy this position by a reserve platoon of the F.F.R. failed, the Jap guns opened up again, and at 1800 hrs. the Mahrattas withdrew inside the box which was now held by their own "D" Company. It had been a wearing day.

"D" Company, 6 Mahratta, were left to hold the box alone for the night of the 23rd/24th and the two following days, with the Japs close at hand. The Mahrattas conducted the defence with great spirit. If the Japs attacked, they were beaten back; if they sniped from the nearby trees, the snipers were brought to earth; and to show that Mahrattas thought little of Japs, on the 24th a patrol discomforted the enemy with grenades, and a two-platoon attack, with the single tank in support, destroyed a bunker and its contents. This kept the Japs at arm's length, but their machine guns were still on the knoll and, as artillery concentrations on the 25th failed to knock these out, an attack was launched against them at first light on the 26th. The leading troops were a company of the Baluch Regiment with half of "B" Company, 6 Mahratta, under command to mop up, but the attack petered out against strong resistance and the force withdrew to the box, where they were joined by a Frontier Force Rifles company. Though a further attack was proposed, the sane counsel of the Mahratta "D" Company commander prevailed—that a hastily mounted attack would be squandering lives.

The Mahratta companies were released next day and returned to the calmer air of Shuganu, their casualties being nine killed, thirty-five wounded. The awards gained included a M.M. to a sepoy for fine section leading in the attack on the 24th and the I.D.S.M. to a lance-naik who, in the gruelling battle on the 23rd, volunteered to lead two others to search out the enemy and persisted in his enterprise, despite an early wound, until he was close enough to hurl grenades at their bunkers.

From the Tiddim to the Ukhrul road and to June 15th, a

sad day for 4 Mahratta, when it rained persistently and little went right and there was nothing to show at the end for the loss of sixty-six wounded and twenty-two killed, among them two fine company commanders who had been with the battalion from the far distant days of 1942. 4 Mahratta, temporarily under command of 20 Div., came back to the Yaingangpopki saddle, which 37 Bde. had cleared two months earlier, to fulfil a task allotted to them when they and 1/16 Punjab formed the Corps reserve. The Japs had dug in on one of the ridges to the west of the saddle and cut off a company of the Border Regiment on a peak to the north from the next British position on a height nearer the road.

The men bivouacked in the open from the 11th–13th, while a series of conferences and recces took place, though the C.O.'s recce was of little use as the enemy were shrouded in mist; hence the reports of 20 Div. patrols on the Jap dispositions had to be taken on trust. At 0530 hrs. on the 14th the Mahrattas moved up the slopes of the nearer peak to the start line, but there was to be no attack this day. On the day before, the unit providing the tank support had been changed and instead of the Lees of 3 D.G., the old, worn out Stuarts of 7 Cav. arrived in the late afternoon of the 13th. Though a bulldozer had scoured out a track up to the start line, the gradient proved too steep for these tanks, which only reached the top at 1400 hrs. after more bulldozing and the use of a tractor. It was too late to attack and the Mahrattas marched down the hill to bivouac under their groundsheets.

At 0800 hrs. on the 15th the Mahrattas were again close to the start line; ahead the R.A.F. were straffing the Jap, behind the tanks struggled to the top of the hill with engines groaning. So exhausted were the engines after reaching the top that the tanks could not surmount the slight final rise to the start line until the driver of an unarmoured, unprotected tractor gallantly volunteered to run the gauntlet of the sniping and shell-fire and dragged each tank to its place in turn. By then the air strike was over and the attack, starting late, had lost the cover of the artillery concentration; much worse, the Japs, who had seen the attack coming and started shelling, scored a direct hit on "B" Company Adv. H.Q.; and, worse still, it was immediately clear that the patrols had erred by several hundred yards in pinpointing the enemy positions, which had been untouched by our aircraft and guns. The tanks might have been able to save the day, but they soon found the country too difficult for them to deploy right or left and in front was a deep and impassable ditch; they had a costly day, for a direct hit put one out of action, a second was bogged and had to be abandoned, and the third was damaged by mines.

The Mahrattas persevered alone, "B" Company right, "A" Company left and "D" in reserve against stiff opposition. There was grand leadership by the two forward company commanders. The subedar of "B" Company, who took over when his H.Q. was wiped out, conducted his advance single-handed; he had to run from platoon to platoon giving orders, always over bullet-swept ground, and he kept the momentum of his attack going for close on two hours before a machine gun opened up murderous fire on his right; neither the tanks nor our artillery could silence this gun. "A" Company at the start made some headway until they were counter-attacked from the left; they beat off this attack and went on once more, only to be held by mortar and machine-gun fire fifty yards from the main Jap positions. It looked as though the attack must fail; the commander, havildar and all section commanders in the leading platoon had been killed or wounded, and the Japs fired unceasingly from their bunkers. A lance-naik thought otherwise—he took over command, rallied the survivors and led a tremendous charge which cleared six bunkers and breached the defences. The company commander could be heard over the wireless urging on his men, and then suddenly, "Christ, I'm hit!" While his men hung on grimly to their gains, he refused to leave them; a little later he fainted and when he came round, he started to walk back to the R.A.P. alone. His refusal to take a single man away from the battle as escort cost him his life. On the way back, a tree sniper hit him in the stomach and he lay in the open for two hours before he was found very weak but still alive; he died during the carry back from the R.A.P. to the dressing station.

With the attack held, two platoons of "D" Company were sent forward, one to the right against the machine gun there, the other to the left to ease the pressure on "A" Company's flank. There was no progress and it was all the Mahrattas could do to hold on. In achieving this the men of H.Q. Company had a part to play by forming parties to bring up ammunition and carry out the wounded; they suffered casualties as they crossed the ridge, but they went quietly on with their task. The Mahrattas made a last effort to break through the breach "A" Company had made; they had not yet committed one platoon of "D" Company and two of 4/10 Gurkhas lent as a replacement for their missing company. It was of no avail—by 1200 hrs. all was spent and at 1430 hrs. the Mahrattas were ordered to withdraw. Was there nothing to show for this day of sadness and failure? There was this consolation—one who watched said that these were the most gallant Indian troops he had seen in action.

It was a rigid rule in 23 Div. that no attack should be launched unless surprise could be achieved, for the Jap mind works along "fixed lines" and proved time after time, in big operations and in small, unable to adjust itself to unexpected happenings. The Mahrattas were not fully their own masters on the Yaingangpopki saddle where surprise had been lost by the abortive attack on the 14th. The next day the Japs were ready.

CHAPTER 17

The Sengmai Turel

THIS chapter would have taken a very different form had 1/16 Punjab not been required as part of the 4 Corps reserve for the clearing of the Kohima road. As it turned out, they were back under command within a week, but by then the damage had been done and the Japs were far down the Sengmai Turel on the doorstep of Div. H.Q. It may be that some will feel that the move need not have been ordered, but such thoughts are unjust; a reserve of two battalions for a big operation is little enough and it might so easily have been the Punjabis' lot to be embroiled in as savage an engagement as 4 Mahratta at Yaingangpopki.

Once we had withdrawn from Ben Nevis, 1 Bde. held a series of positions on prominent peaks along what we knew as the Sita track. There was to the east of Sita a Jif brigade which had long shown a masterly inactivity, but needed a small eye fixed upon it lest, like a dormant volcano, it erupted violently; hence one Kali Bahadur company kept a lonely watch at Sita. Next, coming west, there was Hambone, where the Patialas guarded a valuable O.P. for our gunners. There remained the protection of the supply line to these forward posts. There had been a time during the 1 Bde. advance when a makeshift route was used up the Sengmai Turel, but the rains had brought that to an end and the convoys now had to go the long way round through Nungtak, which was the base for the Kali Bahadur Regiment less the Sita company.

The Division had during these two years been in many uncomfortable places, but few were as forlorn as these peaks on the Sita track. If it was not raining, they were shrouded in perpetual mist and it was bitterly cold living day and night under a cloak of gloom. The health of the strongest suffered from exposure to the elements in these dreary regions, where men lived shut off from the world outside, face to face with a wall of mist. They had in the mule convoys bringing up supplies one regular link with other men and one only.

From time to time casual references may have suggested that our mules, their drivers and their officers led a hard existence. That bare statement in no way falls short of the truth. The men, marching twenty or more miles a day over rough country, were among the fittest in the Division and their work was not done when the march was over. The mule is a willing beast, but he is like any other living creature in having his daily needs, and it is to these that the driver must attend at the end of the day when the time has come to feed, water and groom the two or three animals in his charge. These tasks were not as simple as they are when caring for race-horses in well-equipped stables. When, as often in jungle warfare, the forests were a vast No Man's Land where a convoy was in danger of attack though well behind the fighting, the camp sites had to be chosen for ease of defence as well as for convenience. The water flowed in the valleys, the hill-tops made the safest camps, and if it was not possible to camp in the valleys, the drivers had more marching before the animals were watered. The day was not over—sometimes there was fodder to cut, frequently there was dirty saddlery to clean and always there were defences to dig and a perimeter to defend throughout the night. We relied on the mule, we relied on his driver, we relied on the patience and endurance of both and we did not put our trust in them in vain. Out in all weathers, tramping over rough and steep tracks that were the more difficult because they tried the animals so sorely, the drivers saw the supplies through and carried on their unending task with quiet fortitude.

It was during the events that form the subject of this chapter that a large mule column was required to move the Patialas, less one company, from Hambone to Half Way Hill. Shortly after daybreak, when patrols had reported the tracks clear, the convoy of three hundred mules and two hundred men moved off from Nungtak. Climbing continuously, they covered eleven miles in the first four hours before they stopped for a long halt; in pouring rain the drivers squatted down on their haunches to eat their haversack ration, the reins in one hand and a chapatti in the other. By 1300 hrs. they were at the foot of Hambone, but it was some time before they reached the Patiala positions at the top as the last half-mile of the track was feet deep in thick, glutinous mud.

The march back began at 1700 hrs. and the first Patiala company with its complement of mules reached the rendez-vous where the battalion was to collect in an hour and a half; there they and the other companies waited four hours until they were joined by one last platoon which had been in contact with the Jap. The rain poured down, the wind bit through wet clothing. When the time came to replace the loads the men and animals were numb with cold, and chilled fingers, fumbling with the equipment in the dark, found difficulty in fastening the one hundred and sixty pound burdens securely. Some time after 2230 hrs. the whole column moved on with four miles left to cover. The march took four hours on a night so dark that one man could not see his fellow in front and only kept touch with him by holding on to his bayonet scabbard. This was no march but a shuffle through the night where men and mules slithered along over the mud. By the time Half Way Hill was reached ten mules had disappeared over the edge of the track and had dropped an unknown number of feet into the jungle, where they had to be left until search parties went out in the morning to find the bits of rag that marked the point of the fall. One mule had to be shot as its leg was broken, nine were recovered, though one died at work a few days' later and was found to have a broken neck!

On arrival at Half Way Hill not many hours of the night remained before dawn. The mules were unloaded and tethered, the Patialas went about their business and the mule company, left alone once more, formed a perimeter round the animals; some of the men were required for guards, the more fortunate lay down in the mud to sleep if they could. When day came, after the mules had been fed and cleaned so far as the rain allowed, the men found a little comfort from a mug of "char"[1] while waiting for fresh orders. These came at 0800 hrs.—forty-two mules were to be left

---

[1] Tea.

behind for a fresh task and the rest were to report back to Nungtak. By the end, they had been out thirty hours and had marched thirty-two miles; and they came out of the mist and rain on the hills into the brilliant sunshine below knowing that before very long they would be trudging back again up the hills.

This move of the Patialas was completed in the early hours of June 16th and was occasioned by the need to release 2/19 Hybad for an attack on the Japs, who had come much too far down the Sengmai Turel to be pleasant. The Hyderabads had changed over roles with the Kali Bahadur Regiment on the 9th, and it was that evening the Japs put in the last of their big attacks on Scraggy. Thwarted there, they gave up using their troops like a battering ram against Shenam and moved round the northern flank. They mustered for the task an assortment of gunners, engineers, drivers and others with a leavening of infantry, but, being Japanese, they were tough fighters who moved fast and set about their task with determination. By the 11th they had occupied Ben Nevis and parties had reached Khudei Khunou; by the next day they were dug in there and had brought up guns on to the Phalbung ridge whence they fired an occasional shell into the Div. H.Q. box and on to the airfield, much to the distress of our friends in the R.A.F. who threatened to fly away unless we silenced the disturbers of their peace. On the 13th the Japs had moved yet farther north and had occupied Maibi Khunou and the sharp pointed hill overlooking Langgol.

Such was the situation that confronted the General when he returned on the 14th after a six-day visit to Calcutta for medical attention. He found that Brigadier Andrews had, in his absence, set on foot measures for the removal of our unwelcome visitors who were being watched from Machi and Langgol at the end of their penetration and harried farther east by an ambush company of 5/6 Rajrif which lay athwart the Jap L. of C. along the Phalbung ridge.

The watching from Langgol was done by a battery of 2 Ind. A. Tk. Regt., who were thus employed in an independent role as infantry for the first time since they came to the battle-front. They seized the chance to show that there was no fault to be found with their fighting qualities though they were taking on an unaccustomed task. At the start they remained largely on the defensive and were called on to repel an attack throughout the night of June 16th/17th. It was in this engagement that a gunner, who could not use his rifle because of a shattered arm, remained at his post to throw grenades and carry up ammunition to the forward troops until the enemy withdrew at dawn. Later, as their confidence increased, they sallied forth and launched several successful raids against the Jap who was dug in on a woody peak three hundred yards from Langgol. It was a strong position and the Jap clung to it for some time to come despite the attentions of our artillery, the R.A.F. and our anti-tank gunners turned infantry.

Maibi Khunou, though no easy objective, was less formidable than Langgol, and as its capture would sever the supply line for the Japs to the West, this village was selected as the point where we would attempt to disrupt the enemy's infiltration. The attack ordered on June 14th was due to be delivered by 2/19 Hybad on the 17th, but the weather caused a twenty-four hour postponement; the tracks were ankle-deep in mud after forty-eight hours' incessant rain, and by the time the battalion, less their company at Sita, had concentrated at Machi, all were "wet, dirty and tired." In the early hours of the 18th the hills were veiled in mist and the R.A.F., who had made two effective strikes on the village the previous day, could not support the attack, which needed all the help that could be given. As so often in these assaults on villages, everything favoured the defenders, who could watch their assailants as they stumbled on uphill through the jungle and struggled to reach the carefully sited and well-concealed bunkers where the foe waited; nor was it easy for the preparatory patrols to find out the exact positions and strength of the enemy. The Hyderabad patrols had done their best, and a havildar, who led a party of volunteers in a "blitz" raid, forced the Japs to disclose some of their positions, but not all were located as events on the 18th showed.

The plan of the attack was for "D" Company to assault the main position while a commando platoon infiltrated round the right flank to take the enemy in the rear. This lone platoon was early in trouble against far stronger opposition

N

than expected. Two unsuspected machine guns barred the line of advance, volleys of grenades came from the hill-top, and men struggling forward through this intense fire were picked off by tree snipers. The leading section commander was badly wounded at the start and ordered out of the battle, but he stayed at the head of his men for three hours. Somehow, slogging on amid the bullets, the platoon captured three bunkers before "A" Company came up between them and "D" Company, who were fighting hard to reduce a formidable bunker fifty yards ahead. This was in outline a repetition of the Mahratta struggle at Yaingangpopki, a slow grind where the infantry fought with their courage and their weapons to dig a tenacious enemy out of his trenches one by one. Such close quarter affrays cost lives, and if the enemy holds on there comes a moment when the attackers have no strength left to go on with the laborious, sickly business of killing. The Hyderabads did not lack determination. The havildar who led the patrol was again to the fore; with his men held up by a machine gun, he and a sepoy crawled away on their own until they could see the Jap gunner; the havildar raised his Bren, the bullets found their mark and he rushed up to the bunker. Here he was staggered and wounded for the second time in four days by a grenade which burst at his feet and smashed the butt of his gun, but he did not heed his wounds; there were more Japs ahead and he called for ammunition to continue the fight. Deeds such as this, which won the M.M., were not enough. Though the Hyderabads had gained the knoll to the north of the village, a counter-attack came at the moment when their strength was spent and they were forced back a short way down the hill. They had suffered a hundred and seven casualties before they drew off in the rain to the gloomy, isolated hill-top of Machi.

4 Mahratta less two companies arrived at Machi the next day, June 19th, to take over from the Hyderabads. It was pouring with rain and the whole camp was a morass with four hundred and thirty mules churning up the mud inside the perimeter while the units unloaded and loaded their baggage. The Mahratta comment, "What a day!" surprises only by its restraint. The Hyderabads, freed from Machi, returned to the peaks along the Sita track. These

two moves were part of the plan to exchange 49 Bde. with 1 Bde., who had been fighting the Jap and the monsoon for six weeks and needed rest on the quieter and less unpleasant southern front. 1 Bde. had already reached their new positions when the Jap stepped in and delivered one final stab aimed at our vitals, whereby he effectively stopped the completion of our design.

On June 23rd the Rajrif in ambush on the Phalbung spur reported a company of the enemy digging in on a feature we called Lone Tree Hill, and the Kali Bahadur Regiment, patrolling forward from Bull Box, clashed with another party on a knoll farther west. This thrust south of the Turel was full of menace. At Lone Tree Hill he was behind the Shenam defences and overlooked our gun positions, and his forward troops on the knoll were only two miles from the Palel bridge over which ran the road to Shenam. Though the strength of the Jap forces was not great, we had fought this foe far too long not to recognize in him an obstinate and determined beast, capable of a quick and dangerous raid which might cause no little damage and inconvenience. It was not sufficient to check this intrusion; the threat must be removed with all speed. "B" Company, 4 Mahratta, were dispatched to oppose the more westerly force, and the signal to the Rajrif left no doubt that the expulsion of the Jap from Lone Tree Hill brooked no delay.

That signal read, "You must do everything possible to prevent Japs digging in on Lone Tree Hill," and on its receipt the Rajrif, temporarily under command of Major D. C. Misra, set about the business. There was no time on the afternoon of the 23rd for careful preparations, so that the attack by "A" Company with a platoon of 3/5 R.G.R. as reserve relied for success on nothing but courage and speed. When the first assault failed, a second was pressed home with fine determination and the Rajrif surged to the top of the hill, but the Japs were at their throats again very soon and the Rajrif were hurled out of their gains. In that second assault, the leading section commander did not wait for orders on the hill-top and went pell-mell after the retreating Japs before he was recalled, and when he came back he found his Bren gunner was missing. Once more he went off down the far side, this time alone, and a little later he could be seen staggering up the hill with the man over his shoulder.

A second and more deliberate attack in the late afternoon of the 24th was a hard and bloody affray which cost the Rajrif seventy casualties. After an accurate strike by the R.A.F. and a heavy artillery bombardment, they stormed the hill in four waves, pitting their determination against Japanese bullets and grenades. This time the brunt of the battle fell on "B" Company, with "A" in support; three times they were repulsed in this grim struggle to gain the bunkers, but a fourth effort almost carried the attackers to the crest. The wounded and dead lay on the hillside, the enemy kept up their fire, and those who watched knew that the issue was in the balance. The attack began to waver, and in a matter of minutes hope of success was snuffed out when the Japs counter-attacked the weakened force before it was possible to rush up more ammunition.

War is often hideously ugly and never more so than when it comes to a slogging match like this battle for Lone Tree Hill, which could not cease until the enemy had been destroyed. His strength was now estimated at about two companies and the Rajrif were given orders to attack on the 25th with "C" and "D" Companies, which had not yet been committed. The Rajrif spirit remained undiminished. After a concentration from our guns, the assaulting troops moved forward up the steepest and previously untried route under cover of an air strike, and waited a hundred and fifty yards away from the crest until the R.A.F. had done with pounding the Japs. After the air, the mortars took up the pounding and, as the mortars began, the R.A.F. returned to deliver a series of dummy runs. While our aircraft screamed overhead and the Japs waited for the bombs to fall, one jemadar led his platoon on to its objective unopposed. The enemy were as prompt as ever to counter-attack, but the Rajrif were quicker still; as the Japs charged, the jemadar led forward his men and the bayonets of the Rajrif prevailed. There was furious fighting on the hill-top before the Japs were exterminated and there were many hand-to-hand clashes. One of the company havildar-majors dashed at a Jap who stood on the edge of a bunker preparing to throw a grenade; he reached his man before the missile was thrown, wrestled with him in a brief grapple, wrenched the grenade away in time and took his foe prisoner. Somewhere in the midst of this confused struggle were the C.O.'s personal bodyguard, who had sought leave at the start to take an active part in the affair and had been firmly refused. A few minutes later the C.O. looked round and found the lure of the battle had proved too great; the survivors returned in the evening—ready to resume their uncongenial duties. There had in all been four distinct counter-attacks before the Jap drew off, leaving ninety-two dead behind; the Rajrif losses on this day were twenty-two killed and eighty-four wounded. Throughout the battle the battalion had fought with fine courage and determination, as the General recognized when he ordered on the 26th that Lone Tree Hill should henceforth be known as Rajput Hill.

There remained the Japs on the knoll close to Div. H.Q. a feature christened "Scott's Knob" after the commander of "B" Company, 4 Mahratta. The enemy resistance was not less stubborn here than at Rajput Hill and two attempts to shift him on June 24th were unsuccessful—"B" Company, 4/5 Mahratta, made the first alone, and the second was a joint affair with "B" Company of 6/5 Mahratta, supported by a troop of tanks. The 4 Mahratta company was then given a watching brief from a nearby hill until 6 Mahratta, now under command of Lieut.-Colonel J. A. Mellsop, had completed their concentration from Shuganu and carried out essential recce patrols. One of these had a successful skirmish with a large party of Japs and brought back two wounded prisoners.

On June 27th a double attack was made on the enemy in the area of "Scott's Knob," "A" and "B" Companies, 6 Mahratta, attacking from the west and 3/5 R.G.R., who had relieved the Rajrif, assaulting another feature in enemy hands to the west and north of Rajput Hill. It was a day of mixed success. The Mahrattas met stern opposition from the start and had "B" Company commander wounded early in their advance. Once again the records tell of the gallantry of a subedar who took over the company and recked nothing of bullets and grenades in his efforts to urge on his men. "B" Company did struggle on to their objective and a solitary platoon of "A" Company reached the "Knob," but our guns had not touched the Japs in a nullah behind the feature and, when the customary counter-attack came, the Mahrattas could not hold on. The Gurkhas were more fortunate, though only after a five-hour struggle which long hung in the balance. At the crisis of the battle leadership of the highest order turned the scale. Casualties in the composite force of five platoons had been heavy, for twenty-two lay dead on the slopes of the hill and some eighty had been wounded; night was approaching, the Japs still resisted, and it seemed that the fire had gone out of the attack when the commander ordered the survivors of his force to crawl forward and close with the enemy. The Gurkhas followed his lead. A jemadar platoon commander, creeping forward on his own to silence a machine-gun post firing from a hidden bunker, came upon three Japs evacuating another position; single-handed he killed two and wounded the third. By this and similar acts of bravery the Gurkhas reached the hill-top and set about flushing the enemy from their lairs. Night was already falling before the task was fully over, and the commander, who was awarded a bar to the M.C. he had gained earlier in the month on "Scraggy," consolidated his hard-won gains in the darkness, uncertain how close the remnants of the enemy might be. These were speedily dispatched next morning when a Jap officer was found among the dead with an excellent panorama of Shenam and most of our gun positions in his pocket.

The last Jap thrust at us was well-nigh ended. Shattered by the fighting on June 27th, he made little resistance to the assault on "Scott's Knob" delivered by 6 Mahratta on June 30th, with the R.A.F., our gunners and two troops of tanks in support; the show was over in half an hour. That short and insignificant skirmish marks the end of our defence of the Assam–Burma frontier; for two long years we had waited for this day when the tide of battle should turn and we were free to hound the Jap out of his conquests, and now, unobtrusively and unheralded, the day had come. We had known he was beaten from the moment the Kohima road was cleared, but while we fought the foe at Shenam and within two miles of Div. H.Q., our battle still seemed very much a battle for survival. At last we could put defence from our minds and, however hard the fighting that remained ahead, it would be where and when we chose—we were turning to the offensive, to the break-out from Shenam. The outline plan for that operation was already in the hands of brigade commanders, for the General, knowing that the Japs were in full retreat before 33 Corps through the jungle to the north and seeing the course of events on our own part of the front, had looked forward with his usual foresight to the day when we should be on the move eastwards. The directive issued on June 29th pointed from Shenam to the Tamu road and Burma.

Before that advance could take place, it was necessary to remove the Japs who were lingering on the left flank, and the 49 Bde. operations conducted by 4 and 6 Mahratta at the beginning of July form an epilogue to the fighting in the Sengmai Turel and a bridge to the break-out from Shenam. It was a period that the Jap contrived to make lively for Div. H.Q. for, despite the beating he had taken, two suicide gangs disturbed our peace at nights. The first of these appeared on the Palel airfield in the early hours of July 4th and set fire to six aircraft; this was no fault of ours as the R.A.F. Regiment had taken over the protection of the place a few days earlier, but the firework display on our doorstep became very much our concern; the H.Q. stood to and patrols were sent out, but the enemy made good their getaway. The second gang who turned up in the 49 Bde. administrative area three nights later did little more than disrupt sleep.

The operations to clear the Sengmai Turel had begun on June 28th when 4 Mahratta, who had been recalled from the mists of Machi where they left a detachment, moved off from the Palel area to the long spur running south from Khunbi. Here they paused for a few days while their patrols probed the various pockets of Japs who remained on the hill-tops. Once 6 Mahratta were freed after the end of resistance at "Scott's Knob," they were directed east to Khudei Khunou while 4 Mahratta swung up north to Khunbi. Here there was a stiff company battle on July 8th after "C" Company had approached in the darkness to within four hundred yards of their objective. When daylight came, the weather was so bad that the gunners could not give support and the infantry had to rely on their own weapons. It was a difficult place to attack with the Japs holding the bare terraces and shooting down through the mists at any movement. The Mahrattas, with the company commander in the van, secured all but the last fifty yards, when the advance was held and any movement brought down a shower of grenades from above. Here there was conspicuous gallantry which won the M.M. for a havildar in one of the leading platoons; though a target wherever he moved, he went around collecting the crews of grenade dischargers and 2-inch mortars from other platoons and formed a battery which he directed on to the main point of resistance with a Bren. With the aid of this makeshift artillery, the Mahrattas prevailed and captured Khunbi— just another small company battle, it may seem; but that was so often the way in the Burma campaign, and one of the main reasons the Japanese lost the battle for India is that the infantry, British and Indian, proved masters of the enemy in skill and courage in these countless small engagements when the hazards of war were no less present than in fighting on a larger scale. At this moment 4 Mahratta were mourning the loss of their C.O., Lieut.-Colonel C. J. W. Simpson, who had a few days before succeeded the battle-worn Trim, and of an Adjutant who had served throughout the campaign, both killed outright when a stray shell landed in their trench on July 6th.

From Khunbi 4 Mahratta moved to Maibi Khunou, which they reached on the 11th, and a day later 6 Mahratta were in Khudei Khunou; both places were occupied without opposition, but 6 Mahratta had another of these company engagements on the 7th when "D" Company were held after a notable effort to fork the enemy out of a position west of Khudei Khunou. Here a section commander of the leading platoon, when confronted with an enemy machine gun and two bunkers, ran forward under very heavy fire, fired his tommy-gun through the slit of the first bunker and hurled in two grenades. Satisfied from the silence that there was no further danger here, he then led his men on to the next bunker, which was similarly quietened.

The General had signalled on the 10th that "any enemy withdrawal will be followed and harassed relentlessly," and to increase the Jap discomfiture he had ordered 37 Bde. to establish an ambush astride the maintenance route that crossed the Phalbung spur. Here "A" Company, 3/10 G.R., waged a very successful campaign of their own against small parties of the enemy who, exhausted by the fighting and the monsoon, floundered into the traps laid for them. Between July 8th and 11th the Gurkhas claimed twenty-eight scalps and had only one man wounded themselves.

By now the monsoon had swollen the Sengmai Turel from a two-foot stream to a raging torrent, and even if there had not been other business on hand, operations would have come to a halt from the difficulty of maintaining the troops and the guns which had been lugged far up the Turel in support of the advance. 6 Mahratta pulled out to Palel on July 16th, 4 Mahratta, "very tired and badly in need of rest," a day later when they were on both sides of Khudei Khulen; 2 Hybad, based on Hambone, were ordered to report on enemy movements in the area. These were all in an easterly direction and the day had nearly come when the Japanese at Shenam were to be sent reeling the same way. There was no rest yet for 23 Ind. Div., which was on the eve of the only action it fought with all its troops taking part in one battle.

CHAPTER 18

Operation "Crack On"

HAD the General had his way, "Crack on" or the break-out from Shenam would have been staged a fortnight earlier than it was and the Mahratta operations in the Turel would have been curtailed once the way was clear for the major enterprise. We ourselves were ready for our effort, but we needed additional troops if the full scope of the General's plan was to be achieved, and as these could only come from formations that had been fighting hard, we had to bide our time until they were judged ready for battle. A further reason for the slight delay was the regrouping in the higher command by which 33 Corps was put in charge of the two-pronged monsoon offensive down the Tiddim and Tamu roads, for which 5 Ind. Div. formed one spearhead and 23 Ind. Div. the other. We came under 33 Corps on July 8th and two days later we were told that detailed planning could begin, 5 Bde. from 2 British Div. of Kohima fame, 268 Lorried Inf. Bde. and extra artillery and engineer resources being allotted us for our task.

The General aimed not simply at a break-out from Shenam but at the annihilation of Yamamoto force—"23 Ind. Div. will destroy the Jap force N.W. of the Lokchao crossing and capture the guns and tanks," read his intention. His plan can be described in technical language as "pincers," with the addition of a frontal assault on Shenam. This was to be delivered by 37 Bde., with the Seaforths under command on the day of assault, while 49 and 1 Bdes. formed the two arms of the pincers. Of the two latter brigades, 49 had the more arduous and difficult role as their task called for a long approach march north of the Palel–Tamu road to the Sibong ridge overlooking the Lokchao bridges; these they were to destroy and so block the retreat of the Japs driven out from Shenam. The 1 Bde. hook to the south of the road was a shorter punch directed first at Ralph Hill, followed by exploitation east towards the H.Q. of Yamamoto force near the main road. 5 Bde. was held in reserve and 268 Bde. protected the left flank along the Sita track. This outline of the plan and the diagram are deceptively simple, for they leave to the imagination the weather and the country and take no account of the enemy. Let it suffice to add that the Division had at the height of the monsoon to advance to battle over precipitous ridges where the tracks through the jungle were often knee-deep in mud. We had been set a tough task.

D Day had been fixed for July 22nd, so that the time left to prepare for the attack was short. While the storms raged, a ceaseless struggle went on behind the front to carry out the preliminary movements of men, guns, tanks and stores. Two additional regiments of 25-pounders, a regiment of medium guns and part of a H.A.A. battery had been put under command, and these weapons had to be hauled up to Shenam. In all there were one hundred and thirty-three pieces of artillery in support of the attack, a massing of guns that had been rare in the theatre in the past—certainly we had seen nothing like it before. Besides the guns, there were the Grant tanks of "B" Squadron, 149 R.A.C., to be moved up and all had to be done over an unreliable road while normal maintenance continued and dumps of ammunition and engineer stores were established at Shenam. In the rain and the mud the sappers toiled to keep the road open against the destruction of its surface and acts of God. One of the latter occurred on July 15th when a loaded tank transporter disappeared through a small bridge near Palel and effectively blocked the way, but the sappers slaved throughout the night and by dawn a detour had been constructed across the paddy. The road was open once more, ready for the carefully controlled stream of traffic which went to and from Shenam; each evening the General approved the next day's moves, and the D.A.A.G. was released from his other duties to supervise all movement.

Away to the north, along the track from Nungtak to Sita, another sapper "battle" was in progress. Here a veritable army was deployed wrestling with the mud and the incessant landslides; day after day and for twenty-four hours each day 2 Engineer Battalion less two companies, 2 Bombay

Grenadiers, infantrymen turned into labourers, and a crowd of local coolies worked to keep open the track along which had to pass the supplies for the advanced base being built up at Sita and the maintenance for two brigades. Before the operation was over 800 mules and 120 jeeps were being used to maintain the units dependent on this precarious L. of C., the jeeps working by day (if the sappers decided the road was fit for M.T.) and the mules at night. If the verdict was unfavourable—as not infrequently happened—the mules took the whole load, tramping along at two miles in the hour, their drivers beside them, with the mud over hocks and knees.

There was a further reason for widespread interest in the health of the Sita track. The General had decided that a troop of 6 Bty., 3 Ind. Fd. Regt., and three hundred rounds per gun must be moved to Hambone so that the guns could shoot on to the reverse slopes at "Scraggy." The staff advised that the feat was impracticable, or if by some miracle four guns did arrive at Hambone, they urged that the feat would only be accomplished by an imprudent diversion of effort. The General was not to be shifted and the Division set about carrying out the order. The first stage of the move was child's play and merely necessitated stripping the guns, loading the bits and pieces into four jeeps for each gun and driving along a fairly level track to Nungtak, where the guns reported complete (or, more accurately, in pieces) on July 17th. At Nungtak the climb began, the loaded jeeps "refused" the first genuine hill and three more jeeps had to be attached in tandem as engines before the hill was overcome. At the top nearly all the jeeps gave up the ghost as their clutches were burnt out and alternative means had to be devised for reaching Hambone. The sapper answer was that the guns must be reassembled while they sent for two bulldozers to act as tugs. The dozers arrived, the haul began and on the evening of June 21st the gun sitrep., more eagerly studied than any latest from the course, recorded that one gun was at Hambone; less satisfactorily, a second was reported over the edge and screwed to a tree three miles short of its destination. The next day there was another disaster at the same point when the road slipped under the tractor which was hauling up the third gun. Time was

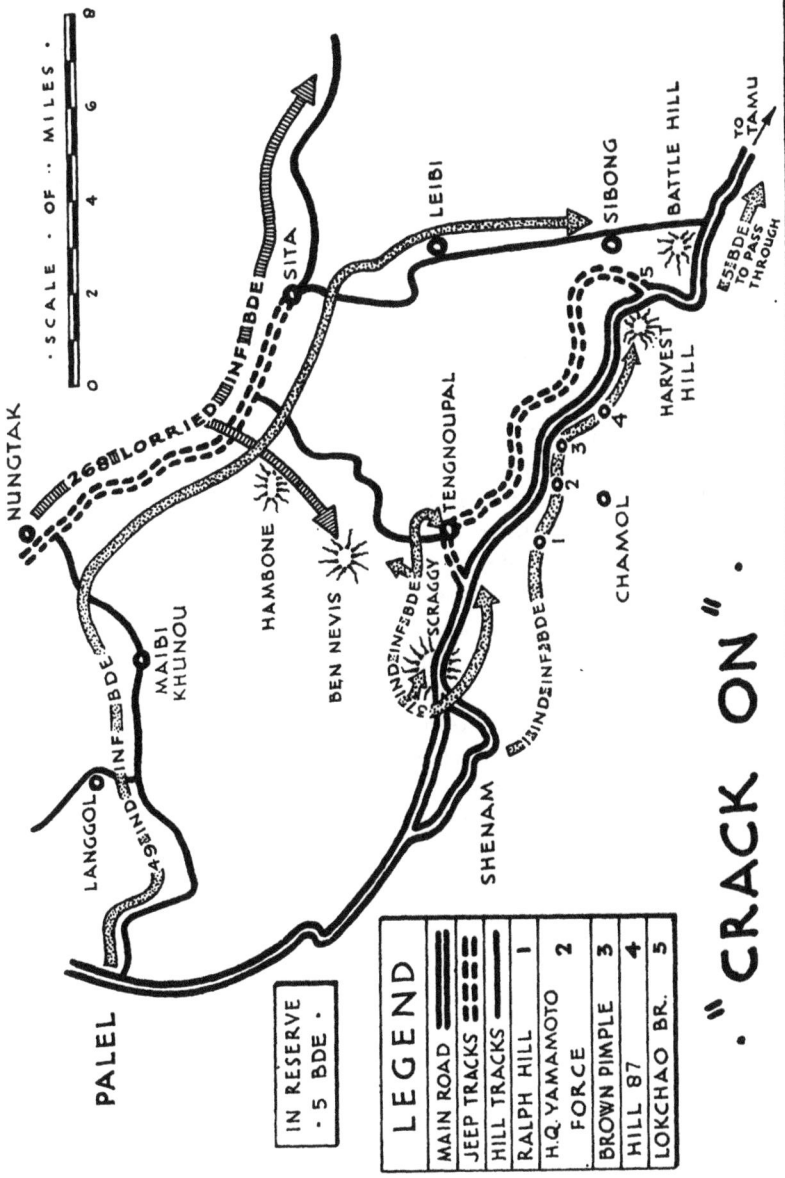

PALEL

NUNGTAK

LANGGOL

MAIBI
KHUNOU

49 IND INF BDE

268 LORRIED INF BDE

HAMBONE

BEN NEVIS

SITA

LEIBI

TENGNOUPAL

SCRAGGY

37 IND INF BDE

20 IND INF BDE

SHENAM

CHAMOL

SIBONG

BATTLE HILL

HARVEST HILL

TO TAMU

5 IND BDE
TO PASS
THROUGH

1   2   3   4   5

· SCALE · OF · MILES ·
0   2   4   6   8

IN RESERVE
· 5 BDE ·

LEGEND

MAIN ROAD	
JEEP TRACKS	
HILL TRACKS	
RALPH HILL	1
H.Q. YAMAMOTO FORCE	2
BROWN PIMPLE	3
HILL 87	4
LOKCHAO BR.	5

· "CRACK ON" ·

running short if the guns were to be in position for zero and the dozers had proved too heavy for the track; it must be jeeps again and somehow sufficient were found to carry the fourth gun from Nungtak to Hambone, and when that was done enough survived to move up the third. Grit had prevailed— three out of the four guns were there ready to give their surprise hammering to the Jap shortly before zero.

Far up the Sengmai Turel 5 Battery of the same regiment were engaged in an equally tough struggle all on their own. They and a battery of 16 Fd. Regt., R.A., had been support- ing 49 Bde., but when the order to withdraw came the Madrassi battery was three miles farther up the Turel and they were faced with twenty-three crossings of this turbulent stream before they could reach a road. They knew what these crossings meant, for one of their lorries had a few days previously been caught by the torrent at the fifth ford and overturned like a cork; but they knew as well that there was a battle coming and they were resolved to be there. The Mahrattas had gone out by a mule track on a ledge thirty feet above the raging stream, and the gunners resolved that their one hope of salvation was to broaden this track and then construct their own road across country; so they sweated and laboured, soaked to the skin, and when opposed by a rock face they brought up a gun and blasted the cliff away from three hundred yards range. The battery commander and his captain took turns at driving the vehicles along the ledge, and then came the "road" where the strength of two hundred gunners was often needed to haul out bogged tractors and guns. When they reached the startled British battery, who were being rafted out by the sappers, 5 Bty. went on their own way, driving their tractors through the torrent and winching the guns across. Sometimes a gun and trailer disappeared completely from view to emerge like "some dreadful amphibious monster," and one gun was overturned by the current and regretfully abandoned; but this and three vehicles were the only losses, while the sappers lost three guns. The end of this minor epic was not as it should have been—the battery arrived in rags, with many covered in sores from the wet and the bites of leeches, two days too late. "Throughout," wrote one who took part, "the men were incredible; we never heard a moan or a grumble. They worked harder than I believed men could work and all in such a cheerful spirit that we, their officers, felt very humble."

So it came about that nine of the one hundred and thirty-three guns did not support the operation, and the rains which caused their absence greatly hampered the massed artillery from carrying out the preliminary programme. It rained for fourteen consecutive days and, with the mists hugging Shenam, the guns were unable to register their targets. There was a break for three hours soon after dawn on the 18th and the next day harassing fire began in earnest. It was comforting to hear the shells screaming overhead at Shenam, knowing that they were travelling east. During these shoots, all guns that could be brought to bear on a target fired one or two rounds simultaneously; after an interval the mixture was repeated elsewhere or, if the directing gunners thought it appropriate, on the same target— anything to lower Jap morale to the depths. This softening continued for the five days before D Day, which had to be twice postponed to give the guns the chance to complete registration; it was not until the 22nd that the weather was sufficiently favourable for this, and our friends in the R.A.F., who had been out during a brief break the previous day, came over again and delivered a number of accurate strikes.

The massed guns were under the overall command of the C.C.R.A.,[1] who had been loaned to us for the occasion. Briefly, the artillery plan for the battle was that our own guns under our C.R.A. would support the 37 Bde. assault except that 1 and 49 Bdes. each had a battery of 28 Mtn. Regt. under command, while the Corps artillery under the C.C.R.A. supported the whole operation; each brigade had with it the commander of one of the gunner regiments as artillery adviser. Except for a few special tasks, there was no timed programme, the artillery being at call once the attack had begun.

When the divisional artillery is supplemented to this extent, the two people behind the scenes who suffer most are the A.A.Q.M.G. and C.R. Sigs., the former having to dump the ammunition where the gunners require it and the latter to co-ordinate a complex signal layout and find the

[1]Commander Corps Royal Artillery (rank, Brigadier)

spare bodies and equipment to assist the R.A. signal section, which is not designed to form the separate signal office required under such conditions. At least the A.A.Q.M.G. was spared one worry—there was no shortage of ammunition. Since the opening of the Kohima road, the administrative situation had vastly improved, and with the Dakotas continuing to defy the monsoon, it had been possible to resume full rations on July 7th. Even before then British troops had been able to taste again fresh meat, indescribably savoury to the palate after months of bully, and for the first time since March it was possible to have the nightly tot of whisky. When such luxuries were available, ammunition was not likely to be short, and the dumping which began on July 15th proceeded with reasonable smoothness.

C.R. Sigs. and his men, with their usual competence, found the answer to each of their problems—all lines were carefully labelled, a special detachment formed to man the important O.P. at Hambone and line parties positioned to repair breaks at once—and he and the A.A.Q.M.G. awaited with interest the move of 49 Bde. as the support of this Brigade was for both a matter of some difficulty. When the Brigade began their march, wireless silence was imposed and they kept in touch with the outside world by listening in to special intelligence broadcasts made three times a day to the W/T detachment established at Sita. This formed an invaluable relay station once the Brigade moved on to Sibong and resumed direct wireless communication with H.Q., for the distance was considerable and the periodic fading, so frequent in the theatre, much in evidence; when this occurred, messages were passed to the relay station by wireless or by phone until line maintenance became too dangerous. Owing to atmospheric conditions, communications were sometimes difficult, but the plan as a whole was successful.

The administrative plan, as so often, depended on the outcome of events, for no one could forecast whether the column would have heavy fighting at the end of its trek or would be able to maintain mule convoys between Sita and Sibong. Hence the Brigade left carrying with it three days' supplies and prepared to pick up two more at Sita *en route;* thereafter it would, if possible, send back its mules to Sita to collect another day's rations or ammunition if there had been heavy fighting; and if the track were closed, air supply would be demanded. Again the plan proved good except for a strange lapse, to be recounted hereafter. Two more points before returning to the battle front—one mobile surgical unit accompanied the northern hook, while a second was stationed behind Shenam, and the divisional carriers were concentrated to form an armoured supply column in case isolated enemy positions held out close to the road after our attack.

While these preparations were going on behind the line, there was continuous patrolling by the forward battalions to gain information about Jap movements. Three Jifs who surrendered at Sita on July 1st said that 15 Div. had orders to withdraw, and it was a sign of the times when a major, who claimed to be second-in-command of the Gandhi Bde., walked into our lines with his orderly on July 6th; he gave 750 as the brigade strength and added that morale was very low, most of the men wishing to surrender. Later there came reports that this formation had been withdrawn on the 17th towards Tamu, so there were indications that the Jap retreat was extending to our part of the front; but an escaped prisoner of 3/10 G.R., who reported on the 20th, had not seen any guns moving back, and patrols on the eve of the battle reported most of the features facing Shenam as still held. An excellent officers' patrol from 1 Seaforth on the 19th, after finding Jap Hill clear, moved on to Nippon, where they took careful note of the wire and bunkers and submitted a report which proved entirely accurate; they estimated the position to be lightly held, and the Japs had not gone two days later when another patrol probed Nippon and Morgan's Peak. The same night, July 21st/22nd, the Gurkhas crept forward in the mist and the rain to the top of "Scraggy" and heard sounds of movement below the crest on the reverse slope.

All the time formations had been quietly moving into position and the build-up for the assault was almost complete. On July 11th 1 Bde. took over the right of the Shenam defences; on the 17th 268 Bde. took over the left flank protection along the Sita track with 2 Hybad under command; on the 20th 5 Bde. concentrated a little east of

o

Palel. We were poised like a hawk with wings fluttering ready to swoop, and as we hovered units began to slip away to their forming-up places.

On the 19th 49 Bde. left Palel on their flanking march to Sibong, their route card reading Langgol, Maibi Khunou Sita and Leibi. It proved an utterly exhausting march; the way was steep, the mud clinging and the men were heavily laden. They pulled their feet out of the mud's grip for hour after hour, trudging on and ever on, their stamina and endurance taxed to the hilt. In the slime, many of the mules slipped over the cliff-side and were lost with their loads, for there could be no waiting and no return on the morrow. The Rajrif, who had been at Nungtak since the 16th, joined the column near Sita and led the way into Leibi on the 21st. On the next day 6 Mahratta were in the van and, marching hard, they gained the Sibong ridge by nightfall without a man falling out on the way. The approach march was over unopposed and surprise had been achieved, but the Brigade was near to having to fight on empty stomachs. Div. H.Q. knew that the mules had been sent back to Sita as arranged and assumed that rations had been collected, but it turned out that the experienced officer in charge of the convoy had drawn ammunition despite clear orders to the contrary. The error was not immediately discovered owing to bad atmospheric conditions, and as the monsoon prevented an air drop on the 23rd, when rations ran out, and only allowed a partial drop the next day, the Brigade was temporarily hungry. On the 25th and 26th the weather was clear enough for drops, and a mule convoy arrived to help rectify an unexpected and unwelcome intrusion of the human element into the battle.

Other units had as difficult marches as 49 Bde. though they were shorter. 3/3 G.R. were speeded on their way by the General when they set off on the morning of the 22nd round the north of Shenam; the next day, as they plodded on through the mist and the rain, sometimes hacking their way through the jungle, they nearly felt the weight of our guns when harassing fire began to fall fifty yards away, but there was no accident and at 2300 hrs. they began to steal forward on a night so dark that the men kept in touch by carrying blocks of phosphorescent wood on their backs.

Simultaneously, the Seaforths were engaged on an equally laboured approach on the south towards Jap Hill; they started on the afternoon of the 22nd and had a hundred and fifty Khasi porters under a British missionary as a baggage train, for the going was too rough for mules. On the morning of the 23rd the C.O. decided to profit from the mist and ordered main H.Q. to join the rifle companies; as the H.Q. was crossing an exposed ridge, the mist temporarily lifted and all had to go to ground for the day. At dusk they moved on and reached a stream which was in spate; the track had in places been nearly perpendicular and the porters could only cross the stream after the sappers had made a bridge; even so several fell in and had to be rescued. Further progress was impossible in the dark and there main H.Q. stayed, huddled together with the rain beating down on them, while the fighting troops moved on. That same day it took the Patialas twelve hours to cover three miles, and the tanks of "B" Squadron, 149 R.A.C., had a hair-raising ride on the night of July 23rd/24th. While our guns concealed the roar of the engines, they crawled along the last four miles of the winding road to Shenam, which was only just wide enough to take the Grants. The smallest error would have sent a machine crashing over the edge through the jungle, so, lights being banned, the rest of the crews laboriously steered the drivers with cigarette ends throughout the journey. The tanks were successfully guided into the positions from which they were to support 37 Bde., and as the hour of zero approached, 0440 hrs. on July 24th, the assaulting troops waited in their appointed places; all were there to time, a very fine, almost a remarkable achievement, for the rains never ceased during the forming-up, and as zero came near the storms still swept Shenam.

The objectives allotted for the assault were these. On the left, 3/3 G.R., after their flank march, were to attack Cyprus from the north and sweep through Tengnoupal village on to Crete East; they had a company of 3/5 R.G.R. under command for exploitation to Morris Hill and their own "B" Company was given the task of forming stops beyond Cyprus. In the centre, 3/10 G.R. took on "Scraggy" and "Lynch"; on the right, 1 Seaforth had as their first objective Nippon, from which they were to exploit to

Morgan's Peak. That was the task set 37 Bde., who had 3/5 R.G.R. in reserve. 1 Bde., reduced to two battalions on D Day for ease of control, used 1 Patiala for the attack on Ralph Hill and kept 1/16 Punjab back for the pursuit towards H.Q. Yamamoto force, last heard of at M.S. 46 on the Tamu road. One point about these objectives must be made clear—the attack on Shenam was in a way a frontal assault, but the attack was so devised that most of the battalions assaulted from a flank; nor were there any special artillery concentrations before the assault, the harassing programme previously described continuing up to zero. By this deliberately restricted use of his guns and by the carefully planned approach marches, the General achieved the complete surprise at which he aimed, and so laid the basis for our success on July 24th.

The day went wonderfully well. 3/3 G.R. were not heavily opposed and, as they charged on to Cyprus, the Japs fled, seventeen falling into the trap set by the ambush company; after a pause they were on again through Tengnoupal to Crete East, and by 0940 hrs. they reported their task completed, for Morris Hill had been found unoccupied.

On "Scraggy" there was for three hours a furious encounter at close quarters. "B" Company, 3/10 G.R., advanced up the hill, three platoons up, the battalion pioneers being used as fighting troops to work round the left of the hill, and they were within twenty yards of the crest when grenades showered upon them. There was no hesitation—in went the assault with the men shouting "Ayo Gurkhali" as they charged, but victory was not to be easily gained. As the first wave topped the rise, they came under heavy fire and from that moment it was a "dog fight" where gains of a few yards had to be forced at the point of the bayonet. The Gurkhas fought fiercely for those slight gains. A section commander with one comrade stalked a bunker just ahead, threw in three grenades and leapt down into the entrance, where he met a Jap coming out with a L.M.G. The naik was the quicker—he seized the gun and had a hand free to give the Jap a burst from his Thompson. Returning to his section, he found he was now the senior man in a platoon where only fourteen remained unwounded,

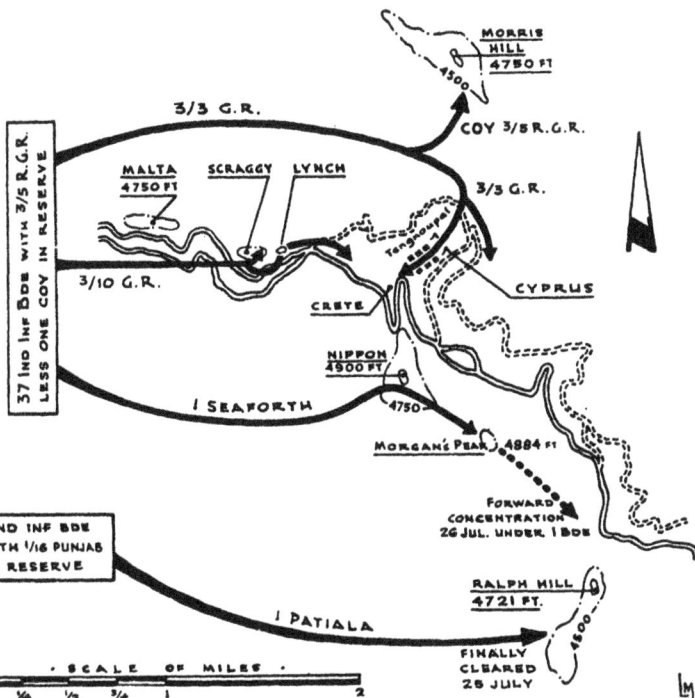

"CRACK ON"
OBJECTIVES AT SHENAM "D" DAY

but, nothing daunted, he led another charge and gained fifteen yards when he was fired on from behind; off he went to stalk this position, armed with a makeshift flame-thrower, and with it he dispatched three more of the enemy. There were other deeds as fine—there was the naik who saw that the left platoon had been pushed off the crest and moved over his section to fill the gap, which he held for two hours against all attacks, exposing himself on the skyline and pouring tommy-gun fire into the enemy when his men began to falter; there was the gallant havildar of the pioneers who, meeting much heavier fire than expected, hung on with five unwounded men; and there was the company commander, dominating the battle by his fearless example. Their efforts should have prevailed unaided, but it was not to be; the reserve platoon had failed to turn the scale, grenades had run out though each man carried ten, and half the company were casualties. In response to a request for reinforcements, "A" Company was sent to assist and after a combined attack "Scraggy" fell—at 0702 hrs. officially, five minutes before "D" Company reached "Lynch"; Crete West fell later in the day. After the battle forty-eight Jap dead were counted on "Scraggy" and the Gurkhas could claim two prisoners, of which one had feigned death before he was restored to life by slaps on the face from the company commander. The Gurkha losses were four-teen killed, ninety wounded, a heavy price that might have been less had the tanks been able to give support, but the mist forced them to listen impatiently to the sounds of battle on the hill-top.

Nippon fell to the Seaforths after a shorter and less savage struggle. The commander of "B" Company, the assault company, had made use of clay models to instruct his men in their task, and he himself led his men through the dark-ness. Near the top of the hill a Jap sentry spotted the attacking troops, but he was promptly dispatched by the commander, who broke into a double and charged at the head of his troops. There might have been trouble from some bunkers on the reverse slope had it not been for the gallantry of a lance-naik in 68 Field Company, who coolly reconnoitred the position from fifteen yards, placed his charges and blew in all six bunkers with the Japs inside.

3/10 GURKHA RIFLES ON "SCRAGGY"
24TH JULY, 1944

It was such episodes that built up the mutual respect British and Indian troops had for each other all through the Division. The Seaforths had captured Nippon by 0630 hrs. and an hour and a half later they were on Morgan's Peak ready to exploit southwards to Ralph Hill, where the Patialas were still fighting.

They had been held up as much by the weather as by the enemy. In the mist it was hard to locate enemy positions, and when the C.O. decided that he needed supporting fire, the state of the tracks prevented the movement of guns. One detachment of 3-inch mortars arrived about 0915 hrs. and with this aid "B" Company cleared the south of the hill, but it was seven at night before the mountain battery had hauled their guns within range—too late for a further attack. This was the only hitch at Shenam on a day of otherwise unbroken success which had laid bare the weakness of an enemy whose resistance had been neither so stern nor so protracted as we had expected. The General's orders that night to the brigades at Shenam ran—37 to secure the ground won, 1 to resume command of 1 Seaforth, clear Ralph Hill and exploit eastwards. After boxing in the enemy with a second company, the Patialas cleared their objective during the morning of the 25th, and shortly after midday 1/16 Punjab passed through—the break-out was complete and the pursuit of the broken Japanese forces down the Tamu road towards 49 Bde. had begun.

All had gone marvellously well, but we could not claim complete success, for the left arm of the pincer had been thwarted and we had not been able to close the trap as the General intended. Down at the Lokchao bridges 49 Bde. were fighting hard. The attempt by 5/6 Rajrif to reach and blow the bridges on the night of July 23rd/24th had miscarried in the darkness and it was soon clear that the enemy were holding this vital position on their line of withdrawal in strength. It was later discovered that two fresh battalions of the Japanese 4th Division had arrived from Sumatra almost at the last moment and these were now guarding the bridges. They would not have been there had "Crack on" come a fortnight earlier as the General wished ... but it is useless to speculate on "might have beens."

Unsuccessful in their attempt to effect a surprise coup, 49

Bde. set about finding a route that would enable them to sever the Japs' life-line farther east while the H.A.A., directed by the 49 Bde. artillery adviser and firing at 18,000 yards' range, made life very uncomfortable on the road. The 24th, when there were jitter raids on the Rajrif, had perforce to be spent in recces, and these were brilliantly conducted by 6 Mahratta. On one, the commander of "C" Company, after finding a key feature christened Battle Hill unoccupied, left the main body of the patrol and wormed his way forward until he could observe the Jap positions twenty yards away; while there, he had an unexpected close-up of a Jap who left his bunker to relieve Nature. This patrol was followed on the way back, but the enemy fell into a cunningly laid ambush and lost fourteen killed. A lance-naik took over another patrol when the commander was killed, skilfully extricated his men and had the coolness and resource to set an ambush which disposed of a dozen more Japs.

This N.C.O., though greatly fatigued, acted as guide on the night of the 24th/25th for a night attack by 5/6 Rajrif on the summit of Battle Hill, but the enemy had taken alarm and were there first. 6 Mahratta were therefore ordered to clear the track east of the hill on the 25th. The fight in the mist, where progress could only be judged by the noise of the battle, was long and bloody. The leading troops of "D" Company were soon held and their quick encircling move to the left brought heavy rifle fire from very close range; "C" Company, put in fifty yards to the left through the jungle, could make no headway and life was made more unhealthy by fire from the main enemy positions on Battle Hill which could occasionally be seen through rifts in the mist. This made it very difficult to use the mountain artillery and mortars, but used they were, the direction being by the sound of falling shells and bombs! With his leading companies held, the C.O. decided to bring up "A" Company to hold his gains and then to attempt to bludgeon his way through. Right nobly did "C" and "D" Companies carry out their orders—in an intense fire fight, "C" were halted three times in fifty yards, "D" four times in the same distance. Casualties began to mount; one section commander, himself wounded, saw three of his men fall, but he fought on; another N.C.O., who was thrice hit, took over a Bren from a wounded man and went on firing from the hip; in the end he carried the Bren, a tommy-gun and a rifle out of the battle, for withdrawal it had to be. "B" Company were ordered up as a second lay back, but before they were in position the Japs were at the Mahrattas and "C" and "D" Companies were involved in a hand-to-hand grapple. Eventually they disengaged and the withdrawal followed in excellent order, assisted by 15 Mtn. Bty., now under a havildar who showed fine skill and powers of control after his commander had been wounded and the O.P. killed. During the withdrawal one of the covering companies was counter-attacked from two sides; the response of its commander has been preserved: "Can we have another fifteen minutes, sir? We're having a lovely time and still killing Japs." The Mahrattas estimated the enemy dead at seventy-eight and their own losses amounted to about fifty. Awards of the M.C. to two of the company commanders and of other decorations followed this gallant affair.

The next day, July 26th, it was the turn of 4 Mahratta; they were tired and greatly reduced in numbers from sickness and exposure to the elements, but they fought as courageously as ever. The plan was to cut the main road about a mile east of Battle Hill and it meant a four-hour approach march up and down steep and rocky ravines. They reached the road, deployed "A" Company to hold it and pushed across a depleted "D" Company, barely fifty strong, on to the high ground beyond. The Japs counter-attacked and, as luck would have it, scored a direct hit on a knoll where the small garrison was obliterated; this exposed the left flank and, though "A" Company was sent to assist, the Mahrattas were slowly forced back to the line of the road. There a detachment of 71 Fd. Coy. were showing consummate gallantry; the Japs had a machine gun fifty yards away and were spraying the sappers with bullets, but these courageous men persisted in their attempt to form a road block of tar barrels and anti-tank mines. Heavily engaged on the front, the Mahrattas were put in further peril when a fresh company of Japs appeared on the right flank from Lokchao; they had no strength left to attack and they could only withdraw away from the road until they could no longer command it with small-arms fire; later they were ordered to rejoin their Brigade by the way they had come. This sort of engagement, coming at the end of a long campaign, puts to the supreme test the fundamental military qualities of a unit; 4 Mahratta weathered the storm, thanks to their toughness and the leadership of their acting C.O., Major W. M. Mackay, who won the D.S.O., and of the "D" Company commander, the only other experienced officer left, who did much more than command his company in the withdrawal and won a bar to his M.C.

49 Bde. had shot their bolt. Though the R.A.F. harassed the Japs at Lokchao on the 26th and 27th and the Rajrif made a further attack against Battle Hill on the 28th, which penetrated to within two hundred yards of the top, they could not close the road and bar the withdrawal from Shenam. The men were exhausted and weakened, many were badly crippled by trench feet, and the Brigade was again straitened for supplies owing to storms on the 29th and 30th which grounded the Dakotas. 4 Mahratta wrote on the 30th: "No air drop for two days; supplies short; all ranks right out of cigarettes. No one has had a wash or shave. With boots and clothes caked thick in filthy mud, unwashed and bearded, we are a villainous-looking crowd indeed—and God, how we stink!"

Their work and that of the Division was nearly done. While 37 Bde. stayed in the Shenam area where General Slim came on the 27th to congratulate the Gurkhas he knew so well, 1 Bde. took up the pursuit with fine *élan.* 1/16 Punjab, temporarily checked close to the main road on the evening of the 25th, sent "A" Company on a wide encircling move through Chamol early on the 26th and soon whisked the Japs off Brown Pimple, though they had to clamber up two hundred feet to a commanding ledge. The next morning, while it was still dark, the jemadar commanding the leading platoon of "A" Company heard from a patrol that the enemy were still holding Hill 87, the company objective; they were at the end of a fourteen-hour march, the enemy strength was unknown and the ground unrecced, but the jemadar was not for waiting; he planned and carried out a night assault which was entirely successful.

Tails were very high in the air! When the news of this success reached Bde. H.Q. they ordered the Seaforths through to Harvest Hill; and finally, on July 28th, the Patialas pushed on with a troop of tanks in attendance to the Lokchao bridges, where they found part of 6 Mahratta had been waiting an hour. The Mahrattas had had an awkward march from Sibong down the east bank of Lokchao; at times they were forced to wade through the river, and when they reached the bridges they found them blown, as they had expected from the explosions heard during the previous night.

The appearance of the tanks with the Patialas and indeed the maintenance of the pursuit was something of a miracle. On the 26th the General had ordered 37 Bde. and the tank column to open the road to Ralph Hill and pass a jeep convoy to 1 Bde., but the advance had not gone far before it was halted by a landslide. We were used to these, but this was a landslide *par excellence*—two hundred yards of road had disappeared. The sappers set to work with bulldozers roaring away, and by midday on the 27th they had excavated on the Shenam side of the break a 1 in 2½ slip, down which selected vehicles were lowered by winches to a track leading on to the road beyond the "break." It was like a famous description of the descent into the nether regions, for it was tolerably easy to go down but there was no return. The supply system established close to the vehicle slip was simplicity itself; ammunition and boxed stores went down a chute, petrol drums were rolled down under their own steam—simple and effective, but very laborious as the stores had to be taken off the lorries on the road, put on their way down the hillside, manhandled at the lower level to dumps and loaded into jeeps. Nor were the sapper troubles confined to the "break"; after they had bridged a slide at Shenam on the 28th, a bulldozer lost its bearings and went over the side of the bridge so that the work had to be done again, and the roads on the Japanese side of the "break" had been so shockingly maintained that it was hard to imagine how their troops were supplied. By dint of working night and day in the rain and howling wind, the sappers and administrative units kept the roads open and supplies moving forward while the fighting troops forged ahead, with the signallers hard pushed to keep pace.

On July 31st, three days after the link-up at Lokchao, the whole of 6 Mahratta used the two remaining cables of the suspension bridge as supports for hands and feet when they crossed the swirling waters of the river to form the southern arm of a further attack on Battle Hill. After an artillery concentration, the Rajrif advanced simultaneously from the north and reached the top two minutes before the Mahrattas. This, our last assault in Burma, was an almost bloodless affair as the enemy had been pulling out slowly since the 27th, and the only excitement fell to the lot of a Patiala company sent out as a stop. One of their sections fell in with an enemy party and after two attacks had on their hands some baggage, a couple of prisoners and two boxes which were full of Div. H.Q. records and orders.

The fighting was over. 268 Bde. had completed their unspectacular but essential task on the left flank—Ben Nevis was occupied on the 27th and patrols of 2/4 Bombay Grenadiers, reaching the head of the Kabaw valley at Mintha, had returned to ground with which old hands in the Division were so familiar. The enemy forces between Shenam and the Lokchao bridges had been utterly shattered and there was no resistance left to bar our way. By now the sappers of 208 Fd. Coy., R.E., and 94 Fd. Coy., I.E., had constructed an aerial ropeway and cradle and a small box girder bridge over the Lokchao, and across the bridge came 5 Bde.

Hot on their heels on August 2nd went the General with a party of officers and an escort. This distinguished force was not on a "mopping-up" operation, but when they saw two Jap soldiers scuttling into a drain under the road they turned into satisfactory infantry. The Japs had not lost their obstinacy in defeat. True to their nature, this couple paid no heed to exhortations to surrender and only budged when a smoke grenade was thrown into the drain. Flushed from their lair, they found the General had made a sound plan for their capture, and if they did not realize what notable prisoners they had become, they can be pardoned for that.[2] Thereafter the General resigned the physical conduct of operations to 5 Bde., who entered

---

[2] There is another and more entertaining version of this story, but General Roberts assures me it is apochryphal.—AUTHOR.

PURSUIT OF THE JAP

MAINTENANCE AT THE "BREAK"

CROSSING THE LOKCHAO

Moreh on August 3rd and Tamu on the 4th, the latter now a revolting place, ankle deep in mud, where putrefying corpses polluted the air and millions of flies took their fill. In the village were numerous half-starved Japs and Jifs who went to swell the bag for the first week in August, when 106 Japs and 80 Jifs passed through our cage, an astronomical figure for this campaign.

There the story of the Fighting Cock on the Assam–Burma frontier comes to an end. We had lived in the jungle for two years and three months and for all but a bare five months of that time we were front-line troops. Eighteen months had gone by since half of the Division had been on leave of any sort, many had been at the front for three monsoons, and all were exhausted and tired from the strain of the fighting since March. There comes a point when the best of Divisions are battle-drunk, when they can slog on mechanically but lack fire, and so it was with us. Nothing but a rest can restore the vital spark, and it was welcome news that on relief by the 11th East African Division we were to regain our strength in Shillong. The brigades began to concentrate for the move out from the beginning of August, and at midday on the 10th we handed over command. We were no longer part of the battle, nor were we ever destined to rejoin the pursuit which, beginning at Shenam, went on and on through the length of Burma until it ended the following May within a stone's throw of Rangoon. Had anyone suggested as we moved out of the battle, that the next time we met the Japanese they would come bowing and hissing before us as members of a defeated race, he would have been laughed to scorn—but the visionary would have been right.

There is nothing very spectacular about our story, no feat of arms that appeals immediately to the imagination like the fly-in of the Chindits or the 2 Div. clash at Kohima, but it is none the less a fine record of long service in the cause of freedom. While it was necessary we waited patiently and won our struggle with isolation and the jungle, and when the battle came we fought tooth and nail. Tough and unyielding in defence, resolute and spirited in attack, masters of the approach through the jungle, we had never been worsted by the Jap wherever we had been called on to fight him. Discipline, courage, endurance, skill in the use of arms—these are prime virtues on the field of battle and these we had shown we possessed. The long list of honours and awards summarized at the end of this book is witness to our quality, which owed so much to the two fine soldiers who were our commanders. Inevitably in war there is a price to pay; our casualties from all battle causes were 2,910, of which 605 were killed in action. Against these losses we could set the 2,400 Japanese who we knew had been killed by our arms, and when we left the front, our total of 127 prisoners was higher than that of any other Division.

CHAPTER 19

A Year in India

THE A.A.Q.M.G., Lieut.-Colonel H. S. P. Hopkinson, and the A.Q. staff were breathless when they arrived at Shillong after extricating the Division from the battle. For the first ten days in August their life had been particularly hectic, as they had to maintain the fighting troops of five brigades over a shocking L. of C. made worse by the monsoon, hand over our commitments to the East Africans and move out our honourable selves in our own not over-plentiful transport; it was a very awkward handful, but "Q" is rarely baffled and under the A.A.Q.M.G.'s efficient direction the hand-over and big movement programme went smoothly. After a day's rest in the Palel area, where there were the simple but great pleasures of hot showers and clean clothes, we trundled away in our lorries and were all gathered at Shillong by the 24th except for the mule companies, who were walking out by easy stages.

At Shillong all thoughts turned to leave or repatriation, the latter a distant dream for most who had come from the U.K. Only a few months earlier it seemed that those who had the misfortune to be serving in the East were cooped up in the jungle to eternity, but a great day had come when repatriation was permitted. At first it affected none but the Regular soldiers, many of them men with seven or eight years' service overseas, and here at Shillong it was the six-year men who were going home, but the prospects of return continued to improve fairly rapidly until by the New Year the period of service had been reduced to four years—quite long enough, but it was a span that the mind could measure.

For our thousands of Indian troops leave presented few difficulties; they had their homes to which they could go as fast as special trains could be provided to take them to railheads which often left a hundred-mile walk to be covered at the end of the train journey. But there was difficulty over leave for British troops, who longed for home and the comforts of home life and longed in vain. After two years in a climate which put an unending strain on a man's strength, the coolness of the hills could provide the refreshment that was so necessary, and there were some who enjoyed their stay in an admirably run hostel at Naini Tal, but the delights of a hill station did not have a universal appeal and many born and bred in towns preferred Bombay or Calcutta, where there were cinemas and shops and all the outward signs of modern civilization; these cities were not so beneficial to health nor were the leave arrangements always good. British residents in both places gave up countless hours of their time to look after the troops, but they were not numerous enough, nor was there sufficient accommodation to provide satisfactorily for all.

While the Division was thus strewn out over the length and breadth of India, those who remained at Shillong were visited early in October by the B.G.S. Training, 11 Army Group. His visit settled the fate of the Division. We had expected that after a period for leave and re-equipment we should return to the jungle whence we had come, but when it was clear that we should not be fully restored until the end of January, 1945, we were consigned to India; destination— Bombay or thereabouts; object of the exercise—training as an assault division for combined operations to repair the gap left since 2 Div., the experts, had been plunged into the battle of Burma. It was a swift turn of fortune's wheel. We could give others useful tips about jungle warfare, but there was hardly a man among us who at this time knew one end of a boat-hook from the other, and the Gurkhas were not the only troops who had hardly heard of the sea's existence.

There was a week at the beginning of December when our future went into the melting-pot again, but "Q" were spared a staff officer's nightmare. 1 Bde. were paddling and conducting other nautical exercises at the Combined Training Centre at Bombay, 49 Bde. were being put through their paces on the Kharakvasla reservoir near Poona, 37 Bde. were at Shillong; our 15-cwt. trucks had reached Jhansi, our jeeps and 3-tonners had been bequeathed to Fourteenth Army; Div. H.Q. were taking their ease in a train; the movement of mules had begun. Suddenly there came a stand-fast order and all wondered what was afoot while one or two high ranking officers disappeared to H.Q., 11 Army Group. It transpired later that the discussion was over the possibility of marrying up all the bits and pieces that were 23 Ind. Div. and sending them back to Burma, where the plan for a gigantic right hook was maturing. It would have been exhilarating to have been part of the 4 Corps sweep down the Gangaw valley and across the Irrawaddy, but none can dispute that it was wise to send 17 Div., who were complete and rested, much as we may regret our lost opportunity and enforced idleness.

We were to be idle much longer than anyone anticipated. In mid-November part of the staff had hastened away to Delhi, where they were joined by the General, who was flown back from his leave at home to join in the hurly-burly of planning an expedition designed to strike at the Jap vitals in the southern extremity of Burma. It seemed then that we should be off again on our travels in a little while, but we had come to combined operations at the wrong moment. The war in Europe had gone more slowly than at one time seemed likely, and the S.E.A.C. resources, which had been whittled away for "Overlord," could not be made good; there were insufficient landing craft available and many of the administrative and special units needed for amphibious warfare were not in sight. By mid-December the planners were back after an experience that could at best be described as interesting. For a month they had lived in a world of strange initials and they returned with S.N.O.L.,[1] P.M.L.O.[1] and L.C.A.[2] coursing through the brain like a tune that cannot be forgotten. They had also learnt another series of initials too vulgar to be recorded here, but very relevant to the upsets that plague the lives of those planning "Combined Ops."

In the middle of April, 1945, these same much-tried planners came back chanting the same refrain. Once again they had been away about a month, but this time our hopes of a move had run high as they had migrated from Delhi to

---

[1] Senior Naval Officer Landing and Principal Military Landing Officer, the naval and army staff officers controlling the landing of a division.

[2] Landing Craft Assault.

P

Bombay, whither they had summoned the brigade staffs. We had been asked to interest ourselves in Puket Island, an obscure place off the Thailand coast between Burma and Malaya, too small to feature on a normal map and therefore thoroughly suitable for S.E.A.C.'s slender resources; but even this operation proved beyond us and exercise "Roger" followed "Bamboo" into the waste-paper basket. The stark and unpalatable truth was clear for all to see—we were grounded until the end of hostilities in Europe.

Wherever we might go eventually, it would be under a new commander and with several new faces among our brigadiers. It was a sad moment for many when they heard that General Roberts had been translated to the command of the newly formed 34 Indian Corps, though all rejoiced in his promotion and knew that merit had been justly rewarded. This was on March 12th and for three days we were left wondering who was to be our new lord and master before it was announced that Major-General D. C. Hawthorn was coming straight from the Arakan, where he had been B.G.S., 15 Ind. Corps, and had recently gained an immediate award of the D.S.O., a rare distinction for a staff officer in this war. We were to find that for the third time we had been fortunate in our General, whose practical experience of the problems peculiar to operating in the chaungs of the Arakan, added to the mind of a soldier who had made a deep study of his art, made him very much the man for our needs.

General Hawthorn had under him almost a new team of brigadiers as only Brigadier King remained of the men who had led us through the Burma campaign. Brigadier N. Macdonald, D.S.O., had succeeded Brigadier J. F. Marindin as the Gurkha commander of 37 Bde. at the end of the battling at Shenam; Brigadier A. W. S. Mallaby, C.I.E., had come from a distinguished staff career at G.H.Q. to take over 49 Bde. from Brigadier C. H. B. Rodham after we had been a month at Shillong; and lastly, General Roberts filched from us Brigadier Andrews, who was replaced by a cheerful gunner from Europe in the person of Brigadier R. B. W. Bethell, D.S.O.

There were during the period various changes in units designed to make us into the "Standard" division which had been evolved as the most suitable organization for jungle warfare. The first step here had been to shed one of our G.T. companies and a mule company before we left Imphal, the units from which we parted being 122 Ind. G.T. Coy. and 61 A.T. Coy. We waited the arrival of reconnaissance and machine-gun battalions, a third workshop company and some light aid detachments; 5/8 and 6/8 Punjab came from N.W. Army[3] in February as our new fighting units; the L.A.Ds. and 135 Ind. Wksp. Coy. we raised ourselves.

Thus by the time "Roger" was cancelled in mid-April, our reorganization was complete, the staff had had ample practice in compiling staff and landing tables, the waterproofers had seen many a vehicle wade ashore and the troops had fully explored the mysteries of assault landings. We wanted action, but there was none to be had for those who sat kicking their heels in the Nasik camps while Fourteenth Army raced through Burma and the defeat of the Hun drew near. There was far too much time to think at Nasik, where accommodation was not of the best and life had few attractions and no excitements to offer. We had been too long out of the line. Indian troops no less than British had had enough of inaction, and the Indians reasonably disliked the drop in their pay caused by the loss of special allowances since they came out of the battle. In curt, soldierly language, the Division was "browned off" and the state of mind was reflected in two awkward disciplinary cases.

A contributory cause to the drop in morale was the absence of senior officers at the critical time when the first phase of training was nearing its end. As the result of the "Roger" planning, it was not until a month after his appointment that General Hawthorn was free to acquaint himself with the Division, and he was quick to sense the needs of the moment. H.Qs. that had become too static were bundled out into the open on a series of exercises—"Cock I" chanced to coincide with VE Day!—and the influence of the firm hand at the top halted the decline. VE Day itself was not without importance in restoring good cheer. The significance of the day was not missed either by British troops of all ranks or by the more educated Indians, and we celebrated

[3] On the N.W. Frontier of India.

the occasion in true style, exhilarated by the victory and by the prospect of a speedier end to our war.

At the beginning of June there came a further fillip when the planners were summoned to Delhi to resume their labours. There had been previous disappointments, but all felt that, with the war in Europe over, we must be on a winner this time—and we were right. There were to be no more small islands as objectives; the task before us in "Zipper" was the reconquest of Malaya, for which we and 25 Ind. Div. were to be the two assault divisions, with 5 Ind. Div. and 26 Ind. Div. to follow up; the whole operation was under the control of 34 Ind. Corps, with General Roberts at the head, so we were in good hands.

Shortly after the planning started, the Government did their best to sabotage the operation by reducing the length of service overseas to three years and four months without warning; the change was regarded by all as an electioneering ramp and it created a fury in the minds of men who saw in this move no sign of the promised full support for the war in the East. So many were affected in our British Field Regiment that the unit was disbanded and 178 Fd. Regt., R.A., came to us in its stead; other units were less seriously hit, but all lost experienced N.C.Os. for whom there were no fully trained substitutes. Had there been a less high proportion of Indian troops in the operation, some alteration in the time-table would have been inevitable, but as it was the planning could proceed uninterrupted. By mid-June the first phase in Delhi was complete and a week later the Division and Brigade staffs gathered in Bombay, where junior officers lived in a deal of discomfort in a building that some judged to have been a lunatic asylum; it was thus, they said, very suitable for combined operators.

It is the immense amount of detail required that makes the planning of an assault landing so laborious and wearisome. When every single vehicle in a division must be allotted a space and almost every man fitted in to a landing table, when precise calculations have to be made of the stores that can be stowed in vehicles and craft, the mind is lost in a maze of figures and diagrams; and it is so easy for tired men working against time to make mistakes which lead to new calculations at a yet hotter pace. One such error occurred in the "Zipper" planning over the number of heavily laden vehicles that could be carried on the transports and led to a grim burning of midnight oil for a couple of nights. The exhausted planners had hardly recovered from this crisis when the Navy caused further excitement by announcing that ten of the precious L.S.Ts. due from Europe were in a state of collapse at various points between Alexandria and Karachi. The loss of these craft would have shattered the plan, and as the concoction of a fresh plan and the mounting of a new expedition would have taken seventy days, by which time the Navy thought their hulks would be repaired, it was decided to adopt a policy of "no change" and hope for better news. In the end, nearly all the L.S.Ts. tottered across the Indian Ocean and there was no change in the date of D Day—September 9th.

By July 20th our plans were complete and it was high time to return to Nasik, where there was an ever-increasing air of expectancy as it became obvious to all that the end of boredom was in sight. The men were in great heart and nothing better could have been devised for giving the keenest edge to their enthusiasm than the great parade on July 13th when the Commander-in-Chief came to decorate those who had gained honours in Burma. It was one of those days of impressive military ceremony that stir the heart and make the pulse beat faster. The low hills behind Mashrul camp formed a natural grandstand from which the Division watched the scene below, where picked detachments from each unit formed three sides of a square. In their midst stood the long lines of those who were to be honoured and facing these, on the open side of the square, were two generals, five brigadiers and a colonel. It was a day of grand reunions, when men who had become friends amid the stress of battle met in happier surroundings, and a day that embraced the whole history of the "Fighting Cock." In the grandstand was a small man with a perky walk—General Savory, the father of us all, was back—and on the same parade ground, whither General Savory was summoned later, stood his two successors side by side and behind them, among the brigadiers, Balwant Singh and Andrews, King, Macdonald and Mallaby.

When General Auchinleck arrived, an order rang out,

followed by three crisp movements as the parade gave the General Salute, and then for a brief space there was a great stillness with the Union Jack, now broken at the masthead, fluttering over the scene. After the inspection of the 2/19 Hybad guard of honour, the C.-in-C. moved to his appointed place and the presentation began—generals and brigadiers, W.Os. and V.C.Os., privates and sepoys, these came up in turn until at last the centre of the square was empty and all stood in front of their units with their medals pinned on their breasts. The General moved forward to the microphone, spoke in Urdu of the noble deeds that belonged to the past and of the tasks that lay ahead, and finally inspected the whole parade. As he turned to go, General Hawthorn called for cheers, which were given right willingly by men who had subconsciously gained corporate strength from a deeply impressive occasion. The chief architect of the day's success was the G.S.O.1, Lieut.-Colonel Mellsop, who was a masterhand at stage-managing big parades; it was not his fault that a certain rivalry between the bands sometimes produced discordant noises.

This parade made a pleasant break in the whirl of planning and gave the staff a chance to spend a valuable day at Nasik before they were free of their duties at Bombay on the 20th. By then there were only nine days before the vehicles of 37 Bde. were due to leave for Madras, where the brigade group was due to embark; for the rest of the Division time was less pressing as all were embarking at Bombay except for a small H.Q. party. This separation of the Division by the breadth of India was only part of the problem of mounting an expedition in a country which, with its vast distances and poor communications, was the worst possible base for a combined operation. In England, if stores were urgently needed at the time of "Overlord," goods traffic was given priority, but there was no such easy remedy in India, where fear of upsetting the population prevented changes in published train services. The equipping of the force was rendered even more difficult by slowness in the depots where the few British officers were urging on their Indian staffs to greater haste in sorting out and distributing the quantities of equipment that had begun to arrive from Europe. Perhaps the remarkable thing is that we left India

THE NASIK PARADE
The C.-in-C. inspects the 2/19 Kumaon Guard of Honour

THE NASIK PARADE
The C.-in-C. inspects detachments of The Rajputana Rifles and
Mahratta Light Infantry

Facing page 214]

"PREDOMINANTLY A DIVISION OF INDIAN TROOPS"

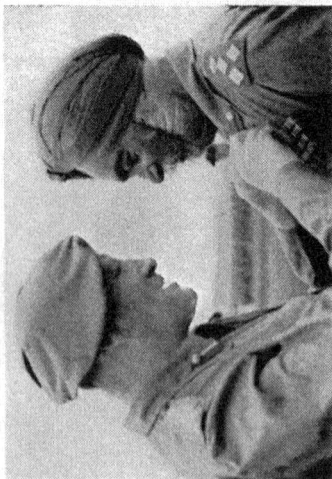

BRIGADIER BALWANT SINGH, SARDAR BAHADUR, O.B.I., RECEIVES THE D.S.O.

JEM. BHAKATBAHADUR RAI, 10 GURKHA RIFLES, RECEIVES THE M.C.

C.S.M. V. STEVENS, SEAFORTHS, RECEIVES THE D.C.M.

NAIK NARAYAN SINDE, MAHRATTAS, RECEIVES THE I.D.S.M.

with so much of what we wanted, a statement that is a tribute to A.D.O.S.,[4] who by his personal efforts extracted many luxuries from the depots, and even more to those in India Command who made a low gear machine work at a faster speed than was customary. In the end, our new acquisitions ranged from the latest pattern rifle to Bergen rucksacks, which came in such numbers that the sapper demands were abundantly satisfied and some officers had a welcome addition to their kit.

Yes—we were better equipped than we had ever been before and we felt that we were ready to give a good account of ourselves as we watched the first vehicle convoy go past the start point in the early hours of July 29th. Four days later the first trainload of Gurkhas steamed out of Nasik station.

The General had been there to see the road convoy off, and as the last tail-light disappeared round the corner he said quietly, "The march to Singapore begins." Little did anyone guess what was in store. Seven days passed, seven perfectly normal days on one of which the General gave a brilliant exhibition in directing a T.E.W.T. On the eighth, the world was shattered by the release of the most ghastly weapon yet devised; two days later a second explosion shook Japan to her knees. There were many rumours in the early evening of August 10th that she had surrendered, and at 2130 hrs. all turned to the wireless. The rumour was true—the scientists had rendered the task we had been set unnecessary. Doubts whether the Japanese would agree to the condition that the Emperor must be under the authority of General MacArthur persisted for a few days until on August 15th, 1945, there came the final answer. The Second World War was at an end. There remained the chance that the outlying Japanese armies would refuse to obey orders from Tokyo, but anxieties on this score were largely set at rest when envoys from the C.-in-C., Southern Army arrived at Rangoon on the 22nd. The invasion had become a peaceful reoccupation.

There was no wild outburst of heartfelt rejoicing at these utterly unexpected events, a seemingly strange reaction to a great moment in world history yet not inexplicable. Partly

---

[4] Assistant Director of Ordnance Services (Lieut.-Colonel).

we were too busy to do much more than pause in the work of preparation, partly some felt that the celebrations in London were premature while the attitude of the Japanese in Malaya and elsewhere was undetermined; but the real reason for our state of mind was a dreadful sense of anti-climax. We had been kept waiting a year, while we listened to the stories of the victories gained by others, and our nerves and minds were keyed up as the hour approached when we should be the spearhead of another great feat of British arms. At the eleventh hour that prospect faded into the realm of "might have beens," and some units, which had previously been denied a tilt at the Japs, were desolate.

So there was in those last few days before embarkation a conflict of emotions, for it would be foolish to deny that there was not also present in the hearts of most of us a feeling of deep relief as the trains rumbled on to Madras and Bombay. Disappointment there might be, but the task of restoring order in a land dominated by the enemy for three and a half years might not prove easy, as General Sir William Slim reminded the officers of 37 Bde. in a farewell address which made it plain that the Jap should know we came as victors. That was on August 30th, and the next day when the troops at Madras began to embark he was there with Generals Roberts and Hawthorn to watch them filing on board. On the morning of September 3rd the Madras convoy formed up outside the harbour ; zero hour was midday and prompt to time we steamed away from the shores of India. The Bombay convoy had started the day before. Some may have wondered whether our journey was, after all, necessary; the future was to prove that it was and that Malaya was only a port of call.

One footnote—the "standard" Division was suited neither to an assault landing nor to our subsequent role in "Zipper" and we left sadly behind in India 28 Mountain Regiment and all our mules. We had hoped to see the gunners and a few of the animals again when they came on a later convoy, but they were among the units that never sailed when the plan was changed—the parting at Nasik had been final, the end of a three years' partnership with the "Fighting Cock."

CHAPTER 20

Malayan Interlude

THE voyage to Malaya was a brief spell of delightful ease. Had it been one of Messrs. Cook's or Lunn's pleasure cruises, the accommodation would have been less cramped, but after a long swell on the first day out, the sea was calm enough to quieten the fears of the worst of landlubbers, the sun shone and the mind was free to relax. The only untoward event occurred on September 6th when the Madras convoy seemed likely to be charged by six fleet carriers. Lamps flashed angrily to and fro and danger was averted by the convoy altering course and steering back towards India for a space. Owing to a miscalculation during the night, the convoy had turned east prematurely and was out of position, an error which aroused the wrath of the Admiral in charge of the operation and caused more flashing of lights. The Army allowed themselves a chuckle when they heard the message read "Your navigation is deplorable, repeat deplorable." Thereafter the steering was accurate enough to avoid risk of collisions and we went peacefully on our way, enjoying the leisure and delighted to watch the lights from hundreds of portholes dancing on the waters at night, a spectacle so different from that remembered by all who had come out from England in blacked-out convoys.

On September 8th, the day before D day, there was a wonderful meeting on the high seas. Far away to starboard were the fleet carriers whom we had met earlier, closer in the cruiser and destroyer escort, and inside these a vast array of small craft which had started before the personnel convoys. War might be over, but here was an unforgettable reminder of Britain's might at sea. Gradually ships and craft fell into their appointed places and all steamed on through the afternoon with the sky stained by black smudges from many a funnel until darkness came and myriads of lights twinkled out like the front of a seaside resort seen from afar. During the night the pace slowed and at last the rattle of chains told us that we had reached the anchorage—the respite was over.

The plan for "Zipper" might have filled many more pages of this book, but though it has little more than an academic interest, a brief account needs to be given for an understanding of the story. The overall design of the Army plan was this: the formation of a bridgehead in the heart of the Malay peninsula between Singapore and the main Japanese forces, which were believed to be in the north, the defeat of the expected attack from the north and, with this flank firmly held, a thrust south to the Johore Straits and Singapore. The areas selected for the assault were at Morib, where it was hoped the 25 Div. landings would lead to the early capture of Port Swettenham and its airfield, and round Port Dickson some miles to the south where we were to land. As the hard fighting was likely to fall on the northern sector, 25 Div. had most of 50 Ind. Tk. Bde. in support and 5 Ind. Div., mounted at Rangoon, were to follow up over the Morib beaches.

The 23 Div. assault could not take place in its entirety on D day as there were only enough landing craft to carry one brigade group ashore. This subsidiary attack north of Port Dickson was entrusted to 37 Bde., with Sepang as the first objective and an exploitation task towards Port Dickson. Our main attack between the township and Cape Rachado had to wait until D plus 3. For this we had under command 3 Commando Brigade, a British formation with a fine record in the Arakan, and they and 49 Bde. were to take the covering position through which 1 Bde. were to pass inland to Seremban the same day. If all went well with the whole operation, we were to turn south on D plus 12 and move as a motorized division towards Singapore. The degree of resistance encountered would decide whether 26 Ind. Div., the Corps reserve, put in a seaborne landing farther down the coast to assist our advance to the Straits, and when we looked over the narrow stretch of water to Singapore Island (as we were sure we would) we hoped to be part of the final assault to link up with an airborne attack by 5 (British) Parachute Brigade.

The collapse of Japan brought about several last-minute changes in the plan. The two main assault landings remained unaltered except that we lost the Commando Brigade, who disappeared at breakneck speed to Hong Kong along with part of 24 Fd. Amb. and one or two other units which we had lent for the battle and never saw again. The other big change, which did not affect us, was the diversion of 5 Div. to Singapore, but a number of fighting units such as tank regiments were cut out of the order of battle and the spaces in the stowage plans filled with Corps administrative vehicles.

So much for the plan which would have achieved complete tactical surprise, as was clear from wireless messages that came from Force 136, our guerillas in Malaya, while the expedition was on the high seas. The Japanese strength was all in the north and there were not more than a few hundred administrative troops in the area of the 34 Corps assault, nor was there anything more formidable on the road to the Johore Straits; Singapore Island was garrisoned by some "Independent Mixed Battalions" and these were not crack troops. It may be of interest to remark here that not only were the Japs completely deceived about the selected point of attack and its timing because they neither gave the British credit for daring to penetrate right inside the Straits of Malacca nor expected an assault during the monsoon, but they had followed the British example and placed their defences at Singapore on the southern side of the island!

The messages from Force 136 removed the last fear that there would be any trouble from the Japs, who had given complete information about the dispositions of their forces and offered no resistance. There was a hint of future trouble in the news that disorderly elements, styling themselves Chinese Communists, were at large up and down the country and had bought arms off the Japanese, but they would hardly disturb the landings. The way was clear for a peaceful "invasion."

The dawn on September 9th was of great beauty. The hills of central Malaya formed a deep blue bastion against the lightening eastern sky which was flecked with red as the sun struggled through the light clouds that hung over the hills. No ripple marred the smoothness of the sea, and those who looked to the east felt the profound peace—broken on a sudden by the rattle of winches as the L.C.As. were lowered to the water. The spell was broken and all turned to the work ahead.

News soon came in to show that 37 Bde. were moving fast inland. There was momentary excitement when a signal reported sounds of firing, but this was merely an eager Bren gunner whose finger had twitched on the trigger. As had happened in the Arakan on a falling tide, the waters swept up the chaung leading to Sepang in apparently the wrong direction and the L.V.Ts.[1] made fast time; by 1400 hrs. the Gurkhas had reached the village. Meanwhile all was far from well on the beaches. The intelligence proved faulty and the firm layer of sand on top gave way at once under the weight of heavy vehicles which stuck fast and then sank into the soft, muddy bottom. Two were trapped on shore; others, caught while wading, were soon submerged and unloading stopped abruptly. The Morib beaches, though not so bad, were also treacherous, and it may occur to some to wonder what would have happened had this been an operation of war with the Japs massing from the north against 25 Div. while a tense struggle went on behind to haul vehicles, equipment and stores to safety across the beaches. Undoubtedly there would have been anxiety during the "build up," which would have been delayed, but from subsequent knowledge about the Japanese strength and intentions, it is clear there would have been no crisis. As it was, we could go to sleep with a quiet mind.

There was no rest that night for 3/5 R.G.R., who marched through the hours of darkness towards Port Dickson. The General heard early on the 10th that the march was near its end and he was off to the shore as soon as the Navy could provide a taxi. By the time he reached the quay, Brigadier MacDonald was there and so was the entire population of Port Dickson, laughing, smiling and chattering. No one on shore knew much about ropes and bollards so there was some delay before the tying-up process was complete, but the Navy were eventually satisfied, set up a ladder and rushed on to the jetty. They were at the top of a lampost and flag

---

[1] Landing Vehicles Tracked (amphibians with tracks like tanks).

· 25 · IND · DIV ·   · 34 · IND · CORPS ·   · 23 · IND · DIV ·

SOUTH MALAYA & "ZIPPER"

LEGEND

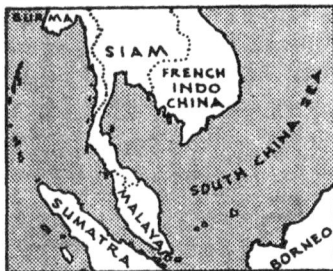

· L E G E N D ·	
STATES	JOHORE
TOWNS	Johore
RAILWAYS	++++++++
23 IND DIV	▷
25 IND DIV	▪▪▪▶
37 BDE	•••••▶

staff in no time; on one they hoisted a White Ensign, on the other a Union Jack.

Greetings over, the General moved on through the throng to the main square, where there was a large American car waiting with a Union Jack on the windscreen. The town was *en fête* with triumphal arches and banners of welcome spanning the streets; the people were transparently full of joy at our coming. They made way as the General drove off to 37 Bde.'s temporary H.Q., where he paused to settle one or two points before moving on to a prisoners' camp a little south of Port Dickson.

There were in this place 1,100 Indian troops who had been captured during the fall of Malaya. They were now living in fair comfort in modern barracks, but they had not long enjoyed a proper roof over their heads. The Japs had in their cunning moved the men to these quarters after the surrender and had given them new uniforms for the rags they wore before. There had been time, too, for the Red Cross aircraft to appear overhead three times, and out of the skies had come razors and soap and food so that some of the signs of confinement's grip had gone—some only. At the entrance to the barracks was a select guard of honour, miraculously smart and complete with arms, but none others in the camp could match their soldierly bearing. The men stood in fifteen groups, divided by religion and regiment, their shoulders bent and a cowed look on their faces as if they were ashamed to be alive and were unsure of their reception, but they had not forgotten their past. As the General approached the first group, there was a command and the men made a supreme effort to show that they were soldiers. They stood there, struggling to stand erect for a few moments before the General bade them stand at ease as he went round their ranks, stopping often to talk. When he paused, some from deep-engrained habit bowed obsequiously and then remembered the time for cudgelling and beating was gone and tried to bring their arm up in a salute. At the end, they were called once more to attention and a voice rang out, "Three cheers for British victory"; some, as they cheered, had tears in their eyes, and some who chanced to be there had to fight very hard to control their emotions. So it went on and always the cheers at the end, one group calling for "His Majesty," another for "Raj victory," a third for "glorious allied victory," and a fourth showing their joy by decking the General with a garland of flowers. Here were men who had come through the loneliness and savagery of imprisonment under the Japanese, held together in adversity by a young Indian captain later awarded the M.B.E., and by a few V.C.Os. who refused to accept defeat as the inevitable end. For some, the ordeal had proved almost too much; in the hospital were eighty gaunt wrecks of men, most so weak that they could not lift their frail bodies as the General walked by. It was not easy to render much immediate help with most of the Division still afloat, but we could and did provide the companionship of their fellow-countrymen.

On the morning of September 11th, after the Bombay convoy had arrived off Morib, the Brigadiers had the novel experience of being taken to a General's conference in launches. As "Zipper" had turned into a peaceful landing, some of the craft allotted to us had been whipped away to other tasks and their loss meant a last-minute adjustment of landing tables. This was done at the conference, but there was no D.R. to take round the copies of the orders, and though officers chugged about in motor boats trying to find units, not all knew of the changes by nightfall, when it was useless to go on hunting further for ships in an anchorage that was a wonderful spectacle for those who could pause to glance at the blaze of lights. The likelihood of some confusion in the landing was increased when a beach report, received in the early hours of September 12th, indicated obstructions on one sector.

The first stages of the landing could not be seen from the ships, which had moved to the Port Dickson anchorage during the night, as a violent squall of wind and rain obliterated the land and would have made difficult close support from ships and aircraft had there been a battle. 4/5 Mahratta were soon put ashore without accident except that one rifleman plugged another in the heel with a bullet, and it was encouraging to hear that the beach seemed firm enough to bear M.T. While the landing of 49 Bde. continued uninterrupted, L.S.Ts. began to move towards the shore and we watched the impressive sight of one craft heading for land full steam ahead; the local population were surprised when its bows ended up among the palms and jungle that fringed the beach. Events proved that we were more fortunate than 25 Div. in our place of landing, though there were a good many runnels and soft patches in which some vehicles were bogged, with a consequent disruption in the unloading. It was here that the alteration in the landing tables began to tell. Sommerfeld roadway was urgently needed, but neither this nor the equally important direction signs appeared, and matters became much worse when some L.S.Ts., diverted from the mud at Morib, were signalled to land in error and began to disgorge Corps administrative vehicles on to unprepared beaches. Among others who were held up were the layout party of Div. H.Q. and the provost, and a good many others had long walks when they landed as rocket craft, finding that shooting was off, kindly acted as ferries and put men ashore at various points down to Cape Rachado.

By the late afternoon some order had been re-established. 49 Bde. having landed ahead of the troubles on the beaches, had occupied the Corps covering position, Div. H.Q. was operating in a school delightfully situated near the shore, 1 Bde. were ready to move to Seremban, and a few vehicles had arrived. That night, September 12th/13th, 1 Bde. repeated the effort of 3/5 R.G.R. and marched to Seremban, where they were installed by 0800 hrs. on the 13th. Hot on their heels came the General—to the discomfort of a few stragglers who had not expected to have their names taken for falling out of the line of march by a General early abroad. The next day the General moved into the Residency at Seremban, the capital of Negri Sembilan, and there on the 15th, after hoisting the Union Jack to the head of the tall flagstaff at the Residency with full ceremony, we held a great victory parade.

This was a fine spectacle to watch and a great achievement so soon after landing. The Corps Commander was at the saluting base with the General by his side, and the entire population of Seremban lined the route. They watched in silence as the tanks and guns rumbled by and were not apparently stirred as the marching columns appeared with fixed bayonets glinting in the sun; first, a party from the

SEREMBAN "VICTORY" PARADE

THE NAVY STEAM PAST

13TH LANCERS APPROACHING
THE SALUTING BASE

Navy, and behind, the Seaforths with their pipes skirling, the Patialas and the rest. But now the crowd had been brought to their feet. Out of the northern sky there had come a squadron of fighters, and each time they roared overhead, dipping their wings in salute, cheer on cheer broke out. As the last of the troops marched by, the fighters disappeared to the north and the crowd wandered slowly away, excited and content with this display of military strength. At the end of a parade which bore the true Mellsop stamp the Navy were a trifle disconsolate. The leader of their party had been so anxious not to steer a crooked course that he and his men had steamed straight past the saluting base without a head quivering!

Our task in Malaya called for a speedy occupation of Northern Johore, Negri Sembilan and Pahang, so that the early appearance of the Army as they rounded up the Japanese should restore confidence, quell any uprising by dissentient elements and lead to the resumption of normal life. The more distant tasks fell to 1 Bde. in Johore and 49 Bde. in Pahang, while 37 Bde. and the battalions directly under Division occupied Negri Sembilan. The troop movements began on the day of the victory parade when 1/16 Punjab, with part of 178 Fd. Regt. and a squadron of 11 P.A.V.O., led the 1 Bde. advance south; the next day they were at Gemas and on the 17th joined hands with a unit of 5 Div. at Kluang. The rest of the Brigade followed on the 18th by road and rail, for trains were already running under military control, and occupied the Segamat area. The same day 37 Bde. set up their H.Q. at Kuala Pilah with 3/5 R.G.R. and 3/10 G.R. grouped round the town and 3/3 G.R. back at Sepang. The start of the 49 Bde. move was somewhat delayed from a lack of vehicles and stores due to the last-minute alterations in loading at Bombay; while they waited a 4/5 Mahratta column entered Malacca, which was subsequently taken over by the Seaforths. The move to Pahang began on the 19th, and that evening Bde. H.Q. were at Raub with 6/5 Mahratta split between Raub and Bentong; on the 23rd a company moved out to Termerloh; on the 24th 5/6 Rajrif reached Raub and pushed out into the wilds to Kuantan, which they reached on the 27th; 4/5 Mahratta had moved up on the 25th to complete the occupation programme.

Q

We all fell in love with Malaya during this fortnight in
September. The quick dispersal of the Division produced
the desired peacefulness and only two disturbances were
reported, one north of Seremban, where 6/8 Punjab and
Force 136 had a skirmish with bandits, and the other at
Tampin, where there was a clash between Chinese and
Malays for which members of the Kempeitai, the Japanese
secret police, were significantly said to be responsible.
Otherwise there was calm in a land where the countryside
smiled and the people smiled. It was all splendidly refresh-
ing after India. Green hills rose and fell in a nice disorder,
wherever the eye turned; streams bubbled in the valleys,
where the fruits of the earth flourished abundantly in the
fields. At midday the sun, though mildly soporific, was not
excessively overpowering; in the early morning there was a
delicious and delicate nip in the air. It was a land that
satisfied eye and body, and a land that had known prosperity. Up and down its length ran excellent roads that were
a wonder to those accustomed to the infuriating trunk road
from Bombay to Nasik, where stretches of concrete had been
laid on alternate sides of the road and a car bumped from
concrete to earth, or switched from side to side and hoped
there would be no opposition. There was nothing so crazy
about the roads of Malaya, while in the towns, where the
streets were broad, the many schools were a welcome sign
of progress and there was not that air of awful poverty that
characterizes India.

A ride through this land was like the progress of a victorious general returning to Rome. Each village had its gaily
decorated arches, and as our jeeps drove slowly through, the
children ran laughing and cheering to the roadside, giving
their version of the "V" sign. Of all the friendly welcomes
none quite equalled the rapturous reception given to "D"
Company, 4 Mahratta, and a squadron of the P.A.V.O.
when they entered Malacca. This town had experienced
after the surrender of Japan a final example of bestial
savagery when the entire staff of a Chinese newspaper were
taken away to a nearby island and shot in cold blood because
the Japanese disapproved of some outspoken comments on
their country's fall. The relatives of the murdered men
went that night to recover the bodies and found among the

dead three who, though horribly wounded, were still alive. Two survived to the day of the Mahrattas' entry, but by then they were delirious and unable to give any coherent account of the island murder before they died. With the memory of this crime fresh in the minds of the townsfolk, it was little wonder that the British force marched amid an exultant crowd through streets festooned with flags and bunting until they reached the Japanese H.Q. in Government Building. The commander was given orders to parade at 1500 hrs. on the sports ground of the Malacca Club with all Japanese in the town, military personnel bringing their arms, ammunition and such kit as they could carry. For the surrender, the tanks were stationed at the four corners of the ground, two platoons filled the gaps between the tanks and a third formed the search party. At 1500 hrs. ninety-six officers and men and forty civilians appeared. As they laid down their arms, the thousands who thronged the parade ground set up a deafening uproar of catcalls, hoots and boos, and the cries of derision broke out afresh when the Japanese were marched off under escort two hours later.

Surrender ceremonies and victory parades were the order of the day. On the 21st the General watched while 37 Bde. took the surrender of the Japanese at Bahau, where the weapons handed in included 260 swords and 1,227 machine guns; the same day 49 Bde. disarmed 272 Japs at Raub. On the 22nd 353 surrendered under the eyes of the Seaforths at Alor Gajah, and other surrenders followed in the 49 Bde. area at Bentong and Kuala Lipis. Once relieved of their arms, the Japanese were not left to sit down in idleness; they doubled to their place of work in the morning, they spent the day on such menial tasks as cleaning the streets, and they doubled back to their quarters in the evening.

Victory parades followed the disarming at Raub and Bentong, and in Seremban there was on the 29th a pleasing display of a less orderly character when each community in the town presented an address of welcome to the General. As he mounted the dais, the official band, composed of one trumpet, one saxophone, a drum and a pair of cymbals, mastered its rivals and gave tongue, selecting for their prize piece, not "See the Conquering Hero Comes," but a prehistoric dance tune. Unfortunately, the band had another and yet noiser rival in an approaching thunderstorm, and as the first drops of rain fell the populace, who were present in full force, stampeded and made for cover like a flock of sheep. The ceremony was now shorn of some of its splendour, with the party on the dais left in solitary state and in danger of a soaking. Accordingly, all adjourned to the pavilion, where efforts were made to resume but it took time to gather enough chairs and longer still to collect representatives of the communities, and by the time the chairs and the representatives were present the rain had ceased, so the bold decision was taken to adjourn again to the open air. This operation was not speedily accomplished, and before all were back there was more rain, but the General said the rain must be endured. After his magnificent bouquet had been toppled off its perch by a gust of wind and restored to its place of honour, the speech-making began to a background of lightning flashes and thunder-claps, with the populace present in moderate strength; they were grandiloquent, flowery speeches, to which the General replied more simply and with dignity. This was the end of the official reception, but the turn of the spectators was to come; they formed up and processed through the town, and there was much to entertain those interested in the survival of primitive rituals like the dragonman's dance.

The superstitious might have seen in the lightning and the thunder and the fall of the bouquet omens for the storm that lay ahead of us. On September 18th, the day when the bulk of 1 Bde. moved to Segamat and 37 Bde. set up their H.Q. at Kuala Pilah, the General summoned an early-morning conference and began by announcing quietly that the Division was bound for Java forthwith. There were vague rumours of trouble in the island, but none foresaw, as they listened to the General in peaceful Malaya, that some of the ugliest days in our story were to come.

The immediate burden fell on the "Q" staff. They had on their hands the prospective move of 49 Bde. to Pahang as soon as enough vehicles were unloaded and the maintenance of a widely scattered Division, and they were now asked to re-embark the whole of 1 Bde. group, including 178 Fd. Regt. over the Port Dickson beaches at high speed—as soon, that is, as the Navy could scrape up enough craft, for operation "Persil" was still in its infancy and nothing had been organized. We were greatly assisted by the P.M.L.O. at Port Dickson, Lieut.-Colonel Bullmore, M.B.E., and by 41 Indian Beach Group, who saw to the victualling and loading of the craft on their arrival. On the evening of September 24th the Seaforths and part of the Bde. H.Q. set sail on an enterprise that began to hint at danger. Almost at zero Brigadier King was sent fresh instructions which ended with the astonishing words, "If it is necessary to use the help of the Japs to preserve law and order, you will do so," and the first message from the G.I.'s tiny advance party flown in to Batavia on the 25th did more to reveal that there was very urgent business on hand.

As the rest of 1 Bde. concentrated at Port Dickson for their departure on the 28th, the C.R.A.'s Bde., comprising 2 Ind. A.Tk. Regt., 5/8 Punjab and 2/19 Hybad, was created to take over some of our commitments, but it was already clear that none of us could be much longer in Malaya. The latest reports presented to the General at a Fourteenth Army conference held at Singapore on the 28th revealed the need for a great acceleration in the movement of troops if a widespread conflagration was to be avoided. There was little shipping to spare in South East Asia, but "Persil" had become top priority in the theatre and vessels were found to mount part of the Division at Singapore. On the 30th the General received orders to leave Seremban and fly in to Java forthwith; on the 1st a column of divisional troops moved to Singapore and plans were drafted for the re-embarkation of 37 Bde. at Port Dickson, the latter a complicated task because it was for some time uncertain whether the Brigade would land at Batavia or in isolation at Surabaya, with a large number of supporting units under command.

It is time to leave the final stages of our sailing from Malaya. Already the Seaforths had landed in Batavia and the curtain goes up on a story of deep tragedy and surpassing courage.

CHAPTER 21

Clouds over Java

BATAVIA, at the end of September, 1945, was a city of flags
and crowds, but there were no triumphal arches gay with
bunting and no wild outbursts of enthusiasm to greet the
arrival of the British. The flags were all of one colour,
horizontal red and white stripes, the emblems of the newly
born Indonesian Republic; and the crowds watched
impassively, a sea of faces devoid of any visible emotion.

To the new arrival from Malaya it was as though he had
come out of the sunlight into the darkness that broods over
the earth before a monsoon storm bursts.

Into this gloom came, on September 25th, the advance
party of 23 Ind. Div., after a slight delay at Singapore
where Press Correspondents flew off in our Dakota before a
staff error could be adjusted. Lieut.-Colonel Mellsop had
with him Capt. L. N. Paylor of 2 Ind. A.Tk. Regt., who had
worked in Batavia before the war, and he steered the party
to the Hotel des Indes. From there a message was sent to
Rear-Admiral Patterson on H.M.S. *Cumberland*, flagship
of the 5th Cruiser Squadron and now lying off Tandjoengpriok, the fine harbour constructed by the Dutch as the
port for Batavia; the Admiral came in person in answer
to the message and he insisted on removing the G.I., A.D.M.S.
and C.R.E. to his flagship for the night. The G.I.
retired late and very bewildered after a long talk with
Mr. van der Plas, the pre-war Governor of West Java, a
deep perusal of the succulent naval signals on the Javan
turmoil and ample hospitality; by the evening of the 26th he
had come to appreciate that "this Bedlam"—the phrase was
Admiral Patterson's—accurately described the situation.

To the outward eye life seemed fairly normal; the trams
ran regularly up Koningsplein, the trains steamed out of the
main station to Bandoeng with innumerable passengers
taking a precarious journey on the footboards in typical

500 MILES

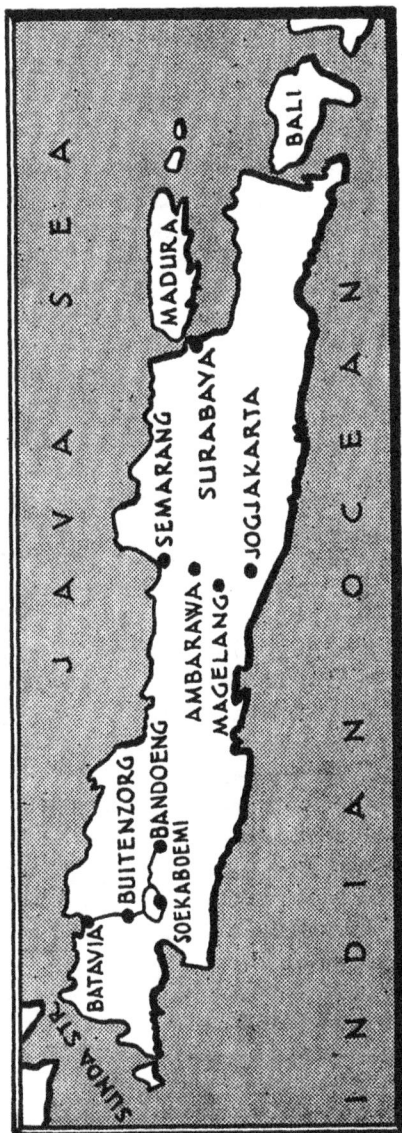

500 MILES

500 MILES

J A V A   S E A

BATAVIA

SUNDA STR.

BUITENZORG

BANDOENG

SOEKABOEMI

AMBARAWA
MAGELANG
JOGJAKARTA

SEMARANG

SURABAYA

MADURA

BALI

I N D I A N   O C E A N

THE TOWNS SHOWN ARE THOSE IN WHICH 23 IND DIV OPERATED, EXCEPT
FOR JOGJAKARTA, THE INDONESIAN H.Q. THE NORTHERN ROUTE FROM
BANDOENG TO BUITENZORG WAS USED AFTER MARCH 1946

12000'

12000'

· APPROXIMATE CROSS SECTION THROUGH JAVA & BALI ·

· J A V A ·

Eastern fashion—but these trams and trains were not quite normal. Through the mass of bodies the eye detected huge slogans daubed in sprawling characters on the sides of vehicles and carriages. "Atlantic Charter means freedom from Dutch Imperialism," shouted one; "America for the Americans—Monroe. Indonesia for the Indonesians," screamed another. Everywhere the signs of rampant nationalism abounded. A caller lifting up a telephone receiver would be greeted by a bark of "Merdeka" (Freedom) from the exchange, and if he chanced to raise his eyes to the walls of a public building opposite he would find "Merdeka" glaring defiantly at him; or it might be "To hell with van Mook" or "van Mook and van der Plas, you can't pull wool over our eyes."

The puzzle did not end with paltry slogans. Out in the streets high-powered American cars sped from place to place with Japanese officers, dressed in sword and full regalia, riding in state in the comfortable back seats. It was the Dutch who more closely resembled a beaten people, most of them just released from a three and a half years' ordeal in concentration camps and forced to walk the streets in a city of which they had once been masters, while the hated Japanese rode by and the Indonesians clamoured that the days of Dutch suzeranity were over.

The newcomer found Batavia like a kaleidoscope in which the glass pieces refused to take shape, a world apparently upside down where people milled round in circles, all of them wanting something but none being sure how to achieve their objects. The Dutch wanted to return to their homes and their rightful heritage, but were without power; the Indonesians wanted freedom and had power of a sort, but were both exhilarated by and afraid of the power they had usurped; the Japanese, so they speciously protested, wanted to be rid speedily of their responsibilities for maintaining law and order, but could find no one to whom they could hand over control. Besides these three, there were other lesser pieces and these also had their wants. R.A.P.W.I. was a phrase that fell frequently on the ear amid the babel, and gradually it merged that this was an organization, part British part Dutch, for dealing with the Released Allied Prisoners of War and Internees, of whom there were tens of thousands somewhere in Java not so much "released" as penned into camps in constant fear of attacks from lawless mobs. Working in some ill-defined relationship with R.A.P.W.I. but distinct from it was a party of the British Red Cross, while more complications arose from the existence of N.I.C.A., the Netherlands East Indies Civil Administration.

For all his bewilderment in a city where no one "really knew anything," the G.I. had rapidly established a few facts and sensed the danger ahead. With N.I.C.A. no more than a name, the Japanese supine and the Indonesians infants in power, Batavia was fast degenerating into lawlessness. All and sundry were helping themselves to houses, cars and the contents of the big warehouses, and there were persistent and wild rumours of impending attacks. In this vacuum no one acted except in his own self-interest—if he was able to do so.

It was clear that our advance party had much more with which to concern themselves than reserving accommodation. With the G.I. acting as Admiral Patterson's Chief of Staff, the Japanese were told to re-exert their authority for the protection of R.A.P.W.I. and the suppression of looting, and it was made plain that the only operative orders they would receive were from the Admiral through his staff officer. These instructions set the Japanese about their proper business and restored a degree of control, but the R.A.P.W.I. fears were not entirely groundless. Already barricades were appearing in some of the streets and there were early signs of the Indonesian extremists' burning hatred of the Dutch. Though the British at this stage always met with courtesy, there were incidents in which Dutch and Eurasians were manhandled and insulted and some panic arose in the camps. In the absence of troops, Admiral Patterson sent ashore every man he could spare, and the Navy's irreproachable turn-out and discipline did much to raise the morale of Europeans besides causing a fluttering in hearts long denied so fair a sight.

The advance party, and all of us as we arrived, had a remarkable variety of tasks to perform. One of the G.I.'s first measures was to freeze accommodation and allow no one to enter guarded buildings and dumps without one of the special passes which the Japs printed for us very quickly. As R.A.P.W.I. and hundreds of civilians were searching for homes, they laid siege to the G.I. and his fellows all day long and wherever they appeared, but the biggest throng swirled round Capt. Paylor, who, with his local knowledge, was appointed house agent in chief.

When the rest of the party could escape, they had plenty to do in their official capacities. The A.D.M.S. controlled the issue of medical stores, visited the camps and advised on hygiene and sanitation which hardly existed in places; the C.R.E. spent hours in visiting and winning over the Indonesian "mayor" of Batavia and the "Ministers" who controlled the public utilities; and our signals officer delved into the intricacies of the telephone system. All were working at high pressure for very long hours, not least the G.I. who on one and the same day issued 60,000 Japanese guilders to start the Dutch civil administration, formally received the Japanese Chief of Staff, welcomed the Consul of a "Friendly Power" when he came to pay a courtesy call, thwarted the skipper of a ship owned by another "Friendly Power" when he tried to remove 6,000 tons of crude rubber belonging to a British firm, and, as a final trifle around midnight, provided a mast for a L.S.T.

It was impossible at times to resist the feeling that this strange mixture was part of one of W. S. Gilbert's most ingenious plots, with the "Fighting Cock" cast for a major role. Fully in keeping with this impression was the incident which occurred outside the H.Q. of the first Seaforth company to arrive. This came a day before the rest of the battalion, a hundred and twenty men representing the might of the victorious United Nations in a none too friendly city. By the strangest of coincidences, the ancestors of our Jocks had visited these parts in the years gone by. In 1811, during the Napoleonic Wars, a British force had landed in Java, and among the troops who routed the French were the Seaforth Highlanders. It is very doubtful whether any who stood on guard that evening in late September, 1945, felt the impact of history, and certainly no such thoughts filled the minds of the large crowd of Indonesians and Chinese who watched from a distance in stolid silence. As East gazed at West, a loud hooting began in the distance and all eyes turned to watch a Japanese patrol which was moving fast down the main road. The patrol was led by a gimcrack armoured car, followed by two lorries full of troops; another worn-out monstrosity brought up the rear. The British shouted to the Japanese to stop, which they did very quickly—too quickly, in fact, as the second armoured car crashed wholeheartedly into the back of the rear lorry. For the first time the crowd showed some emotion and raised a cheer as the Japs explained at length why they had trespassed into "our" sector and then drove away with the wounded vehicle in tow.

The urge to laugh might sometimes be strong, but the laugh very soon turned into what was at best a wry smile. It was obvious from the outset that tragedy lurked round the corner every minute of the day in an island where passions were running dangerously high. Had it been possible to divert two of the "Zipper" divisions to Java at the time of the landings in Malaya, it is likely that the troubles we had to face would never have occurred, but many reasons will occur to the reader why this could not be done. There is one point, however, that may escape notice, and it is this—the readjustment of the boundary between Admiral Mountbatten and General MacArthur through which the Dutch Indies fell under South East Asia Command was a recent event. Up-to-date intelligence about the former Dutch possessions was lacking and the hints of crisis came unexpectedly to a Command whose resources in men and, every bit as important, in ships were at full stretch. Even when the news filtered through, it was not easy in peaceful Malaya to appreciate immediately either the urgent need for haste or the immensity of the trouble, and the original plans for the resettlement of Java and Sumatra envisaged 23 Ind. Div. being able to restore peace single-handed by landing one brigade at Batavia, a second at Surabaya and a third in Sumatra. In the end, three divisions were able to hold a few key towns in both islands, nearly all of them on the coast.

To these reasons and the precipitate end of the Japanese war must be ascribed the delay in sending occupation forces to Java and the slowness of our own build-up. Meanwhile the independence movement, headed by Dr. Soekarno, had seized an opportunity that comes to few revolutions. Nippon surrendered on August 14th, 1945, three days later Soekarno proclaimed the establishment of the Republic of Indonesia, and he and his party were given six weeks to consolidate their authority before 1 Ind. Inf. Bde. began to arrive piecemeal. Actually there were no more than the Seaforths ashore until October 4th, when the rest of the Brigade and 178 Fd. Regt. disembarked and enabled us to take over the policing of Batavia, a slender enough force even for that task and quite incapable of influencing the course of events in an island of 45,000,000 inhabitants in the hands of leaders full of the first flush of power.

The Japanese had done their work hideously well. To some of the lands they conquered they had made early and specious promises of independence, and everywhere throughout the Far East, through insidious and unending propaganda, they filled the minds of intellectuals and hotheads with a bitter hatred of the Western races. On the surface, there was little to show that the Indonesian independence movement was Jap inspired; but those better acquainted than the ordinary soldier with Japanese methods saw clearly the product of a policy which aimed at leaving the United Nations a legacy of disturbance as the immediate aftermath of war, and looked to an eventual return to the islands when Japan had recovered its power fifty or more years ahead.

Indonesia was not one of the countries to which the Japanese had promised independence soon after its occupation. When Dr. Soekarno and Dr. Hatta, the leaders of the comparatively insignificant pre-war nationalist movement, went to Japan in 1943, they were told they must bide their time. The Japanese continued to run the Dutch Indies much as the Dutch had done before them except that Indonesians were given more important posts in the administration. It was not until the end of 1944 that a formal promise of future independence was given, a promise the Japanese never in fact fulfilled except in so far as they did not oppose the declaration of a Republic on August 17th, 1945, and surreptitiously assisted in military training. Thus by the time the British arrived, Java was in the throes of a popular uprising and the Indonesians had assumed control of the public utility services. They ran the railways, the post and telegraph services and the water supply; copying the Japanese precedent, they commandeered cars that were not theirs and they seized buildings to house the staffs of their "ministries"; the police were all Indonesian, the wireless and Press distorted the truth and hurled abuse at the Dutch, and local labour refused to work for their former masters so that ships lay unloaded in the docks. For better or for worse, the Indonesian Republic existed and could not be disregarded.

The Dutch were taken utterly by surprise at the course of events in Java. When our advance party reached Singapore, they had met a cheerful Dutchman who assumed that he and his countrymen were coming back to the peaceful reoccupation of their Empire. There were very many similarly minded, for they were men out of touch with the trend of events. During the war they had been shut up in concentration camps and used as forced labour by the Japanese, or, if fortunate enough to escape that fate, they had wandered about the world as exiles.

It was impossible not to sympathize with them in their present predicament. Their position is best understood by imagining that the British at the end of the war had been dependent on some foreign power for the recovery of one of their richest possessions where a nationalist leader who had sided with the enemy held sway. As the British would have been in similar circumstances, so the Dutch felt helpless and frustrated. With great stakes at issue, there was nothing they could do. At best, they could muster about two companies of their own nationals, all of them men who were undernourished and ill-trained after their captivity, and a few companies of native Ambonese troops, who were loathed by the Indonesians because the Dutch had used them in the past to suppress risings and disturbances. There was no prospect of Dutch reinforcements arriving at any date that could be forecast as all their shipping was in the Allied pool and none had been earmarked to convey Dutch troops from Europe. To crown their troubles, they could never forget the thousands of their women and children who eked out a horrid existence in the internment camps at Batavia and in Central and Eastern Java.

Perhaps it was not surprising that the Dutch government thundered from Europe that Dr. Soekarno and his party were "a Japanese puppet government of totalitarian character," and that Mr. van der Plas in Batavia said, "I do not recognize the Soekarno 'government' or Soekarno himself as having any official capacity." Unfortunately, such pronouncements took no account of happenings in Java and only increased the hostility of the Indonesians to the return of the Dutch and to co-operation with them in any form. Those of us who came to Java came to a troubled land, to a powder magazine where one act of carelessness or one false step would be fatal.

There was nothing pleasant about the task we had been set, and we came simply to fulfil a duty that fell to S.E.A.C. in accordance with the Potsdam agreement. It had there been decreed that the enemy armed forces could only surrender to one of the four signatory powers, so that in the course of time it was inevitable that British troops should come to Java to disarm the 55,000 Japanese who were supposed to be maintaining law and order in the meanwhile. It chanced that we of the "Fighting Cock" were the first who could be spared for the task, and so we found ourselves burdened with a very awkward baby which on closer acquaintance became quite repulsive.

At the start we were almost an independent command. Our immediate superiors were H.Q. 15 Corps, now translated into H.Q. Allied Forces, Netherlands East Indies (A.F.N.E.I.), under their old commander of Arakan fame, Lieut.-General Sir Philip Christison. He arrived in Batavia with General Hawthorn on September 30th, but there was no shipping to bring over much of his staff so that, while he was naturally responsible for decisions on major policy, the whole of Java remained our province for a month or more. We were soon styled H.Q. Allied Land Forces, Java, Madura, Bali, and Lombok, a high-sounding title that raises a smile when one recollects how small a part of Java was under our control.

As has been said, our first task in Java was to disarm the Japanese, but this was not the end of our mission. We were next bidden to rescue and succour prisoners of war and internees, and on us devolved the responsibility for maintaining law and order while carrying out our two main commitments. There was also one negative instruction which ran in the words of a statement issued by General Christison: "We have no interest in their politics. British and Indian troops will not become involved in internal politics."

There lay the rub, for every act in Batavia had a political significance or was liable to be so interpreted. What was there to say when an angry Dutchman demanded back his car which he saw being driven about by a fellow called Soekarno? In his view this Soekarno was a quisling and no "political" necessity could justify the man being allowed a car that was another's property. Difficulties of this sort occurred all day and every day, and the wisdom of ten Solomons would not have sufficed to bring order out of the chaos. As we watched in those early October days, it became clear that unless the Dutch made some broad-minded proposals for a settlement, blood would begin to flow very soon, for Batavia was an armed camp.

By day there was an uneasy quiet, but the lorry loads of Indonesian police and Ambonese troops always had the threat of a catastrophe. Both parties rode about fully armed with their weapons pointing over the sides and backs of the vehicles, and every finger was on the trigger. Not infrequently their lorries chanced to follow one behind the other, and the onlooker felt that a jolt over one of the many potholes in the streets of Batavia would be enough to start a set-to. In the streets, the Dutch released from the internment camps walked about in an assortment of uniforms, all of them carrying arms against an emergency. The tension was inescapable, and it was in an endeavour to produce a calmer air that the British troops walked about unarmed unless they were engaged on a military operation. (It was not long before this order was rescinded after our padre had witnessed two women murdered in cold blood.)

By night, shots were already beginning to ring out, many of them fired by our own troops at looters who raided the godowns in the northern part of the city, but by no means all. Sometimes our search parties were hindered by barricades guarded by Indonesians, who were more frequently armed with pikes and swords than with rifles, but a formidable enough foe, whatever their weapons, if the whole city rose against us. Even after 1 Bde. was complete, we had not enough troops to ensure satisfactory policing of the city, and wide gaps separated the Seaforth keep in the north from the Patialas in the centre, and the Patialas from the Punjabis and the Gunners in the south where were the main R.A.P.W.I. camps. These dispositions left little to spare for the protection of the port which was our life-line with the outer world.

It was this lack of strength which prevented our beginning to discharge our first task of disarming the Japanese. So far from being able to disarm them, we needed their help in Batavia and the interior, a state of affairs as remarkable as it was unwelcome. In Batavia, our resources in man power were swallowed up in internal security duties, and it was necessary for the Japanese to continue guarding their large dumps of arms, ammunition and equipment which had to be kept out of Indonesian hands. Outside Batavia we could not raise a finger, and even when we were strong enough at a later date to occupy Semarang and Bandoeng, we had for a time to order the Japs to fight for us, an event hushed up at home, but readily explicable by men on the spot who were responsible for the safety of defenceless women and children and of their own troops against a bloodthirsty and far more numerous foe.

The Dutch did not favour the use made of the Japanese and there were below the surface other causes of friction. This was to be expected. The man-in-the-street, who in peace time only leaves his own country as a tourist, does not realize how much the races of this earth differ in temperament and outlook, and the unusual stresses and strains accompanying the reoccupation of Java cast a vivid light on such differences. The British had not come to Java to reconquer an empire, and when they found among the Dutch a diehard party whose only policy was to use force, some began to be less sympathetic to the Dutch. No one denied their legal claim to the islands of the East Indies, but the Second World War had been fought for the right of men to determine their own form of polity, and it seemed hypocritical even to toy with the idea of a war of reconquest at the end of a struggle for freedom. Even if the "whiff of grape-shot" policy were not considered outmoded, the demand for its adoption paid no regard to our strength in Batavia or to the ghastly slaughter that would occur in the internment camps if it failed; equally it left out of account the effect on public opinion in Britain and in an India on the threshold of independence if British and Indian troops were used in such a role.

To the soldier caught up in the rush of events, compromise seemed both sane and necessary as increasing contact with the Indonesians revealed that they were incapable of running the country without assistance. Here was a further cause of misunderstanding with the Dutch, who regarded such contact as a recognition of the validity of Soekarno's "government." At first we had tried to avoid meeting "ministers" and their satellites because of the political implications, but this resulted in the grossest absurdities. It was nonsensical to have to tell the Indonesians, who came to offer the use of the railway system, that all our orders would come to them through the Japanese, who would remain in control until we had an adequate staff to relieve them. We could not exist without the co-operation of the Indonesians: having nothing but half a pioneer company, we needed their labour to unload the stores ships; having no railway personnel, we needed the use of the railways to clear stores from the docks to the Field Maintenance Area. So it came about that common sense prevailed and we began to deal direct with the Indonesians.

These friendly meetings were instructive in the light they threw on their political and administrative capacity. Few of the "ministers" showed ability and fewer still any understanding of modern political thought. There was much truth in the Dutch assertion that the Soekarno constitution was totalitarian in character. Certainly there was no trace of democracy in the very wide powers reserved to the President, though one is apt to forget that democracy on the Western pattern is impossible in the ill-educated East.

Whatever the colour of the "government," its financial policy was puerile. The currency in use at the time of our arrival was the worthless Japanese note issue which had no backing. Great efforts were made to persuade the Indonesians to accept the N.E.I. guilder, but no argument could

R

shift their determination to reject these notes which bore the head of the Queen of Holland. When asked how they intended to avoid economic chaos, they murmured at regular intervals "we have a plan"—the plan turned out to be the primitive method of barter, and it was not very easy to put this into practice without shipping! Nor was Indonesian administration very inspiring. Though politics may have had something to do with the difficulty in marrying up the right number of trucks and an engine at the docks, the comptrollers of the railway were little more than boys and seemed better suited to the management of toy trains.

In the end most things in Java came back to politics and politically there was an impasse. The Dutch refused to recognize or treat with the "quisling" Soekarno and his "government"; the Indonesians refused to approach the Dutch, whose help they needed. Between the two contestants stood a few thousand troops of 23 Ind. Div., embroiled in a political quarrel that was no concern of ours and outside our control. The position of middle-man in such affairs is never enviable and we knew, as we waited for the explosion, that we could expect the thanks of neither side, and were likely to have the open hostility of the Indonesians. At the start they had been ready to welcome our arrival, partly because they distorted a remark of General Christison's into meaning that he recognized the Soekarno "government," but our position soon became compromised because of our association with the Dutch, so that friendliness changed into the suspicion that we had come to cover the return of the hated overlords, and suspicion became a certainty.

The shooting began in earnest about October 4th and along with the bullets came a spate of alarmist rumours about impending attacks on the Batavia R.A.P.W.I. camps. There was, of course, no declaration of war—officially there was never war in Java—but incident followed incident by day and night and the ear was continually assailed by the sound of small-arms fire. Usually the telephone bell would ring to report another murder, and out would go the patrols on a fruitless search. The work was exhausting for the troops and it was nerve-racking. In a hole-and-corner business of this sort in a large city, the calls on patrols were so many that few men had two consecutive nights in bed, and there is an obvious strain on the nerves when there may be an ambush round every corner.

Unfortunately, it has to be recorded that the provocation was not all on one side. On October 11th the peace of the afternoon was shattered by a sudden outburst of firing in the main street. The G.I. sped round in his car to investigate and there, outside the Dutch C.-in-C.'s Residence, he found the body of an Indonesian; as the sentry gave no reason for shooting, and an officer in the building could do no better than suggest that the dead man might have been armed, the only surmise possible was that this murder was due to blind hate or to uncontrolled fear. This incident was followed half an hour later by another close to our own H.Q.—this time two corpses lay slumped in the dust. Sometimes one felt that the Dutch wanted to provoke war and thereby force us to fight on their behalf, but any such thought is unfair at least to the policy of the Lieutenant Governor General, Dr. van Mook, who had arrived on October 3rd and began his part in the long struggle to reconcile the two sides; but his presence did nothing immediately to reduce the tension.

The undeclared guerrilla war went on, barricades and road-blocks appeared all over Batavia, and the discomfort of the Dutch increased when the Indonesians boycotted the markets. The only cause for thankfulness in a crisis that threatened to develop into open war was that no British or Indian lives had so far been lost in the shooting. On October 11th the worst occurred. A British officer and V.C.O. of 1/16 Punjab went ahead of a platoon patrol and were slaughtered in an ambush—the Indonesians had drawn blood. Later that evening there was a pitched battle between ourselves and the Indonesians and numerous arrests were made, but arrests could neither settle political differences nor avenge the dead. They were the victims of a policy of drift.

This double murder was followed on October 13th by a proclamation from General Hawthorn amounting to the virtual declaration of martial law in Batavia. Whether by design or chance, the next day produced an Indonesian declaration of war on the Dutch, but this was not taken unduly seriously as among the weapons recommended were "all kinds of poison, blow-pipes, arrows, knives, spears, wild animals like poisonous snakes, petrol, and other incendiary materials." More important to us was the arrival of the leading troops of 37 Bde., who were urgently needed.

All reports from the interior showed that Dr. Soekarno had lost control over the extremists, who were terrorizing the countryside and roving about in bands lusting after blood and plunder. Three stations on the line to Bandoeng were in the hands of frenzied mobs, who cut to pieces two Dutch travellers; others were kidnapped elsewhere on the same line and were never heard of again. In Surabaya and Bandoeng, Semarang and Ambarawa the Japanese had either deliberately quit their responsibilities or been overwhelmed. In these towns were the main R.A.P.W.I. camps outside Batavia, and they were now exposed to the whims of fanatics who had thrown off the veneer of civilization and reverted to the savage. Humanity demanded that succour should be sent with all speed and, in answer to the call, the rest of the division was scattered throughout the length of Java.

A visit to any of these camps seared the heart. They were the "homes" of 100,000 Dutch and Eurasian women and children who had already endured three and a half years of lonely captivity, apart from their menfolk. By the end of November, 1943, even boys of sixteen had been swept away to act as human beasts of burden and there was no able-bodied man left to ease the strain of unending manual labour. If a cess-pit had to be dug, the internees did the work watched over by Japanese soldiers who were ready to strike anyone who faltered. On one occasion, women and girls worked from five in the evening until two the following morning erecting a fence as a punishment for bringing illegal food into the camp, and the offence had been a trap set by a vicious commandant. These Japanese had shown no mercy as conquerors. Every morning and evening they displayed their superiority over the Western races by forcing all to bow before them. No one was safe from their sadistic brutality. A woman was knocked down for some trivial offence and when she rose was told to "walk quicker"; unable to respond, she was sent reeling to the ground, her skull and jaw broken. So these hapless women and children lived, if the word can be rightly used for an existence such as this where the staple food was a modicum of rice and fifty-five centimetres was the allotted sleeping space on bare boards.

One who had endured wrote at the end: "We heard that we were free on August 23rd, but it took us much longer to realize that we were free because things did not alter very much, and we did not know any more what it meant to be free, to think and say what you liked and to go where you liked. But after I have been out of the camp for almost two months now I do know what it means and you do not need to ask me if I enjoy it. It is too good to be true." Yes—too good to be true, but what of the thousands less fortunate in the central Java camps? They had no song in their hearts. They still had to endure the pungent odour pervading those camps, they still lived hugger-mugger on top of each other, the children still scampered about shoeless and half wild in the mud, there was still only rare news of the outside world and that all too often full of sadness. Every day some woman would be convulsed with sobs as the news of her husband's death in Siam came through. Peace had brought medical supplies which helped to reduce the death rate from thirty to three a day, but little else except more misery. The need was for comfort, happiness and, more materially, for proper feeding, and none of these could be provided. The Indonesians banned the sale of fresh food, and at Ambarawa and Semarang they arrested the British and Dutch officers of the relief organizations. The awful truth was that fear of the Japanese had been superseded by a new and greater fear—the dread of wholesale massacre. Peace had come, but it had proved a shadow for those imprisoned in the camps, where the fortitude and understanding of one or two women miraculously prevented thousands from sinking into hopeless despair. It was a crime against humanity that such danger and misery could exist two months after the Japanese surrender, but protests to Soekarno were of no avail. His unruly followers were out of control and we could only hope there would be no disaster before the rest of the Division arrived.

By October 16th, 37 Bde. was complete. Two companies

of 3/3 G.R. had already been sent to Buitenzorg along the Bandoeng road on the 15th, and the Brigade less 3/10 G.R. moved to Bandoeng two days later; 5/8 Punjab took the place of the third Gurkha battalion. The arrival of the Brigade in Bandoeng did not lead to hostile disturbances against us, partly because the Japanese, after giving way to the extremists on October 3rd, had been ordered to reassert their authority. This they succeeded in doing by the 11th, and the ease with which the task was accomplished suggests that their main garrisons had ample strength to prevent the Indonesians gaining the upper hand. 37 Bde. thus came to a town that was fairly quiet for the moment. The Indonesian contact committee expressed surprise when they heard that, under the terms of the General's proclamation, all illegal arms and looted property were to be surrendered, but they raised no difficulties over our guarding the R.A.P.W.I. camps and permitted the sale of fresh food. For a brief space the extremists were lying low—watching and biding their time. The first hints of trouble came on the 24th.

3/10 G.R. had been kept back at Batavia to answer the calls for assistance from Semarang. As they disembarked there on the 19th, a new and ugly prospect opened before us. The Japanese opened fire on the Gurkhas, killing two and wounding seven, and it seemed that the "Fighting Cock" might have to face their old foes once more. There was relief when it was learnt that the Gurkhas had been mistaken for Indonesians who had been fighting the Japanese for the last three days. The Indonesians had been greatly assisted in Central Java by an order signed by the Japanese commander, Major-General Nakamura, who instructed his men to hand over control and arms to the Republicans. Having acquired power, they turned against the Japanese and butchered a hundred and fifty civilians in the Semarang gaol. This wanton bloodshed roused some of the Japanese to a fury, and the Gurkhas chanced to arrive at the end of the resultant battle which the Japs won.

The barbarity of this episode was a feature of the Java scene. 3/3 G.R. rescued one community of 1,250 Christian and Eurasian women and children who were packed into three buildings, and the G.I. disclosed a worse horror at Buitenzorg, where 770 men were packed into a gaol that had room for 100. When discovered they had been living in squalor for ten days at the mercy of guards who beat and mutilated their prisoners as fancy dictated. Ghastly to relate, rumour reached H.Q. that the Dutch were responsible for a similar outrage in Batavia itself—and the rumour proved true. Human nature had run amok in an island that was economically and politically in chaos.

Throughout all the disturbances, difficulties and disappointments, the General remained splendidly imperturbable and wise. As the commander of the land forces in Java, it fell to him to have many dealings with both sides in the dispute. It was his task to send for Dr. Soekarno and demand the cessation of violent outrages against civilians, his to curb the vehemence of the Dutch, his to weigh the claims of humanity against military necessity. The position he held was abnormal and called for broadmindedness and firmness, tact and courage in the highest degree. It is not only the officers and men of 23 Ind. Div. who stand greatly in his debt.

As the General surveyed the scene towards the end of October, he began to see the first glimmering of hope for the future. Batavia was noticeably quieter, the docks were safely guarded by 6/8 Punjab, the tanks of the P.A.V.O. were a valuable addition to our strength, and there was on the airfield the comforting support of two Thunderbolt squadrons and some Mosquitoes; further, the disarming of the Japanese had begun and 1,000 were working as coolies in the docks. H.Q. C.R.A. Bde., 2/19 Kumaon[1] and 2 Ind. A.Tk. Regt. had followed 3/10 G.R. to Semarang, and the Gurkhas had moved inland to Ambarawa and Magelang. They and 37 Bde. afforded reasonable security for the internees in Central Java, so there remained only Surabaya, where 49 Bde. under Brigadier Mallaby began to land on October 25th.

At this moment, even the political outlook appeared brighter. True, a carefully worded and unconstructive statement made by Dr. van Mook on October 15th was followed by two outbursts from Holland inveighing against the Republicans, but the appearance of Mr. Dening of the

---

[1] The title of 2/19 Hyderabad Regiment was changed when the Battalion was in Java.

Foreign Office as political adviser to General Christison led to a meeting between the British and the Indonesian "Cabinet." This gave the Indonesians cause to think as they discovered that the British recognized the legal claim of the Dutch to the East Indies and had nowhere supported a Japanese-sponsored government. The next move was a feeler from the Indonesians to see whether the dispute might be settled through the mediation of a third party. Hopes began to rise. Very gradually the moderate-minded men on both sides were coming together and approaching the deadlock in a more practical spirit. When it was announced on the evening of the 28th that Dr. van Mook had asked the Indonesians to meet him in conference, hopes mounted higher still. It was too late! The crackle of rifle fire could be heard over the G.I.'s telephone as Brigadier Mallaby spoke from Surabaya. The East of Java was aflame! Time is rarely kind to those who linger.

CHAPTER 22

Surabaya

THE port of Surabaya, the Dutch naval base in East Java, presented a forlorn appearance as the vessels carrying 49 Bde. felt their way forward into the anchorage on October 25th. The masts and funnels of scuttled ships protruded everywhere, silent witnesses of a bygone activity. The flourishing pre-war port was dead—but the quayside was very much alive, as those who gazed through their binoculars saw. The walls of the warehouses and dock installations were covered with the customary unfriendly slogans, the people stood watching in silence, and there was another unwelcome onlooker in the form of a machine gun trained on the leading ship.

The machine gun did not open up and there was no interference with the landing or with the first stages in the occupation of the town, which in shape somewhat resembles Batavia. Both wander away from the coast on a narrow strip of land a little higher than the low-lying countryside so that their length is greater than their breadth. Roughly, the commercial buildings are in the north, the principal administrative offices in the centre and the residential district away to the south. Batavia is drained by a system of canals familiar to those who know Holland; in Surabaya the Kali Mas cuts the town in two and fulfils naturally the function of the canals.

By the evening of the 25th, 5/6 Rajrif moving on the west of the Kali Mas and 6/5 Mahratta moving up the east side had reached the Ferwerda drawbridge. Colonel L. H. O. Pugh, the Brigade second-in-command, had held a friendly meeting with the Indonesians, headed by one Moestopo, and the Mahrattas had held converse with a certain Atmaji who that night styled himself second-in-command Indonesian Navy; this man was in fact one of the leading revolutionaries. For the moment he was full of smiles, as was everyone else, and there was no hint of coming trouble or cause for nervousness except that there was subconscious anxiety in living in a town controlled by Indonesians, all of them armed.

Discussions between Brigadier Mallaby and Moestopo continued on the 26th, and as goodwill seemed to prevail, some of our troops moved south to the Darmo area, about seven miles from the docks. Here lived the R.A.P.W.I., some concentrated in the hospital and others scattered about in numerous private houses; here also were important installations such as the waterworks. 5/6 Rajrif, 3 Ind. Fd. Regt., 71 Ind. Fd. Coy. and the bulk of 47 Ind. Fd. Amb. were sent to this area, the intention being to use the gunners in an infantry role as at Batavia.

So far, though the Indonesians were very quick to check on our movements, all had gone well, and when, on the morning of October 27th, "B" Company 6 Mahratta took over the airfield, the Indonesian commander made himself popular by providing cases of lemonade and beer. That was almost the last friendly act towards us; the storm clouds were driving up fast. During the day leaflets had been dropped over Surabaya identical, except for the necessary local variations, with the proclamations issued at Batavia, Bandoeng and Semarang. The clause demanding the surrender of unauthorized arms created a furore and Moestopo hastened to Brigadier Mallaby to express doubts about the Indonesians accepting the order. After argument, it was decided to extend the time limit for handing in arms to October 30th, and Moestopo promised to broadcast. That he failed to do, his place being taken by an extremist who in an inflammatory speech incited the town to fight.

It has sometimes been made out that the dropping of the leaflets was the prime cause of the rising at Surabaya. That is not true. No disturbances had occurred after the issue of the proclamations in other places, nor was there reason to expect trouble over their issue in Surabaya. The drop undoubtedly afforded the Indonesians a pretext of which they made full use, but the real causes of the rising lie deeper. In Batavia, the Japanese continued to guard their arms and ammunition until we arrived; in Surabaya every single round and every weapon, including light tanks and armoured cars fell into the hands of the Indonesians, thanks

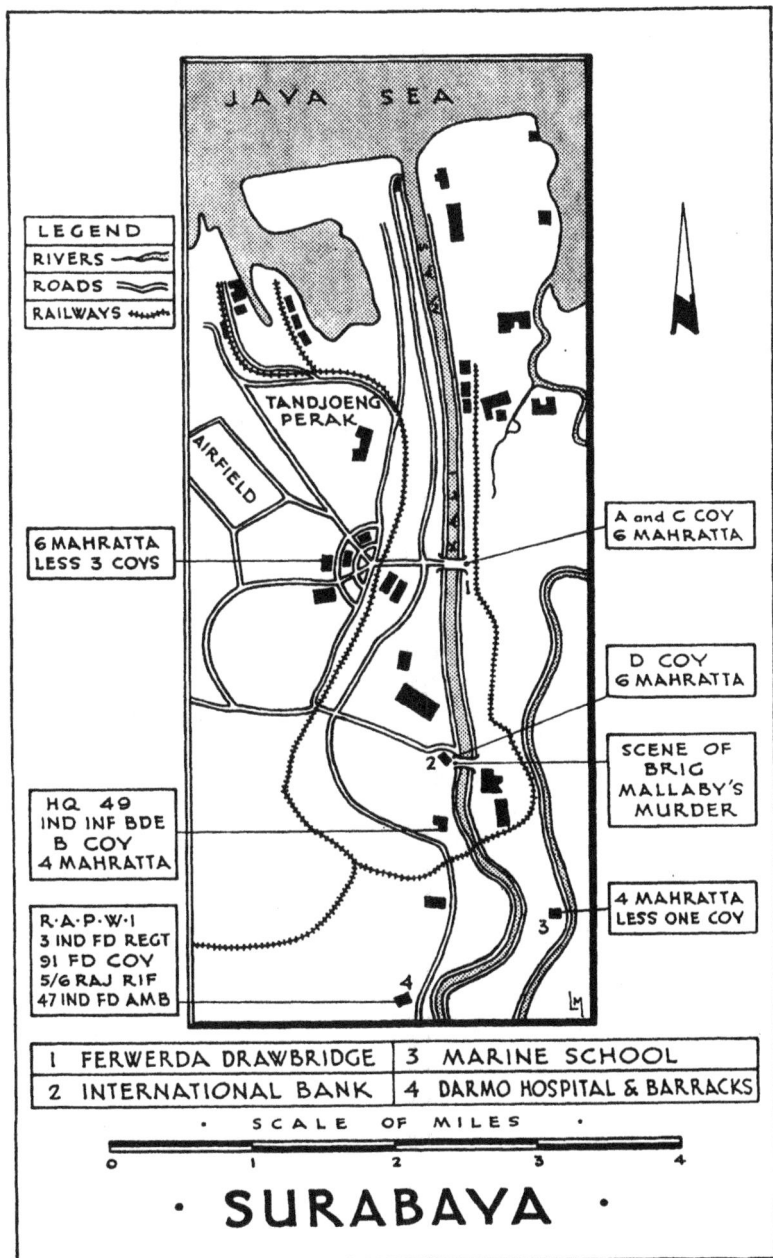

LEGEND
RIVERS
ROADS
RAILWAYS

JAVA SEA

TANDJOENG PERAK

AIRFIELD

6 MAHRATTA LESS 3 COYS

A and C COY 6 MAHRATTA

D COY 6 MAHRATTA

SCENE OF BRIG MALLABY'S MURDER

HQ 49 IND INF BDE B COY 4 MAHRATTA

4 MAHRATTA LESS ONE COY

R·A·P·W·I
3 IND FD REGT
91 FD COY
5/6 RAJ RIF
47 IND FD AMB

| 1 FERWERDA DRAWBRIDGE | 3 MARINE SCHOOL |
| 2 INTERNATIONAL BANK | 4 DARMO HOSPITAL & BARRACKS |

SCALE OF MILES

0   1   2   3   4

· SURABAYA ·

to a lamentable act of stupidity on the part of a Dutch naval officer, who took the surrender of the Japanese though he had no troops to guard the dumps. The Indonesians thereupon imprisoned the man as reward for his folly, seized the arms and equipment and waited for our arrival with their ears close to the ground. They heard the mutterings from Batavia that the British had only come to pave the way for the Dutch, and there were in Surabaya many violent people ready to listen to counsels urging the use of force. Whatever one might think of Dr. Soekarno and his subordinates, they were not thirsting for blood, and the presence of these men in Batavia meant that there was a chance wild excesses would be avoided. Soekarno had his nominee as Resident in Surabaya, but the town was also full of out-and-out revolutionaries—men like Soetomo, leader of the Youth movement, and Atmaji, a commander in the recently formed Indonesian army, the T.K.R. or People's Defence Army. It is not an unfair inference from the subsequent course of events that there was a struggle for control going on in Surabaya between the moderates and extremists, and that the extremists had decided on an armed rising from the moment we landed. Hence the inflammatory broadcasts which said that Dutch troops were landing with us and represented the clearing of civilians from the dock area as a move to conceal this fact.

All through the night of October 27th/28th the town was full of the sound of cars moving from place to place, each of them a moving arsenal, like the vehicle captured by 6 Mahratta at the Ferwerda drawbridge. On the morning of the 28th the people were walking the streets as usual, but there was in the air a sense of impending doom, that strange but inescapable atmosphere which man communicates to man as a crisis approaches. 49 Bde. went about their normal business. During the morning, 4 Mahratta, who had just landed, moved to their billets in the Marine School in the south of the town and east of the Kali Mas; they left "B" Company at the Central Post Office to guard Bde. H.Q. In the afternoon "A" Company of 6 Mahratta took part with two platoons of "C" Company in an operation to clear the docks. Officers and men were all over the town, some engaged in sequestering cars which the Indonesians had failed to hand over, others in moving R.A.P.W.I. to more comfortable quarters.

Suddenly, about 1630 hrs. on the afternoon of October 28th, the whole town rose in arms against us, a fanatical mob over 140,000 strong and 20,000 of them Japanese trained, whipped up to an uncontrollable frenzy and armed to the teeth against 4,000 troops, many of them in isolated company and platoon posts. The bestial scenes that followed in the name of freedom rivalled the vilest moments of the French Revolution.

At the time of the rising there were on the road twenty 3-ton lorries of 123 Ind. Coy. R.I.A.S.C., full of women and children who were being taken to Darmo; the escort found from "B" Company 4 Mahratta, numbered twenty-two and was commanded by a lance-havildar. About 1830 hrs. the leading vehicle was halted by a road-block and the crowd behind the barrier opened fire, killing instantly the officer in charge of the convoy and some of the internees. Almost simultaneously the trap closed at the back, though one driver managed to reverse his vehicle and drove through a hail of bullets to safety. Inside the trap about sixty Indian soldiers remained to defend four hundred women and children against a mob lusting for slaughter; they had for the defence two Bren guns, one at the front and one at the rear, their rifles and their courage.

Inspired by the R.I.A.S.C. subedar at the rear and by the lance-havildar, the defenders fought for two and a half hours to save the women and children, who had been taken from the lorries and put into the houses fringing the road. Up and down the convoy went the havildar, cheering his men and distributing ammunition. The Brens continued to speak, the piles of dead at the barricades mounted, but more and more Indonesians came forward trampling on the fallen. By now night had come and the mob surged round the barriers into the gardens, uttering blood-curdling screams as they saw their prey within their grasp. Where ammunition had run out, the knives, swords and daggers did their devilish work, and the cries of the maimed and mutilated mingled with the attackers' yells of triumph while the flames from burning lorries cast a livid light over this ghastly battle.

The lance-havildar saw that the end was near and, in a last desperate effort to save something from the carnage, decided that he must try to restart the convoy. In the uproar, his voice could not be heard, but he found his driver and hoped that others would follow his lead as he drove full speed past the vehicles. With the windscreen shattered by bullets, he crashed through the heap of dead, crashed through the road-block and struggled on to a Rajrif post. The subedar followed and broke away with three loaded lorries. Wherever he turned in a town that was strange to him, there were road-blocks, but at last he met a friendly patrol. Taking his party into an empty house, he tended the wounded and gave them his haversack ration while he waited for the help which came at midnight. At the battlefield, the mob, glutted with blood, had begun to move on elsewhere, but the struggle was not quite over—one R.I.A.S.C. naik, with superb endurance and determination, held on in his house for two days.

Throughout the city mob rule prevailed. Some officers who were out on lone missions when the storm broke were never heard of again. 4 Mahratta had a solitary platoon guarding the wireless station which had just been visited by the company commander. His men watched his jeep disappear round a corner, heard an outbreak of firing and then —silence. The officer's body was later found floating down the Kali Mas, as were many others—often wantonly and hideously dismembered and defaced. The Adjutant, trying to reach the same platoon and ignorant of the insurrection, met a similar fate. A party from 6 Mahratta, who had been visiting Bde. H.Q. to report the clearing of the docks, were more fortunate. Warned by meeting a road-block on the way in and by seeing the Field Security Officer carrying his wounded havildar into H.Q., they moved back in convoy with Indonesians sitting on the head-lamps. The Mahrattas forced some of these men to dismount as they reached the replaced block where a burst of fire killed the Indonesians to a man, but not before they had cleared a big enough gap in the barrier for the Mahrattas to escape.

A severely wounded gunner officer owed his life to a lance-havildar who put the officer in a safe place when four Indonesians attacked, sent them packing and rejoined his party, carrying the officer on his back. Equally gallant was the conduct of a havildar-major of 3 Ind. Fd. who saved the battery guns. Caught on the road while nearing their allotted position, the men left their vehicles to fight off the attack. The N.C.O. dashed out into the midst of the battle, started the leading vehicles and drove the first gun to safety. Seven more guns remained, but one by one they were hauled away out of danger.

49 Bde. were fighting for their lives and for the lives of the internees they had come to protect, with the odds weighed heavily against them. All their major units except 6 Mahratta were in the south of the town and none was complete; the guns could not affect the battle, Bde. H.Q. was in the middle of the enemy; most serious of all, there had been no time to move up the reserves of ammunition and food which lay useless in the docks. It was a situation to try the nerves of the most hardened, but many of these men were veterans of Shenam and Sangshak, of Gibraltar and Rajput Hill, and they knew how to fight.

Fight they did with magnificent gallantry—in some cases until their ammunition was gone, when the frenzied mob was free to swarm in for the killing. 5/6 Rajrif suffered the worst, for this battalion was the most dispersed, and already by midnight one of their platoons had been obliterated. There were desperate battles all over the town. The naik in command of one Rajrif section took over the Bren when the gunner was wounded and saw seventy of the enemy fall in front of the post. At the Darmo hospital no respect was paid to the sign of the Red Cross. There Colonel Pugh, who had been visiting the Field Ambulance, sited the defences under heavy fire and by his bravery converted a mixed garrison of Rajrif, gunners and medical orderlies into an organized and confident force which beat off attack after attack. Away to the north, "C" Company, 6 Mahratta, were as hard pressed; owing to the operations to clear the docks, there were only thirty-five bodies to hold the position at the start, but the thirty-five held on until the other two platoons arrived. Every post was surrounded. When a 4 Mahratta company patrol attempted to fight its way out of the Marine School to go to the aid of Press correspondents, the attempt had to be abandoned. One dead and two wounded I.O.Rs. lay on the pavement outside, covered by the enemy's fire, but a naik was not going to allow two of his comrades to fall into the clutches of a brutal enemy. This was one of those suicidal missions which seemingly must end in death, but bravery had its due reward. Both men were saved and the naik was untouched.

Midnight came without any pause in the fighting. The Indonesians took no account of their dead; when one man fell, another came forward, drunk and half crazed at the sight of blood. The hours ebbed slowly away and, as each hour passed, the plight of the defence worsened. A Rajrif platoon, after incessant fighting, beat off another attack in the half-light of the dawn and yet another two hours later. On this occasion, two tanks came within five yards of the post and a naik, after throwing many grenades at the tracks, crawled forward to drop more down the turrets; these were closed, but the tank crews withdrew a short distance and later abandoned their vehicles when the naik pumped bursts of L.M.G. fire into the slits. A sweeper helped to keep another post intact by crawling on his stomach carrying mortar ammunition across a twenty-foot gap exposed to snipers who had previously wounded three men. Then there was the Bren gunner of 71 Ind. Fd. Coy.; about 0445 hrs. on the 29th, he was so severely wounded in the mouth, neck and both legs that he could no longer fire his weapon, but he lay there acting as No. 2 until he was dragged away five hours later.

The sands of time were running out. Some time during the morning, three isolated platoon posts of the Rajrif in the waterworks area had nothing but their bayonets with which to ward off the foe. 4 Mahratta, who had beaten off three major attempts to break in through a gap at the north-eastern corner of the School, were wondering how much longer their ammunition would last and were anxiously awaiting the return of a company patrol which had tried to reach the scene of the R.A.P.W.I. disaster. These troops fought their way for three hours through a thousand yards of hostile streets before they were recalled. There was more anxiety at the 71 Ind. Fd. Coy. position where a crowd six hundred strong was being held at bay, fire being directed by an officer who established himself as an O.P. forty yards from the enemy.

This heroic resistance could only end in the extermination of 49 Bde. unless somebody could quell the passions of the mob. There was no such person in Surabaya and all hope rested on the influence of Soekarno. Genuinely distressed and even shocked on the evening of the 28th when the G.I. first told him of the bloodshed, he had readily agreed with the suggestion that the R.A.F. should fly him to Surabaya next day. He arrived at H.Q. 6 Mahratta on the 29th at the precise moment they were dispersing an attack by 3-inch mortars, and having had a glimpse of the battle, he was dispatched towards the town in a truck. Two hundred yards farther on, the truck was stopped by an armoured car and Soekarno disappeared from the ken of 6 Mahratta.

About 1600 hrs. when the fighting was still fierce, a British intelligence officer, who had accompanied Soekarno, stepped into the office of "B" Company, 4 Mahratta, next door to Bde. H.Q.; he said that the "President" had come to confer with Brigadier Mallaby. The company commander and this officer set off together, escorted by a fully armed mob. Half a mile down the road stood Soekano, to whom the company commander was introduced, feeling a little uncomfortable because several bayonets and two machine guns were pointed at his back. They went into the Court of Justice together, where it became apparent that Soekarno thought he was talking to the Brigadier. After the mistake had been rectified, Brigadier Mallaby and Soekarno conferred for an hour, agreed to a truce and set off to the Broadcasting Station.

At the end of the conference, O.C. "B" Company took part in one of the few light incidents in the sad story of Surabaya. As he stepped out on to the street, he was unceremoniously bundled into the back of a waiting car which was full of armed Indonesians. The car was driven fast away from his own H.Q. for five miles, and when at last it stopped, crowds swarmed round. The officer had no illusions about the fate coming to him in the next minute, but the sword did not descend. Instead, there were handshakes all round and drinks, an hour's hospitality and a safe return to Bde. H.Q.

S

The presence of Soekarno in the town and his broadcast did something to calm the populace, but it did not re-establish control over a mob which was far too intoxicated by its orgy of murder for words to suffice. According to the terms, ambulances were to be granted safe conduct, but as soon as these tried to leave Bde. H.Q. they were driven back by snipers. The only vehicle that moved carried O.C. "D" Company, 6 Mahratta, who had been at Bn. H.Q., cut off from his men; the hazardous journey was successfully accomplished and the ambulance returned safely with a few wounded. Elsewhere, the wounded could not be moved and many suffered grievously from lack of attention.

Throughout the night of October 29th/30th there was desultory firing and pitched battles continued in a few places, among them at the wireless station, where a jemadar commanded the 4 Mahratta platoon. By 1600 hrs. on the 29th they had fought an all-day battle to hold a four-storey building with big plate glass doors and windows on the ground floor. They had driven off a series of vicious attacks and put two tanks to flight, but now two more had come up, the upper storeys were ablaze and ammunition was low. Some of the defenders were burnt to death when the top floors collapsed; the survivors took off their burning clothes and continued the fight on the ground floor, where the jemadar quietly collected his men for a last stand. In intense heat, which scorched the eyes, the Mahrattas fought on until the last round had been fired. Choked by the fumes and smoke, some of the men charged blindly into the street, where they were hacked to pieces; the rest stood grimly watching, and when the Indonesians called on them to surrender, the jemadar replied that they would stand fast and die at their posts. The mob rushed in from all sides and carried the survivors away in exultant triumph to the gaol. Here, the jemadar was taken aside and bayoneted to death; of the rest, who were all badly burned, some were taken to the hospital and later came back to tell the tale, others just disappeared.

The night was followed by an uneasy morning. When General Hawthorn landed about 0915 hrs. on the morning of October 30th, the fighting was threatening to flare up once more. He was met by O.C. 6 Mahratta, who remarked "I think I can hold the airfield for half an hour," as he took the General off to his H.Q., there to await the arrival of Brigadier Mallaby and Drs. Soekarno and Hatta. It was some time before they appeared, and when they did come, the conference proved abortive because Soekarno, who was nervous and unsure of himself, said he had no confidence in his ability to fulfil his promises without the approval of the full Indonesian committee. The General then agreed to a meeting in the Government Buildings and the party set forth under a flag of truce, the General standing up beside Soekarno and Hatta. As the car threaded its way along the streets, past many road-blocks, the crowds rushed down to the roadside, brandishing every kind of manufactured and home-made weapon and shrieking "Merdeka!" "Merdeka!" In the background the noise of firing continued.

Because of the "truce" arranged the previous night, orders had been given that no unit was to open fire unless it were actually attacked. That order was obeyed although the troops could see the Indonesians moving up to more favourable positions, a supreme testimony to discipline. The situation was particularly threatening round "C" Company, 6 Mahratta, but they were not allowed to fire. Suddenly 6 Mahratta H.Q. heard that the Indonesians were massing against "D" Company, and when a second message said that firing had begun, several 3-inch mortar bombs were put down on the mob.

Those bombs, quite rightly fired, were nearly disastrous. General Hawthorn had gone to the full conference with a very weak and difficult hand to play. He knew that if the fighting were not stopped his forces would be overwhelmed, and if a disaster occurred the effect throughout Java was horrid to contemplate; his only strength was that the Indonesians were not fully aware of our plight. From the start it was a stormy meeting. On one side were the General and Soekarno, on the other a collection of young hotheads, the real revolutionaries who had the taste of blood on their lips; the older and more moderate Indonesians hardly spoke. The first clash came over the dropping of the leaflets and the surrender of arms; the local leader of the T.K.R. rose in a fury and was only quietened when he was told that this force was now recognized and could carry arms. Soekarno went on to explain the plan for the British to control two zones, one at the docks and the other in the R.A.P.W.I. area, while the Indonesians controlled the centre of the town and allowed free movement between the two British zones. This brought Soetomo to his feet, a veritable fire-brand with fanatical, protruding eyes which rolled incessantly and glinted with hatred and unreason. Ironically enough, his argument was that the Indonesians were being hemmed in and Soekarno could do nothing to calm his ranting. In the end he was quelled by the General, who warned him that his obstinacy would bring down the full weight of British military power on his head. The need for a Contact Bureau to implement the peace terms was more easily established, but this was followed by another agonizing and protracted wrangle over the guards for the R.A.P.W.I. camps. The General would naturally have no Indonesians there, the extremists demanded there should be. Once more negotiations threatened to break down as Soekarno became more and more impassioned in his efforts to control Soetomo, but at last sanity prevailed and agreement was reached.

Precisely at that moment the deafening roar of mortar bombs bursting in the streets near by rent the air. Pandemonium broke out in the conference room and it seemed that not only was the ground so laboriously won lost there and then, but that the General and Brigadier Mallaby and Lieut.-Colonel Doulton, the A.Q., who were now behind the Indonesian lines unarmed and alone without escort under the flag of truce, would be assassinated on the spot.[1] Quickly the General turned to Soekarno and said "We must stop the fighting or there will be more useless loss of life." Soekarno took up the cue and there was some semblance of order restored before Soetomo came dashing back into the room to say that the British fleet were shelling the town. The General laughed at him, Soetomo subsided after a further heated altercation, and the truce was agreed; the Contact Bureau was to meet in one hour's time. The last act in the drama was the sight of Soetomo dashing across the street to prevent reinforcements going into action while the General

---

[1] Added on the insistence of General Hawthorn.—AUTHOR.

and Soekarno stood outside the conference building, waiting to go to the airfield in a car which the Indonesians took a quarter of an hour to find.

These two men had between them gained the day, though for minutes on end the extremists had threatened to set the sword above reason and humanity. In an affair so critical as this it is hard to say what finally turns the scale, but nothing counts more than the subconscious effect exerted by individuals. Without Soekarno's presence there would have been no conference and no hope of success, and he strove for peace throughout. Yet important as was his influence, the calm bearing, quiet firmness, courage and sound judgment of General Hawthorn was ultimately decisive and went far to saving 49 Bde. even though some of the most dastardly happenings were yet to come.

As the two aircraft taking the General and Soekarno back to Batavia left Surabaya, "D" Company, 6 Mahratta, in the International Bank building, signalled that they must return the enemy fire. Half an hour later, about 1430 hrs., Brigadier Mallaby drove up to the square in front of the building and dismounted. Carrying a flag of truce, he walked alone and unarmed right across the square to "D" Company while the Indonesians continued to fire. He explained to the company commander that all efforts were being made to implement the truce and ordered him not to fire unless the position were assaulted. A similar conversation took place with some of the Indonesians who went over to pacify their followers while the Brigadier went back to his H.Q. On his return, he sent his Brigade Major and another officer to the Indonesian H.Q., but they never arrived; stopped by an angry mob, they were rescued by a T.K.R. official who took them to a house for safe custody, but the mob broke in and murdered the officers in cold blood.

The next flare-up occurred round "C" Company, 6 Mahratta, where the long-expected attack developed at 1500 hrs. To help in repelling this attack, "A" Company on the right set fire to some wooden barracks which separated the two companies. In these barracks there was a petrol dump and as the drums exploded a column of thick, black smoke rose into the air and spread over the northern part of the town like a funereal pall. It was as though fate had decreed the setting for the final scene of the tragedy.

At 1600 hrs. a message reached Bde. H.Q. that the crowds were again massing in the International Bank Square. The Mahrattas were told to hold their fire as the last details of the truce were nearly settled, and when Brigadier Mallaby arrived with Indonesian officials about 1630 hrs. he found the opposing sides cheek by jowl. The Indonesians, packed tight in front of the Bank, clamoured for surrender, the Mahrattas stood waiting defiantly. The crowd refused to let the Brigadier enter the position, and he talked to his men from ten yards away while the mob swirled and screamed around him. The Indonesians were then ordered to quieten the mob, and they stood on the roofs of their cars haranguing the turbulent throng for half an hour.

When part of the crowd had dispersed, the convoy of cars moved off towards the bridge over the Kali Mas, where another crowd was assembling. There the Indonesian officials began to speak again, but an agitator leapt on to a car and began to incite the mob to violence. The mob surged forward towards the Brigadier and his officers and laid violent hands on them while the Mahrattas watched angrily; they also saw their own danger. The enemy had brought up a machine gun to point-blank range, some had climbed on to the veranda of the Bank, a few were inside the building. The company commander gave the order to fire.

During the shooting the Brigadier and two junior officers with him lay down in the car, feigning death. They had between them two cigarettes which they shared out, murmuring "This is it," and one grenade. After a time the firing died down, and when the Brigadier heard someone calling his name, he sat up in the car. A shot rang out and he slumped back in his seat—dead. The assassin fired twice more, missing both times, and the surviving officers hurled the grenade into the road. In the confusion they had just time to rush out of the car, cover the ten yards to the Kali Mas and leap into the river, down which they swam to the Mahrattas near the Ferwerda Drawbridge and to safety.

This murder sated the blood lust of the Indonesians, but after so terrible an orgy there could be no confidence in any promises made by the enemy. Days of anxiety and strain lay ahead during the negotiations conducted by Colonel Pugh. Hearing of Brigadier Mallaby's death, he had resolved that he must go at once to take over command of the Brigade. Fully conscious that he too might be overwhelmed by the mob, he set off on a five-mile journey through the streets of Surabaya. The sheer audacity of his ride succeeded. Faced at one point by a road-block, he set his jeep at the obstacle like a tank and crashed through to the farther side. On and on he sped, while snipers' bullets whistled past, until he reached Bde. H.Q.

The ensuing negotiations for the concentration of 49 Bde. and the evacuation of R.A.P.W.I. were protracted and exhausting. The Indonesians were truculent, evasive, dilatory and unco-operative and there were many hitches. It was only after long argument on October 31st that they agreed, in accordance with the terms of the truce, to allow the assembly of the Rajrif, gunners and sappers at Darmo, while 4 Mahratta and Bde. H.Q. joined 6 Mahratta near the docks. 4 Mahratta, out of food and short of ammunition, spent an anxious morning as the Indonesians kept on approaching to ask for surrender. There was a real fear that hostilities might break out again, but a message to H.Q. brought Wing Commander Groom out to the School. This officer, who had worked in Surabaya before the war, was well known to the Indonesians and much respected by them. Relying on this respect, he moved fearlessly about from incident to incident throughout the rising, using his influence to restore order. Earlier in the morning he had been at hand to smooth out an awkward moment when 6 Mahratta shot at an Indonesian staff car and killed one of the passengers; and the magic of his presence at the Marine School sufficed to dissolve the crowd there. When 4 Mahratta moved down to the docks in the late afternoon they were unmolested.

As the other troop movements were not interrupted, the military position on the night of the 31st was better and would improve further as reinforcements came. A squadron of P.A.V.O. tanks had already landed and the leading troops of 5 Ind. Div., together with H.M.S. *Sussex* and others of His Majesty's ships were due on November 1st. All through that day a long wrangle went on over the evacuation of R.A.P.W.I. The Indonesians prevaricated, hedged and raised every kind of obstruction; they would not even allow food to be taken to the half-starved women and children, who had had nothing to eat since hostilities began except the rations surrendered by the troops in the area. An air-drop on the 1st afforded some relief, but the aircraft were wide of the target on the next day and all fell into Indonesian hands.

While the negotiations were in progress, a lone figure was driving unarmed about the southern part of the city. For six days and nights Lieut.-Colonel J. F. S. Rendall, the commander of 3 Ind. Fd. Regt., went on his errands of mercy to bring in internees from outlying houses. The town was in the hands of riotous bands out for pillage and destruction and he knew that one false step would mean death. His tact and patience, his physical endurance, courage and judgment led to saving the lives of many women, whose fortitude equalled his own.

The stoicism, the calm bearing and the bravery of these Dutch and Eurasian women had been something at which to marvel. When the rising began, one lady led a party of twenty children to the nearest British post. At first she moved safely through back gardens until she reached a point where she was forced to run the gauntlet down a bullet-swept street. She shepherded her flock together, encouraged them and set off at their head in a race with death which all escaped but one. At the post she offered her services as nurse, an offer gladly accepted for there were several seriously wounded and none to tend them; throughout the fighting she went on with her self-imposed task, never flinching at sights that made the battle-hardened pause.

This brave lady was one of very many, and now the moment had arrived when they must go out through the streets again to the docks, where British warships were waiting to take them away from troubled Java to Singapore. The lorries were ours, the drivers ours, the guards Indonesians; but there was no questioning of orders despite the nervousness they must have felt. They waited quietly for their turn to leave through all the delays and disappointments. On November 1st the delaying tactics of the Indonesians prevailed; on the 2nd 1,500 went aboard; on the morning of the 3rd another 1,100 before more excuses brought movement to a stop. On the 4th the drivers waited in their lorries all day while a battle of words took place to break down pettifogging objections. The 5th was a better day. To and fro went the lorries on this and subsequent days until by the evening of the 9th all who wished to leave were in safety. The estimate was that there would be something over a thousand to be carried; in fact, near eight thousand were rescued.

By November 9th, 5 Ind. Div., under Major-General Mansergh, had landed two brigades strong and had taken 49 Bde. less 6 Mahratta under command. The Mahrattas had left for Batavia on the 5th, the day the troops at Darmo had been concentrated in the north of the town, and their loss was made good by the loan of 3/9 Jat. The stage was now set for carrying out the warning issued by General Christison on the day following Brigadier Mallaby's murder, when he threatened to bring "the whole weight of my sea, land and air forces and all the weapons of modern war" against the Indonesians of Surabaya unless those responsible for the crimes surrendered.

This warning was followed by an ultimatum from General Mansergh which was dropped over the town on the 9th, together with a statement from General Christison making plain that his forces were taking action only against the extremists of Surabaya and were not attempting to impose a political settlement by force. When the ultimatum was unanswered by the time stipulated, all the guns and mortars of 5 Div. bombarded the town on the morning of November 10th and our advance began. This reoccupation of Surabaya was a slow grind in which 49 Bde. played its part; the Indonesians resisted and had to be driven from their positions, but wherever we pressed firmly they gave way. As great care was taken to avoid unnecessary casualties by careful planning and skilful conducting of the operations, progress was not fast and it was near the end of November before the town was cleared.

5 Ind. Div. rightly received a notable message of congratulation from the C.-in-C. A.L.F.S.E.A. at the end of their task, but some felt 49 Bde. should also have been honoured. In the long and glorious history of the Indian Army, there can have been few battles where the odds were greater and few that gave finer proof of the loyalty, discipline, courage and endurance of the Indian soldier. It was his steadfastness, his determination in support of the gallant lead given by his officers, that had staved off disaster, and the great tradition of his Army, created under British guidance, was never more magnificently revealed than in the stand by those lonely platoons which had no officer at their head.

Still, the deeds of 49 Bde. did not go unrecognized. Many were decorated for their feats of arms and there were two letters which are worthy of record. The first from Dr. van Mook to General Christison read:

"I have just read the report on the happenings in Surabaya by Brigadier Pugh. Both from this report and from the stories of eye-witnesses I am deeply impressed by the extremely gallant behaviour of your officers and troops who executed the initial occupation.

"I would like to assure you that their sacrifices, which in the end assured the safety of thousands of my compatriots, shall never be forgotten and will constitute a lasting claim on our gratitude.

"I would like you to convey these sentiments to the Brigade both in my name and that of my country."

The second, addressed to General Hawthorn in answer to a message from him, ran:

"Women of Surabaya, now slowly recovering at Singapore from what they have gone through, asked me to express their deep gratitude towards you and your brave officers and men for rescuing them from the Surabaya inferno. They feel that if you praise their behaviour during the evacuation, such conduct was only possible by the stimulating courage and calmness of your officers and men never wavering under appalling odds which made them proud to co-operate with your troops. Past events have created a strong tie between our countries and an everlasting memory in their hearts."

The losses in this "inferno" were grievous enough; 220 killed and missing and most of the latter gone without a trace being left of their fate, with more than 80 wounded, but there would have been far more grievous casualties to mourn had the fighting lasted a few hours longer.

CHAPTER 23

The Flames Spread

As October turned into November, the British military commanders, caught up against their will in a nationalist rising which they had no means to quell, watched almost helplessly as the tide of violence swept westwards. They had nothing on which they could rely apart from their own courage and that of their men, who were nowhere numerous enough to hold out against a massed insurrection except possibly in Batavia. Our position was precarious, especially in Central Java, where Brigadier Bethell held Semarang with 2/19 Kumaon and 2 Ind. A.Tk. Regt., while 3/10 G.R. had two companies twenty-five miles inland, guarding the R.A.P.W.I. camps at Ambarawa and Banjoebiroe, with the rest of the battalion nearly fifty miles from the coast at Magelang.

The Indonesians struck next at Magelang. On October 30th, the day of Brigadier Mallaby's murder, while reinforcements hurried up from the south to swell the ranks of the mob, a van drove through the streets of the town broadcasting the ominous message, "We have defeated the British at Surabaya, now is the time for all to rise." 3/10 G.R., at most five hundred strong and inevitably scattered in two groups to protect internees, waited for the attack to come.

The next morning, while Colonel Pugh wrangled with the Indonesians in Surabaya and none could tell whether he would succeed, battle was joined in the streets of Magelang. The fight was hottest round "A" Company, who were early cut off from the rest of the force, and though a carefully delivered air strike, the first of the Java "war," helped to ease the pressure in the afternoon, night came with the isolated company fighting desperately and more out of reach of help than ever as the rest of the force had been compelled to relinquish some ground in the north of the town. The Gurkhas were fighting with their customary toughness. One lance-naik, cooped up with his section

268

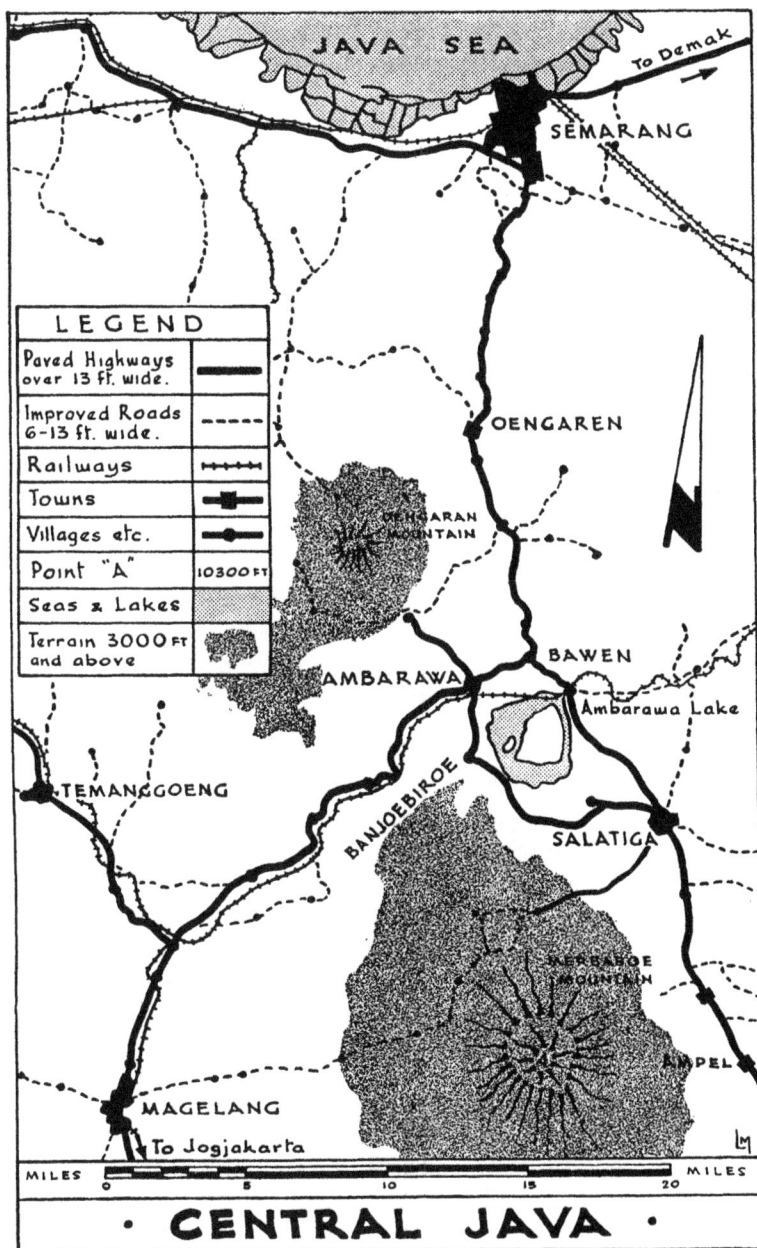

JAVA SEA

To Demak

SEMARANG

LEGEND

Paved Highways over 13 ft. wide.	
Improved Roads 6-13 ft. wide.	
Railways	
Towns	
Villages etc.	
Point "A"	10300 FT
Seas & Lakes	
Terrain 3000 FT and above	

OENGAREN

N

OENGARAN MOUNTAIN

AMBARAWA

BAWEN

Ambarawa Lake

TEMANGGOENG

BANJOEBIROE

SALATIGA

KERBABOE MOUNTAIN

AMPEL

MAGELANG

To Jogjakarta

MILES   0   5   10   15   20   MILES

· CENTRAL JAVA ·

inside a building ill designed for defence, drove off repeated attacks for thirteen hours; once the shrieking, maddened horde was ten yards away, but the naik appeared at an open window in full view of the attackers, who fell back in the face of repeated bursts from an automatic. Another naik held his post for thirty-six hours before relief came.

During the morning of November 1st, a small force of anti-tank gunners, with two platoons of Kumaons and one of 3/10 G.R., joined the defence after fighting its way through a series of road-blocks on the road from Ambarawa. They brought with them one prisoner, which they owed to a lance-naik of the Kumaons who was clearing a house near one of the blocks. When his companion was wounded, he went on alone, dispatched one man who came at him brandishing a Japanese sword and a second armed with a rifle, and then found himself embroiled with two more men and a woman. The men met their appointed end, but the naik had mercy on the woman and contrived to haul her back to his platoon, though he was encumbered with two rifles and four knives besides his own weapon.

Though this small force had won through, "A" Company's danger increased hourly despite astonishingly low casualties —first reports on the morning of the 1st gave only one man wounded; but ammunition was running out and a signal received at Batavia in the early hours of the morning had given 1200 as the latest hour they could guarantee to hold out unless supplies were dropped by air. As there was no air supply organization in Java, this should have been a request beyond the resources of a "Q" staff which was always ready to attempt conjuring tricks; but the crisis at Surabaya had brought into being a make-shift packing team in Singapore, and the first loaded aircraft were due to call at Batavia on the morning of November 1st for final briefing. So it chanced that not long after midday the parachutes began to drop out of the sky above Magelang. It was an uncomfortable drop for the pilots, who found that the tales of "war" in Java were no idle rumour; the Indonesians potted at the machines on the run in, and two aircraft returned to Batavia pierced by a dozen or more bullets.

The drop had been preceded by a second controlled air strike which dampened the ardour of the Indonesians enough for the Gurkhas to recapture some of the ground they had lost, but the situation remained critical, with the force still split in two and completely outnumbered in a hostile town. Though the attackers might have suffered losses enough to give them cause to respect the Gurkha spirit, it would not be long before firebrands whipped up their followers to renewed assaults unless their fanaticism could be allayed.

Dr. Soekarno was not lacking in courage, and when news came of these fresh troubles at Magelang he agreed on a second air trip; he landed at Semarang on the 1st, found the extremists in the town unwilling to parley and set off alone for the interior. His presence in Magelang did not bring immediate peace; there was sporadic firing all through the night of November 1st/2nd and, as the Indonesians claimed they had not been given sufficient warning of the terms, the hoped-for truce did not come into effect at 0900 hrs. on the 2nd. By midday the Gurkhas in the north had linked up again with "A" Company, and it must have been about this time that Soekarno's influence prevailed with his followers enough to bring them to H.Q. 3/10 G.R. for a conference which Brigadier Bethell and Soekarno attended.

The result of this meeting was called "peace," but there was no peace in Central Java in November, 1945. Though the Gurkhas now had the support of a squadron of P.A.V.O. tanks, their arrival at Magelang did not suffice to impress the Indonesians. Wonsonogro, the "Governor" of the district, had very soon to be called in to settle a dispute, and the evacuation of R.A.P.W.I. began against a background of alarmist rumours and acts of violence which boded ill for the safe removal of all who wished to leave. Armed bands ranged over the countryside spreading terror and destruction, and other gangs of desperadoes pillaged and looted in Magelang, where the Indonesians watched scowling as the convoys carried women and children to the grossly overcrowded camps at Ambarawa.

The extremists were long past caring for humanity. Thwarted at Magelang by the resistance of the Gurkhas and the intervention of Soekarno, they sought a fresh outlet for an intense racial hatred originally directed against the Dutch, but increasingly aimed by this time at

British forces. Nothing could illustrate better the cold, unrelenting nature of this perverted nationalism than the incident which served as a prelude to the outbreak in Semarang on the evening of November 17th, when three Kumaon officers were murdered as they escorted some Dutch friends to their homes. The criminal, who was tracked down and caught, made no effort to conceal his action and openly exulted in the glorious example he had set to a people rapidly reverting to the crazed fanaticism of the savage.

Fortunately, there had been warning of impending trouble at Semarang, and as soon as this outrage was reported our troops carried out a series of pre-arranged moves which included the seizure of the telephone exchange. Brigadier Bethell was not the sort of man who believed in half measures, and he acquired a valuable hostage early on the 18th when he impounded Wonsonogro. His next act was to stage an operation to clear unruly elements from the north of the town, and it was here for the first time that the Japanese, under the command of a British officer, rendered important aid. During this action, the Kumaons were held up for a time by heavy fire from the Indonesian H.Q., and after one unsuccessful attempt to storm the building, a company havildar-major lay grievously wounded somewhere within. A junior N.C.O. repeated the gallantry of the Mahratta on a similar occasion at Surabaya; he took a small party of three, dashed across the road and hunted around for ten minutes, a continual target for snipers, before he found the body and hauled it to safety.

Despite Brigadier Bethell's vigorous action, the Indonesians were not easily to be subdued and they launched on the 19th an all-out effort which cut our forces in two. All day long there was hot fighting throughout the town, while we struggled to stem the tide and to ensure the safety of the internees who were being concentrated in the dock area. Once a mob surged forward to overwhelm the Kumaons' H.Q., and left the road strewn with dead and wounded when at last they were beaten back. None of our positions was lost during the day, but the Indonesians remained in control of the town centre, and it became vitally necessary for us to regain command as the news from Ambarawa revealed the possibility of a ghastly massacre. After warning leaflets had been dropped on November 20th, air strikes followed on selected targets, and with this support some semblancè of order was restored in Semarang. The next day the leading company of 4 Mahratta was flown in from Surabaya, and hardly was it complete before it was ordered forth as part of a mixed column of tanks, guns, infantry and sappers bound for the relief of Ambarawa.

Though all the R.A.P.W.I. camps that came within our province were places of gloom, in none were conditions quite so appallingly uncivilized as at Ambarawa and Banjoebiroe, two miles farther south, and into these forsaken and forlorn dens came the refugees from Magelang. Once again these were more numerous than expected, their numbers being swollen by countless Eurasians who fled the terror, and 3,000 remained when 3/10 G.R. received the order to close on Ambarawa. After an appeal from the Gurkhas had brought a twenty-four hour respite, all through the morning of the 20th mixed convoys of army lorries and derelict cars lumbered down the road, ladened with bedding and chattels among which the refugees found a precarious hold. Shortly after midday came disaster. When all the transport was north of a level crossing at Ambarawa, the Indonesians let down the crossing gate and trapped every vehicle. There was to be no more evacuation from Magelang. As the sun rose on the morning of November 21st and the mountain tops of Central Java peeped out above a blanket of cloud, 3/10 G.R. had the utterly harrowing experience of setting out on a forced march to the north while they left behind some 2,000 Eurasians and three brave Dutchmen who choose to stay.

The need to protect Ambarawa and Banjoebiroe was urgent. There were not less than 10,000 internees herded together in the camps, and Major Meikle had for their defence two companies of Gurkhas, dispersed in small detachments, and a reserve of fifty Japanese. At 0345 hrs. on the 21st the Indonesian attacks began in earnest, but their only success was the firing of one camp, where there was a long struggle to bring the flames under control. All through the heat of the day the force from Magelang marched to the rescue, well aware of the issues at stake,

T

and they learnt of the growing threat as they spoke to Meikle late that night on the wireless; his slender force was still intact, but he was full of anxiety for the outcome and especially for one camp in a convent which was unguarded.

O.C. 3/10 G.R. (Lieut.-Colonel H. G. Edwardes) meditated on the hazard of sending one of his companies on in advance through the darkness, but he deemed the risk too great as his advanced guard had recently been in action, and he decided to halt until dawn on November 22nd. By then his rearguard was engaged in a battle where the speed of the Gurkhas and their prowess with the khukri proved distasteful to the Indonesians, but it was 1100 hrs. before the march was resumed. On the way a mined bridge caused more delay, and darkness was falling with the force still two miles short of Ambarawa. As they pushed on through the night, the tanks in the lead swept round every corner with automatics firing, while behind a trail of flaming huts marked the line of the road. Against a different foe such tactics would have been fatal, but the Indonesians had no stomach to resist men driven on in their weariness by the urgency of their mission. Even so, the Gurkhas came too late wholly to avert one tragedy. After nightfall extremists broke into the convent, lined up the defenceless internees against a wall and tossed grenades into their midst. Nine were murdered in this wanton blood-letting and twenty mutilated before the Indonesians fled from this heartless entertainment at the sound of approaching tanks.

For the next three days Ambarawa was a battlefield where the discipline and courage of 3/10 G.R. and the troops of the relief column prevailed after hard fighting. The Indonesian resistance centred on the gaol, a veritable fortress which was pounded unavailingly by anti-tank guns and tanks for some time before one of 178 Fd. Regt.'s 25-pounders was brought up to point-blank range. Five shells went hurtling against the main gate and the walls near by, the smoke cleared away and 3/10 G.R. went storming through the yawning gap. During the fighting, in which our losses were happily low, the R.A.F. Thunderbolts gave fine support, and it was tragic to watch one aircraft dive into the Ambarawa lake through an error of judgment; more help came from the guns of *Sussex* which arrived at Semarang before the end of November and helped to keep the L. of C. open by very accurate shelling on Oengaran.

By now our position was altogether stronger for, with the end approaching at Surabaya, 49 Bde. less 6 Mahratta had been released for the Semarang "front." As already recorded, the leading troops of 4 Mahratta were flown more or less straight from one battle to another, and when the "build-up" was complete, Brigadier A. de B. Morris, D.S.O., who had succeeded Colonel Pugh, became responsible for the evacuation from Ambarawa while the C.R.A. held the Semarang base. 3/10 G.R. remained at Ambarawa, with 4 Mahratta to the east guarding the left flank against marauding bands which constantly threatened the main road; the Mahrattas had one company on this road at Bawen, and 5/6 Rajrif garrisoned Oengaran on the route back to the sea and safety.

Before the evacuation began on December 1st, the Indonesians, resentful of missing their prey, had recourse to their last expedient for harassing the internees. Bringing up a field gun, they fired ninety-five rounds into the town on one day, and, if it was any satisfaction to them, they could boast that eight more women lay dead and twenty wounded; five of our own troops were killed during the shelling and fifteen wounded. After an air strike in support of a 4 Mahratta action had silenced this gun for a few days, the convoys travelled unmolested to and from Semarang, though not without the need for several minor operations to protect the road. By December 14th Ambarawa was clear and our troops fell back to Semarang, with 5/6 Rajrif and two companies of Mahrattas at Oengaran to cover the base.

At the cost of much blood and sweat another large-scale rescue had been accomplished, but where were these desperate races against time leading? They contributed nothing to the peace of Java and less than might appear to the safety of the rescued. Some of those who had escaped from Ambarawa were on their way to Holland, and for these the nervous strain and discomfort of life in Java were horrid memories; but these were few, and the less fortunate who had been flown to Bandoeng had gone to more disturbances, and even those bound for Batavia came to no haven of rest and quiet.

All through November, few nights in Batavia were free from the rattle of small-arms fire, and several day-time shooting affrays developed into small-scale battles. Most of these arose out of encounters between Indonesians and Dutch forces, largely composed of the ill-disciplined and trigger-happy Ambonese, who never hesitated to shoot; and where-ever the fighting flared up, there went the "Fighting Cock" to part the combatants. One of the worst of these clashes occurred when some Ambonese, driving through the city to visit their families, claimed they were fired on by Indon-esians. Both parties were at each others' throats in an instant, the guards on a nearby hospital joined in, and when the Patialas and P.A.V.O. arrived to restore order, the two sides were so inextricably involved that it was hard to concert joint action with the Dutch. It was little wonder that the C.O. of the Patialas bitterly lamented the loss of brave men killed in such affairs.

We had no chance to clean up Batavia until more troops arrived, and we could only fume helplessly when a ship called the *Esperance Bay* appeared off Tandjoenpriok from Australia carrying 1,400 armed Indonesians, who were only kept in order because the guns of an accompanying destroyer were trained on the ship! These cut-throats were persuaded to leave their arms on board when they disem-barked, but Batavia was not a city where it was difficult to acquire weapons to taste. In one raid on an Indonesian police station, our provost laid bare a cache of three tons of arms and ammunition which would one day have been used against us.

It is hard to do sufficient credit to the forebearance and self-control shown by the men during this period. Living in a city full of extravagant rumours and called on to participate in a struggle which to the Indian, at least, was hardly intelligible, they could have been pardoned for an occasional lack of restraint or lapse in the superlatively high standard of discipline, but the need for pardon never arose. Even when the Indonesians tried to tamper with the loyalty of Mohammedans by calling on their Muslim brethren of the "Fighting Cock" to desert, the response was negligible. The superb discipline of these men, British and Indian, was about the only bright feature in the Javan scene during those grim November days when time slipped away fast and the whole island seemed about to descend into anarchy without anyone trying to arrest the decline.

How often did the soldier onlooker pray that the politicians might show a little of that sweet reason which could bring order out of the chaos! There had been a glimmer of hope at the end of October when General Christison and Mr. Dening brought the Dutch and Indonesian leaders together for discussions, but this hope vanished when the Dutch government promptly repudiated Dr. van Mook and their Colonial Minister enunciated once more the principle of "no dealings with the rebels." In the face of this intransigeance, Dr. van Mook's detailed proposals for a settlement were not worth the paper on which they were written, and it was no surprise that they were rejected by Soekarno, to whom the "offer" gave no guarantee of the independence for which, rightly or wrongly, he was striving.

A fortnight later, some allowed themselves the luxury of a quarter hope, which proved too much, when the Indonesians altered the basis of their government and separated the office of President from the Executive, which was to be composed of a Prime Minister and Cabinet. This change brought upon the stage in the office of Prime Minister Mr. Sjahrir, a man of moderate views, and a further meeting took place between the main parties under British chairmanship. Three and a half hours' talking far into the night ended without one inch of progress towards reconciling the two sides, and the soldier was reduced to despair when, at the end of a Nationalist Convention in Batavia where the public speeches had been marked by moderation, the Colonial Minister fulminated from the Hague that the Dutch were fully prepared to reoccupy Java by force.

Similarly, many of the Dutch in the island were still thinking in terms of reconquest, and these men and their supporters at the Hague, to whom British policy was anathema, accused us bitterly for our dealings with Soekarno and his colleagues and for our failure to take firmer action against the increasing disorders. So the split among the Dutch continued and the Indonesians, playing for very high stakes, showed all the dilatoriness of the Eastern races in negotiation; but time was no longer wholly on their side as

their inability to control the extremists and to prevent barbarous outrages was most damaging to their claim to repre-
sent all Java and to their reputation in the eyes of the world.

Politically there was a deadlock, and as long as the politicians jockeyed for position, nothing could be done to restore
the old prosperity of Java. Once one of the wealthiest of
islands where rice, rubber, tea, sugar, quinine and other
valuable gifts of Nature flourished bountifully in a volcanic
soil enriched by plenteous rain and a warm sun, her interior
economy was ruined for years. The rubber and tea planta-
tions lay idle, their European managers and native workers
scattered to the four winds, and the gangs roaming the
countryside had in their lust for plunder turned to the
destruction of buildings, equipment and stocks. Communications had broken down, roads went unrepaired, the railways,
when the extremists allowed them to function, were short of
coal which the Dutch could have provided. All this was
bad enough, but there was one feature in the economic chaos
which was positively dangerous and it came from the fear in
the heart of the simple peasant; he, like millions of his fellows
elsewhere, asked only for peace and a steady livelihood and
cared nothing for independence movements, but so long as
the terror remained, his means of livelihood was threatened.

His staple diet was rice and he spent his life in the carefully
terraced fields, but their fertility depended on control of the
sluice gates and irrigation channels which his pre-war
Dutch masters and their Eurasian assistants had worked so
successfully. One day these men had vanished, and the
peasant farmer, not knowing the secret, found the fertility
of the ground decreasing; he noticed, too, that instead of
being able to sell any surplus crop for money which bought
attractive goods in the market, his new, yellow master
commandeered the surplus without recompense. The next
year, the farmer sowed less ground, and the year after less
still, until in November, 1945, there was a danger of widespread famine, a danger greatly increased by the terrorists,
who kept the peasant from his fields and barred the way into
the towns. With the staple food supply menaced, the
Indonesian "ministers" came, cap in hand, to ask if they
might "borrow" from captured Japanese stocks.

Ultimately, the devastation of the island and the legacy of

hatred came back to the Japanese, and as, during our stay in Java, we learnt more of their schemings, the deliberate intent of their activities became the more apparent. They had gone much farther than "fostering" the Indonesian rising. In the true Nazi style, they had impregnated the youth of the country, both male and female, with their pernicious doctrines, and this "schooling" led on to a period of military training and service in the "Home Guard." Later, when the days of the "Co-prosperity Sphere" were clearly numbered, the glorious thought of independence was quietly planted in receptive minds, to be followed, in the hour of defeat, by the incitement to insurrection.

It was for their part in the last offence that Lieut.-General Yuichiro Nagano, commander of the Japanese 16th Army, and his Chief of Staff, Major-General Yamamoto were arrested on November 14th. Once more Lieut.-Colonel Mellsop proved himself the born stage-manager. In the drive outside Div. H.Q., guards from 1 Seaforth, 6/5 Mahratta and 6/8 Punjab lined the road; on the broad, carpeted stairs inside stood men of 3/3 G.R. and 1 Patiala. General Hawthorn drove up alone to the entrance with the guards at the present and then, after a short interval, came the Japanese. Slowly they walked up the stairs, the doors of the General's office opened and the Japanese came into his presence. The charge was read in English, and translated to the Japanese, whose faces hardly moved as they listened to the order to hand over their swords. Each stepped forward in turn after unbuckling his sword and handed it to the General; withdrawing a pace, they bowed stiffly, turned to the right and were gone to await trial in Singapore, but their unfrocking in this simple, dignified ceremony, could not make good the damage they had done.

At the end of November, open war lurked round the corner and many felt that they were sitting on a smouldering powder magazine without a chance to escape the explosion. With the Dutch and Indonesians unreconciled and obstinately pursuing their separate courses, the British had become the target for both sides and earned little gratitude for the skill and courage with which they performed their task. 23 Div. was fighting hard at Ambarawa; fighting at Bandoeng, which had hitherto been quiet; fighting in and around Batavia, where the arrival of 6 Mahratta from Surabaya and 13 Lancers from Malaya, with their Sherman tanks, increased security, but led to no greater control over the surrounding countryside.

This was disastrously clear from events on November 23rd when a Dakota, carrying Kumaon reinforcements to Semarang, turned back because of engine trouble and made a forced landing three miles from the Batavia airfield. When R.A.F. officers reached the scene, they were driven off by a hostile mob and darkness fell before they could return with a Patiala guard. The next day 6 Mahratta and P.A.V.O. tanks took up the search; they found ugly signs of a skirmish near the aircraft, but the occupants were gone. It was a week before the hunt took 1/16 Punjab and supporting arms to Bekassi and then it was too late; the British crew and their Indian passengers had been murdered by a gang in which the local butcher played the part of chief executioner. It was a sad column that came back with the exhumed bodies on December 1st, and no one felt that anything but justice had been done when a punitive expedition razed the Indonesian part of Bekassi to the ground a fortnight later; but such "reprisals" were banned for the future on orders from home.

Two months had gone by since we landed. Of the tasks we had been set, we had in part discharged the first in the succour we had brought to the internees, but the disarming of the Japanese had hardly begun and the prospect of so doing looked remote. Our troops were at full stretch holding the few cities and towns we had occupied, and it seemed, in the mounting tension, that they were to be yet more highly taxed. The only consolation that could occur to anyone, as he meditated on events with Kipling's famous lines running in his head, was that living in Java was very cheap. Since the Indonesians persisted in their refusal to accept the Netherlands guilder—and thereby made a further contribution to the economic disorders—wads of the worthless Japanese note issue had to be doled out, under control, to all ranks. This weekly bounty, which enabled us to purchase food and other necessities in the markets, continued until the Dutch currency was firmly introduced in February in spite of protests from Sjahrir.

CHAPTER 24

The Turn of the Year (1945/1946)

THE powder magazine did not explode and the storm clouds gradually drifted away to the horizon. That is not to say that Java became a peaceful place in which to live, because the reverse was true, but the danger of a major rising, in which discipline would fight out the issue against overwhelming numbers, began to disappear. The first cause of this happier state of affairs was the increase in our strength in December when the accommodation authorities in Batavia had to find room for two more brigades. These were 161 Ind. Inf. Bde., under Brigadier Grimshaw, from Surabaya (1/1 Punjab, 4/7 Rajput, 3/4 Gurkha Rifles), and the British 5 Parachute Brigade from Singapore, under Brigadier Poett, D.S.O.; in addition, 36 Ind. Inf. Bde. (5/9 Jat, 8/13 Frontier Force Rifles, 1/8 Gurkha Rifles) passed through Batavia on their way to Buitenzorg. All three formations came under our command.

Simultaneously with the arrival of these reinforcements, the more moderate Indonesians came to see that no "government" worth the name could avoid the responsibility for preserving law and order, so that before the month was many days old we were offered the help of the T.K.R. in some special enterprises. This unlooked-for support was apt to be embarrassing because, as our Intelligence Staff repeatedly pointed out, there were "good" T.K.R. and "bad" T.K.R. and it was not always easy to distinguish between the two, nor in our experience did the "good" T.K.R. come near outnumbering the extremists, but the mere thought of Indonesian co-operation would have been an idle dream a month previously. The T.K.R. were to prove helpful and their activities must have had some influence on their West Javan compatriots, who were beginning to learn the real power of modern weapons because more use was made of the R.A.F. when trouble arose.

For these reasons, when disturbances began in Bandoeng towards the end of November, the situation never became as critical as it had been in Surabaya, Magelang, or Ambarawa, though 37 Bde. were to have much stiff fighting. With its invigorating climate, Bandoeng was the ideal hill station for the 60,000 R.A.P.W.I. gathered there; so far they had enjoyed comparative peace, but they too have their ordeal. After a boycott of the markets, whereby the internees were unable to buy fresh food, the cases of looting and kidnapping increased and everything pointed to a large-scale rising on the normal pattern.

Brigadier MacDonald had with him only 3/3 G.R., 3/5 R.G.R. and 1,500 Japanese—his third battalion, 5/8 Punjab, was at Buitenzorg on the L. of C.—and his anxieties increased on November 21st when the supply train from Batavia arrived looted without its small Gurkha guard. There had always been a danger that this would occur, but the Indonesians had surprisingly not interfered previously with the running of these R.A.P.W.I. trains. Now, at a very awkward moment when our hands were full elsewhere, the Brigadier faced an armed insurrection with inadequate troops to oppose it and his L. of C., on which he depended for feeding the women and children in his charge, open to attack.

The rising began on the evening of November 24th when armed bands appeared in four separate parts of the town and snipers started to operate against some of the R.A.P.W.I. camps and buildings; the next night the public utility services were cut. Brigadier MacDonald took firm measures, and the Indonesians, who found the Gurkhas little to their liking as opponents, issued an appeal on November 25th for less violent action. When the Brigadier's demand for the removal of all road-blocks was not met, the Gurkhas continued to display admirable vigour which brought forth a second squeal. The Brigadier's answer came in the form of an ultimatum which required the Indonesians to evacuate the area north of the main railway line which ran from west to east and bisected the town; they were also required, among other terms, to withdraw their forces from an important R.A.P.W.I. building south of the railway.

When the General flew up to Bandoeng on December 1st,

the town was still much disturbed and his meeting with the Brigadier, who was in great heart, took place on the airfield. The Indonesians had in fact begun to evacuate the northern area, but they were going at leisure and some hard pushing was needed to expedite their departure. At the same time, the R.A.P.W.I. left south of the railway line were in sorry plight and their extrication involved more fighting. Hence 37 Bde. struck out alternately north and south in operations designed to strengthen their positions and rescue internees. On December 3rd they were engaged in destroying an Indonesian H.Q. in the north, on the 6th 3/3 G.R. went to rescue 500 internees from the south; both operations were supported by Jap tanks, and the second, which was a stiff encounter, went the quicker for a very accurate air strike on a fortified building.

The Gurkhas were retaining a firm hold in Bandoeng, but the maintenance of the town was giving cause for much anxiety. With the railway in the hands of the extremists, all army and R.A.P.W.I. supplies had to be sent by road with a strong infantry escort, and convoys of a hundred and fifty lorries wound their way from the coastal plain to the hills along a route where there was ample opportunity for ambushes. There had already been one incident when a down convoy had been attacked and a Mosquito covering the operation blew up in mid-air, but this was a minor affair compared with the battle which broke out on December 9th.

An up convoy, escorted by 5/9 Jats, who were newcomers to Java, had begun the long climb through the hills when the leading vehicles were halted by a road-block. The hillside was alive with Indonesians, many of them, in the Japanese fashion, occupying fox-holes, from which they lobbed an endless supply of Molotov cocktails on to the vehicles. It is no easy task to fight out of an ambush where an unseen foe commands the high ground and the infantry escort is spread over eight miles of road; moreover nightfall was not many hours away. The Jat C.O. was seriously wounded in the first brush, one vehicle was ablaze, several others were badly damaged and a number of drivers had slumped over their wheels, either dead or grievously hit. There were fine acts performed as the Jats sought to dislodge the foe and officers and men reorganized the convoy. The R.I.A.S.C. captain in charge of the vehicles moved up and down the road amid the bullets, arranging for the towing of damaged vehicles; he was wounded in both legs but continued in his task. Eventually the way was cleared and the journey resumed, but the convoy was far from safe. Snipers lay siege to the road for miles ahead and sometimes a bullet found its mark; on one such occasion, when a driverless vehicle blocked the road, a naik in the next lorry dashed through intense fire and restarted the first vehicle. So the convoy limped into Soekaboemi near midnight with the rearguard company still fighting miles back on the road. The Jat officer commanding this party fought the enemy for four and a half hours and it was 0200 hrs. on December 10th before the fury of the attacks lessened sufficiently for him to close up the rear vehicles; at dawn he went on his way, driving the leading vehicle himself until he reached Soekaboemi, where the convoy spent the day while the R.A.F. delivered the heaviest air strike of the Java "war." On the 11th the convoy was joined by a relief column of 3/3 G.R., who had to contend with one block in the form of a steam-roller on their way from Bandoeng. Together, the Jats and Gurkhas took the convoy in on December 12th, leaving behind only the one lorry which had caught fire. Our twenty-four dead included the R.A.F. officer who was the ground contact to the supporting aircraft and the drivers of three of the four ambulances.

It was at this point that the Indonesians gave some evidence of a change of outlook. Sjarifuddin, the "Minister for Internal Security," taking on Soekarno's role of peacemaker, had arrived in Bandoeng on December 7th, and at his instigation the T.K.R. ensured the safe passage of the return convoy. As a further proof of their more friendly intentions, they also undertook to run a supply train from Batavia with their own guards; there was some delay over this owing to the difficulty of collecting sufficient "good" T.K.R., but a smart party appeared at the main station on December 11th, with a powerful Indonesian Press escort, and the train steamed out at 1700 hrs. It reached Bandoeng intact about the same time as the battle-worn convoy.

This was better, and better still was a public statement by

the head of the Bandoeng T.K.R. recommending strong measures against the extremists in the north even to the extent of full military action. 37 Bde., reinforced by 6 Mahratta and 3 Ind. Fd. less one battery, had already planned a series of operations for this purpose and they went about the business in their customary manner so that by Christmas reasonable security had been restored in the north of the town; among the less dangerous arms captured were some blunderbusses and an antique gun dated 1831.

The extremists, driven out of their northern lairs, retaliated in the south against the Chinese, who began to flock across the railway to our sector where they reported that the Indonesians were obstructing this flight to safety. Hence the Gurkhas occupied Christmas Day, 1945, in a fierce encounter south of the railway. The Indonesians at first tried to thwart our advance by using panic-stricken Chinese as a screen, but when this inhuman device failed they fell back on their prepared defences. Bitter house-to-house fighting followed and, with each fortified building hotly defended, it took the Gurkhas twelve hours to cover eight hundred yards; but their mission was successful, for 5,000 Chinese were enabled to escape to the north, where their presence aggravated the shortage of food. Thereafter one half of Bandoeng became a tolerable place in which to live, but there could be no full sense of security until the south was cleared, an operation which had to wait until more troops were available after the cleansing of Batavia.

Early in December there had been an important conference at Singapore, where the C.I.G.S. met, among others, Lord Louis Mountbatten, General Christison and Dr. van Mook. After their discussions on troubled Java, the British task was widened to include the establishing and maintaining a régime of law and order in the areas occupied by them, thus producing a political atmosphere in which it would be possible to hold conferences and discussions from which a peaceful conclusion to the present difficulties might arise. That was a right and proper decision and the first step in carrying out this new policy was to make Batavia secure. If this was to be achieved thoroughly, a large number of extra troops were needed as the modern cities in the Dutch Indies have grown up round the kampongs or native villages which remain as islands in the midst of twentieth-century buildings and roads. Hence there was always a refuge for the extremists—their technical name in these parts was "Pemoeda," though some styled themselves "Black Buffaloes"—and it was difficult to search kampongs effectively unless several could be cordoned off simultaneously; at the same time, if a large Pemoeda hunt was to be undertaken, it was vital to avoid a break-down of the Indonesian-run public services in sympathy, and more troops were wanted to prevent this. As already recorded, the build-up was complete by mid-December and the stage was set, General Dempsey, recently appointed C.-in-C. A.L.F.S.E.A. giving his final blessing to the plan when he flew from Singapore on December 21st.

There was first an entertaining preliminary which illustrates the strange variety of tasks which fell to us in Java. The maintenance of all troops in West Java depended on shifting stores by railway from the docks to the depot in North Batavia, and it became apparent that the Indonesians intended to prevent this by removing the engines. Hence 1 Bde. were called on to mount an operation for the capture of railway engines, and an animated discussion developed at the preliminary conference about the proper hour to capture engines, the point at issue being whether a dawn attack, when the engines would be raising steam, was preferable to one at dusk, when their day's work was done. The discussion ended with one of Brigadier King's inimitable flashes of ironic humour: "Well, old boy, make up your mind. I'll do it when you like, but you're the expert and must say when. I'm not a boiler man." The expert opted for a dawn attack, and the event proved him right as a pleasing number of engines fell into the bag.

The more serious part of the clean-up, known as operation "Pounce," began on December 27th after a much quieter month marred by three or four ugly incidents such as that in which a gunner of 178 Fd. Regt., due for home the next day, was killed by a shot from a passing train when his vehicle stopped at a level crossing. There were no such unpleasant episodes during "Pounce," which turned out to be the first bloodless operation of our stay in Java. On the first day 161 Bde. put a cordon round the city, on the next illegally owned cars were impounded, and on D plus 2 all public utilities, except the railway and fire brigade, were taken over and the civil police disbanded. This was the day likely to lead to disturbances, and when the early morning quiet was disturbed by volley after volley of rifle fire the outlook was black; but this was the Ambonese celebrating their belated removal to the Dutch area south of Batavia by a *feu de joie* as they passed 1/16 Punjab. Not a shot was fired during "Pounce," the public services continued to function, and where Indonesians were called on to co-operate with the Dutch, all went smoothly. Careful planning and speedy execution of the plan had won the day.

5 Para. Bde. started clearing the kampongs on December 30th, and after they went to Semarang early in January to relieve 49 Bde., 1 and 161 Bdes. took on this task; 1 Bde. had a particularly fine bag in one raid when they returned with forty Pemoedas in tow. By mid-January five out of the six markets in the city were open and, though shots did occasionally ring out, Batavia was fast taking on the appearance of a busy place where men and women could go about their lawful business without fear.

Simultaneously with the clearing of Batavia, 36 Bde. operated in Buitenzorg, where 5/8 Punjab had been alone since they changed over with 3/3 G.R. early in November; they had several brisk and successful engagements with the Indonesians, more particularly on the Bandoeng road, but they were not by themselves able to dominate Buitenzorg. This was a task left to our G.I. when he arrived to command 36 Bde. on December 12th, and it was much to his liking. According to the extremists, Brigadier Mellsop's appearance on the scene coincided with a period of all-out attacks which were to end with a victory parade through the streets of Buitenzorg, on December 15th. In fact, the only attack came in the early hours of the 15th when a large body approached 5/8 Punjab on guard at a R.A.P.W.I. camp and called on their "Muslim brothers from India" to join their side or be slaughtered. As we were no longer allowed to publish the figures for Indonesian casualties, the subsequent communique read "our troops fired on them and dispersed the mob"; one may now be permitted to record that the "dispersal" caused sixty deaths.

As had happened so often before, Brigadier Mellsop's first step at Buitenzorg was to provide greater security for the internees, and it was in an action fought with this object that a company havildar-major of 5/8 Punjab performed one of the finest individual acts of gallantry in our story. His platoon was carrying out a flanking attack on a position which was thought to be weakly held as a number of the enemy had been seen to fall when our tanks had opened fire. But the Indonesians had feigned death, and as the Punjabis reached the objective they were surrounded by a mob five times their number and all armed with swords, spears and knives. A tremendous hand-to-hand struggle ensued in which the company havildar-major, though bleeding profusely from four wounds, held his men together and killed six of the enemy single-handed. Looking round at the height of the fight, he saw one of his men desperately engaged with eight Indonesians and he charged in to the rescue, despite his wounds. His action cost him his life, but his superb courage and skill in close fighting saved the platoon; at the end eighty of the enemy lay dead, while our casualties were the company havildar-major killed and three others wounded.

This notable action was followed the next day by another vigorous engagement, and the Indonesians, who had previously refused to come to the Brigadier's H.Q. for discussions, thought better of their previous decision. The arrival of 1/8 G.R. and 8/13 F.F. Rif. at the end of December released 5/8 Punjab for Bandoeng and enabled Brigadier Mellsop to widen the scope of his operations. After assisting in "Pounce" by seizing the headworks of the Batavia water supply, the Brigade carried out a number of local operations like the 1/8 G.R. raid on a suspected arms factory, where large quantities of gelignite and saltpetre were found. By mid-January the Indonesians had come to heel and Buitenzorg was sufficiently secure for the Brigadier to lead a column farther afield in connection with the disarming of the Japanese, which was proceeding apace with the improved security in west Java; on this two-day march there was one slight brush and the T.K.R. met were friendly.

Altogether 1946 gave much better promise than 1945, though politically there was a vacuum after Dr. van Mook had flown to Holland in mid-December for consultations with his own and the British government. The continued hostility to his more liberal policy was shown soon after he left, when a band of armed Dutchmen raided Sjahrir's house and drove off our provost at pistol point. A week later another band stopped a car in Batavia's main street and hauled out the occupants; this time the provost arrived as one of the attackers, raised a pistol and fired at an Indonesian's head at point-blank range. Had the pistol gone off, Sjahrir would have been dead, for he was the Indonesian though the Dutch assailants were unaware of this. It was, indeed, a providential escape, but Sjahrir remained imperturbable; while waiting for Dr. van Mook's return he and other "Cabinet ministers" toured the interior, and the only disturbances were the "noises off" emanating from the Russians and their satellites in the Security Council.

Whatever might be the outcome of the political impasse, we had our own work to do; Batavia was quiet, Buitenzorg was quiet, but Bandoeng remained a place of two halves where there was no normal life and to Bandoeng our orders led us. The plan was this: 1 Bde to relieve 36 Bde. destined for Batavia where with 161 Bde. they were to come under command A.F.N.E.I.; 5 Para. Bde. to relieve 49 Bde. at Semarang, and 49 Bde. with many of the divisional troops to Bandoeng.

The first move was the change at Semarang, where 49 Bde. had had a far from quiet month since they took over from the C.R.A. after the evacuation of Ambarawa. There was never any peace either at Semarang or in the outpost position at Oengaran, and the four battalions left to hold our area, insufficient to undertake a major operation to chastise the extremists, led an uneasy life. There were repeated searches of the kampongs to east and west of the town, but searches, however vigorously conducted, could not prevent the Indonesians infiltrating back. Right to the end, Semarang was an uncomfortable place; the water supply was subject to interruption, shells fell on the airfield, aircraft landed under small-arms fire, and there was little entertainment to relieve the monotony. With the assistance of the Navy, a cinema was organized, and there were parties in the messes and with the children over Christmas, but 5/6

U

Rajrif were in action all through this supposedly festive season—that was just Semarang. 49 Bde. had few regrets when they handed over command on January 14th, 1946. Just over a month later, on February 16th, Div. H.Q. opened at Bandoeng with the reorganization complete.

It may seem to readers unacquainted with our stay in Java that life was not only dangerous and exhausting but highly tedious. For most parts of the island that holds true, but those fortunate enough to be in Batavia found ample entertainment and it was not uncommon to be dancing in the evening after dodging the bullets by day. So strange a mixture was all part of the oddness of Java, where a guest, bidden to dine at a brother officer's mess some way from his own, might find on arrival that he had driven into a battle and was needed to man the defences. A rigid curfew parted friends at an earlier hour than some desired, but it could not prevent us having some richly earned and highly enjoyable relaxation.

The Y.M.C.A. took over the Harmonie and had Batavia's most exclusive pre-war club open for B.O.Rs. within a month of our first landing, a fine effort on the part of the enterprising manager, who had another palatial building open for Indian troops a few days later. Officers, British and Indian, gravitated to the Box Club, the old centre of the British community, where there were dances twice a week and pleasant music on Sunday mornings to help down a draught of local light ale. This came from an Indonesian-run brewery, which once threatened to withold supplies because a few Dutchmen were obtaining bottles, an illustration of the dismal way in which politics intruded into the most unlikely spheres. There was never a shortage of partners at the dances for, besides the ladies of the British Red Cross, many Dutch girls helped to bring into our lives a long-forgotten attraction which later led some to the kirk.

Perhaps this is the place to mention the very varied activities which the Red Cross performed with unruffled calm and unending pleasantness. Was there not one occasion when one lady was summoned on official business to the presence of a very high ranking officer and asked at the end to darn his socks? While the lady rocked on her heels, the officer dived into a drawer of his desk and produced two pairs of socks—like everything else in Java, the holes were abnormal—but the socks were handed over with an accompanying "Here you are! I'm on my beam ends." Another dive produced a needle and thread, but the lady must still have shown doubts on her face, for the officer added a final recommendation, "They have been washed." The lady departed in haste—with the socks.

So there were the Red Cross to darn socks, and dances and beer and other attractions as well. Two cinemas were soon open for British troops and R.A.P.W.I. and a third for Indians, with a change of programme twice a week. Another early starter was Radio Batavia, with which we had much to do; but, though not strictly entertainment, it was our own newspaper, "The Fighting Cock," which appeared first in the field on October 23rd. Beginning with the enormously important function of disseminating accurate news and early developing an extensive section in Urdu, it acquired its own home correspondent and became a pot-pourri of world-wide news and articles as the troubles in Java simmered down below boiling-point. Printed under the auspices of 68 Ind. Fd. Coy., this paper was from the early days one of those rare concerns in which British, Dutch and Indonesians co-operated in a friendly spirit.

As the tension lessened towards the end of 1945, some of the battalions gave magnificent parties which were attended in full force by the powers that be, both British and Dutch. The Seaforths set the ball rolling when their pipers and drummers, in the splendour of full dress, gave a heart-stirring display, and the Patialas followed with a magnificent "tamasha" in honour of His Highness the Maharajah's birthday. These parties were valuable because politics and policies were forgotten for a brief while; not that it was easy to forget for long the sadness of the turmoil in Java, as those who thought at all were conscious as Christmas came round. The General spoke for everyone when he wrote in his message:

"This time last year, how many of us thought we should be spending Christmas 1945 in Java? We have travelled far and fast in the last twelve months through Burma, Malaya, and now we are in this troubled land where strife and bloodshed are the order of the day. This is the Division's fourth Christmas, and in many ways it will be the saddest when we think of all the good comrades who came to Java with us, thinking the war was over, and now are dead or wounded. Sad too we cannot help but feel when all around us are thousands of Dutch men, women and children, our gallant friends and allies in the war, now, in the common cause, bereft of all they once possessed: it will not be a very happy Christmas for most of them.

"But Christmas is a time for happiness, and happiness is best achieved by making other people happy. So let all of us in 23 Div. do all we can this Christmas to make our less fortunate Dutch friends, especially the kiddies, as happy as we can. Let us help them to forget the past and look to the future. Then indeed we shall have had a good Christmas.

"All that remains is for me to wish you, officers and men of the Division, and all our friends who read the 'Fighting Cock,' a Happy Christmas, and let us hope by Christmas 1946 that peace and good will will prevail in Java and that once again we shall be spending Christmas at home."

Our Div. Signals mounted the first children's party. Under "Situations Vacant" they had advertised in their Mess for "Fathers and those anxious to learn how to handle small children," and under the genial presidency of Lieut.-Colonel Atkinson, that veteran of Burma, a right merry gathering brought forth in abundance one of the most glorious sounds in the world, that of young children abandoning themselves to the delights of a party. The General and others were not far behind with their own entertainments, and on January 7th the freshly painted curtain at the opera house went up on our own revue, "Cocktales of 1946," which played to full houses for its week's run and owed no little to the dancing of some Dutch girls.

Altogether, Batavia was far from dull, and those who enjoyed their exercise could find that in abundance. A.F.N.E.I. had a soccer league under way in mid-November, and the Seaforths, remembering the roar at Hampden Park, long remained at the top of the ladder. They contributed several members to the forces' side which met the Indonesians on January 2nd. It was a gala day; General Christison attended, the Seaforth band proved a great attraction and the "mayor" of Batavia kicked off; the

JAVA

THE SURRENDERED JAPANESE SWORDS

CHRISTMAS PARTY, 1945
General Hawthorn (left) entertains Dutch children

Facing page 292]

Indonesians, awarded a penalty, side-tapped the ball wide of the goal and were given a "Big hand"; the British later did the same. The friendliness that prevailed on such occasions only underlined the rift which kept the politicians apart.

Soccer is not a game which has greatly attracted the Indian, but his prowess at hockey is world-famed, and there were many good games played in Java. He is equally not addicted to rugger, at which the R.A.F. reigned supreme, but he made his mark on the cricket field or such of the Box Club ground as was left after that ignorant race, the Japanese, had put down hard tennis courts on the outfield.

It is time to leave Batavia for Bandoeng, but before taking the hop it is necessary to record that January, 1946, was a month when the growing tide of release and repatriation began to leave a noticeable mark on the Division. Among those who turned for home was Brigadier King, the last senior officer left from Imphal days; skilful and courageous as a commander in Burma, unperturbed amid the storms of Java, he left behind many who recalled with affection the twinkling eye and swift shafts of humour which lightened many a dull and some awkward moments and helped so much towards the happiness of the British and Indian troops of 1 Ind. Inf. Bde. Later in the month General Christison also went on his way after three years of command in the East, ending with the most unenviable of all jobs, the senior Army commander in a foreign country torn asunder by internal dissension. His successor was another of the victors of Burma, Lieut.-General Sir Montagu Stopford.

CHAPTER 25

Bandoeng and "Exodus"

THIS book is not the place to discuss the interminable negotiations between the Dutch and Indonesians on the future of Java; talks were resumed on February 10th with the recently appointed British observer, Sir Archibald Clark Kerr, presiding, and Sjahrir soon went off to consult his colleagues on the Dutch proposals handed to him by Dr. van Mook. We were not affected by these comings and goings of the politicians—the February stir at Bandoeng following the arrival of 49 Bde. was due to Indonesian resentment at the extension of our zone—but, inevitable though the decision to land Dutch troops was, we lived to regret this new move on the political chessboard as we had always feared (and almost known) would happen.

37 Bde. had been long in Bandoeng and the General decided to complete the regrouping of the Division by moving them down to Buitenzorg and transferring 1 Bde. to the cooler air of Bandoeng. The resulting moves at the beginning of March coincided with the landing of four Dutch battalions, and Sjahrir, who had agreed that one should land in December but had not been warned of any fresh decision, protested to the Allied C.-in-C. The Indonesians of West Java were not content with words. Since the first convoy battle, the road to Bandoeng had not been attacked though the route had been used less because of recourse to air supply, but the increased force in Bandoeng was more than the R.A.F. could maintain so that a large convoy was on the road on March 10th, escorted by the Patialas under command of Lieut.-Colonel Bikram Dev Singh Gill.

Eight miles west of Soekaboemi the convoy was halted by a road-block and the C.O. reported that he expected a fight, but he was allowed to proceed after a parley and for a time all went well though the Indonesians were out in force on the hills. At 1830 hrs., as the leading vehicles neared Soekaboemi, the attack began and the convoy was in travail. Fighting hard, the Patialas brought most of the long, snake-like column into harbour, but, as before, the rearguard company was cut off, several of the drivers were killed and the attackers swarmed in from all sides. The Patialas gave of their best and the company commander managed in the midst of the battle to organize a fresh team of drivers and collect his wounded; with the block cleared, he gave the order to move, but he was forced to stand and fight four more times before he reached harbour at 2100 hrs.

The Indonesian blood was up and the attack on the harbour continued throughout the night of March 10th/11th. The Patialas might have been resisting an all-out attack on "Scraggy"; at one section post which suffered heavy casualties a badly wounded sepoy went out under intense fire with his commander and dragged in two dead men; at another a havildar who was pinned by fire, rushed out in the confusion caused by a grenade burst and hauled a wounded man and his rifle out of the clutches of the Indonesians. When dawn came, the Patialas had lost eight killed and had twenty-five wounded.

The events of the 11th were depressing. The Patialas with the main convoy advanced only eight miles, battling hard the whole way; a relief column of 5/6 Rajrif from Bandoeng, supported by guns and aircraft, was brought to a stop before it reached the Patialas; and a half squadron of 13 Lancers, ordered to hasten up from Buitenzorg, was itself ambushed west of Soekaboemi when the leading tank struck a mine and damaged its tracks. There were thus three separate forces isolated on the road that night, with the tanks and their small escort of 2 Indian Grenadiers in most danger. It was against this body that the Indonesians directed their main effort on the 12th. Several of the tanks were damaged, ammunition was short, and the Lancers would have been in grave peril had not the R.A.F., who gave magnificent support throughout, come to the rescue with a very accurate air drop—those without experience of air supply will not realize the difficulty of "hitting" a small, isolated detachment. But there were no repairs on the morning of the 12th, when the Lancers were fighting hard and their wounded lay unattended because their Medical Officer was a serious casualty.

The tanks, which had been sent to the rescue, themselves needed rescuing, and two companies of Patialas turned back while the main body remained stationary for the day. No one could tell how stiff would be the opposition to the relieving companies, but it turned out to be less than expected—the Indonesians were at full stretch elsewhere. The two companies reached the tanks at 1600 hrs. after the subedar of the leading platoon and some of his men had coolly cleared four hundred yards of mine-strewn road in three-quarters of an hour, and about 1745 hrs. the whole force was on the move to the east. After harbouring for the night on the road, they joined up with the main force at 0930 hrs. on March 13th and the convoy resumed its march towards the Rajrif, whose C.O. had reached the Patialas the previous day in a tank. This meeting had an unfortunate end, for the C.O. was badly hurt when the tank plunged into a ravine on the way back to his battalion, which was protecting an important bridge on the route ahead.

Brigadier N. D. Wingrove, who had come from H.Q. A.F.N.E.I. to command 1 Bde., had by now been put in charge of the battle and a strong force set out from Bandoeng on the 13th to link up with the Rajrif. This column had only twenty-odd miles to cover to the bridge, but the way was strewn with road-blocks, and the force was continually halting, taking up defensive positions and brushing aside small packets of enemy. They did not reach the Rajrif until 0830 hrs. on March 14th, and two and a half hours later the Patiala advanced guard came in sight. The Indonesians still had not done—the Patialas and the main convoy had to run the gauntlet of snipers all the way to Bandoeng, and when 1 Bde. turned back they were so strenuously resisted that they were forced to harbour for the night.

In this five-day battle, fought seven months after "peace" had come to the world with the surrender of the Japanese, we suffered a hundred and fifteen casualties, of which twenty were killed, among them three ambulance drivers. Two of these were replaced by officers from H.Q. A.F.N.E.I. who had come on a sight-seeing expedition.

Happily for us, this battle was the end of heavy casualties, but it was no final storm which left the air clear and there was not much rest for the troops. We had moved to Bandoeng to make the area more secure, and operation "Sam," the name given to the cleaning-up process, was hastened forward after the convoy struggle. For political reasons Sjahrir was given ample warning of the operation and was ordered to have South Bandoeng clear of troops by midnight on March 24th/25th; the extremists made the most of the warning. Shells landed on the airfield on the night before the operation, mortars opened up on our forward positions and the sky to the south was livid with the flames which followed the dull roar of explosions. The Chinese population in the south were terrified and many were streaming across the railway line with that strange and sad assortment of belongings which refugees bring when 49 Bde. began to advance on the morning of March 25th. The extremists had taken heed of the warning and gone, leaving behind a trail of wanton destruction—public buildings and Chinese property had suffered the worst—and by 1130 hrs. 49 Bde. had completed their task, the clearing of the southern district east of the River Tjikapoenoeng, which runs through the town from north to south. This rapid progress could not be forecast, but when it was clear there was to be no opposition, 36 Bde., who had been sent up from Batavia to form the western pincer, were ordered into action a day early. They reached the river line before dark and Bandoeng was clear.

That was the last major operation in which we took part. A degree of order was brought back to Bandoeng, some shops reopened and the number of incidents decreased. The T.R.I., as the old T.K.R. were called, threatened an assault early in April, but nothing worse happened than a few small raids which spluttered like damp squibs. The occasional cases of arson were promptly dealt with by the enthusiastic and efficient fire brigade organized by 49 Bde. out of their pioneer platoons, and when the Netherlands "V" Bde. took over the defence of the whole south sector on April 15th, something approaching calm prevailed.

This did not extend to the L. of C., which never recovered from the upheaval after the landing of Dutch troops.

Since the convoy battle, we had avoided Soekaboemi and used the steeper but shorter northern route from Buitenzorg to Bandoeng over the Poentjak pass, but this too required protecting and the units along the route had to endure persistent sniping; 36 Bde. performed this task until 1 Bde. were released from Bandoeng by the arrival of the Dutch. Though three battalions were used, they could not keep the route clear from raids by Indonesians, who one night in mid-May dug seven large craters, which they filled with water diverted from adjacent fields, and supplemented this effective piece of work by felling forty large trees.

The general disturbance of an area that once seemed to be settling down extended to Buitenzorg, where 37 Bde. had as uneasy a time as the troops on the L. of C. Racial hatred still led to uncontrolled acts of violence, and two Australians and a R.A.F. officer comprising a War Crimes Investigation Team were murdered near Buitenzorg on April 17th; the Indonesian police were gracious enough to put one of the bodies in a coffin and send it back to Batavia by train. 37 Bde. handed over their troubled area at the end of April to a resuscitated C.R.A.'s Bde. and withdrew to the calm of Batavia, where they came temporarily under command of A.F.N.E.I.

One word should be said about the grouping within brigades. This had long remained unaltered, but the precarious situation when we landed in Java led to a partial break-up of the old order, and after the move to Bandoeng, the General fulfilled his intention of having a Gurkha battalion in each brigade. The order of battle from March onwards thus read: 1 Bde.: 1 Seaforth, 2/19 Kumaon, 3/5 R.G.R.; 37 Bde.: 6/5 Mahratta, 1/16 Punjab, 3/3 G.R.; 49 Bde.: 4/5 Mahratta, 5/6 Rajrif, 3/10 G.R.; C.R.A.'s Bde. under Brigadier F. C. Scott, C.B.E.; 2 Ind. A.Tk. Regt., 5/8 and 6/8 Punjab, and 2 Indian Grenadiers, who were on loan to the Division.

More and more Dutch troops were landing in Java and by mid-June they were ready to take over in Bandoeng while we withdrew into the Batavia bridgehead. There was just time for us to hold a momentous race-meeting on the Bandoeng course, with the provost in charge of the tote, before Div. H.Q. closed on June 20th and returned to the humid atmosphere of Batavia. 49 Bde. H.Q. followed five days later, and, in early July, 1 Bde. were brought back from the L. of C.

We had returned at a time of pessimism on the political front. About the time the Patialas were struggling through to Bandoeng, Sir Archibald Clark Kerr, now Lord Inverchapel, had flown to Holland with Dr. van Mook and three Indonesian "Ministers." When the party returned in May, the new Dutch proposals proved unacceptable to Sjahrir, and the rift between the two sides was emphasized when he declared that a "state of emergency" existed. Hence the countryside remained disturbed, so disturbed in fact that Sjahrir himself was kidnapped at the end of June by a gang of his own compatriots, who did not know how big a fish they had caught.

Sjahrir was restored smiling on July 1st, less all the notes of his conversations with van Mook, but this did not assist our units on the fringe of the Batavia bridgehead, which extended about fifteen miles from the city to Tangerang and Bekassi on the west and east respectively and to Buitenzorg in the south. Within the perimeter there had for some time been real peace and quiet. Men and women went happily about their normal business, crowds thronged the streets of Batavia to watch the fine ceremonial parades on VE and VJ Days and the birthdays of Royalty, 37 Bde. were only bothered by looters, and Tommy Trinder and his E.N.S.A. party played to carefree audiences. On the outskirts it was different. Armed gangs continued to terrorize and massacre the inhabitants and hovered on the fringe of the bridgehead ever ready to make a raid into our territory, where 49 Bde. held the west flank, 1 Bde. the east, until another Dutch brigade took over much of their area, while the C.R.A.'s Bde. kept watch at Buitenzorg. Patrolling went on continuously and as late as mid-August 3/5 R.G.R. lost an officer who had won two M.Cs. in Burma.

September was a calmer month, but it was not until October that a genuine hope of peace arose when, partly through the good offices of Lord Killearn, the British Special Commissioner to South East Asia, the Commission General sent out by the Dutch Government met the Indonesians in full conference. Within a week it was agreed that a military truce was desirable, and orders went forth to all troops to desist from hostilities while the details were arranged. A certain Commander Soetomo of East Java, who has figured before in this story, chose this moment to broadcast an appeal to the people and the Army not to trust the Allies and to continue fighting. We could afford to disregard the threat of yet more trouble ahead, for by now operation "Exodus" was in full swing and the last British troops were due to leave Java by November 30th, 1946.

It would have been fitting had General Hawthorn been with us to the end of our stay in Java, but when he came back in September from the conference held by the C.I.G.S. at Camberley, he broke the news that he was destined to leave us almost at once as he had been appointed Director of Military Training at G.H.Q. (India). After a long round of farewell parades and receptions, the final ceremony took place on the Batavia airfield on October 4th. As the General's car drove up, the "Fighting Cock" broke at the mast-head and the men of 1/16 Punjab, the Royal Netherlands Navy and the Dutch Army forming the guard of honour came to the Present. There were handshakes with all his staff, handshakes with representatives from our brigades and battalions, farewells to his colleagues of the Navy and R.A.F. and lastly to Lieut.-General Mansergh, now C.-in-C. A.F.N.E.I., before he stood in the door of his aircraft giving a parting salute.

Eighteen months before, General Hawthorn had come to us of the "Fighting Cock" to lead us in an amphibious operation because of his experience in the Arakan. Those who worked under him during the planning for "Zipper" had ample opportunity to approve the choice, but as chance would have it there was no battle, and it was in quite unexpected circumstances that the Division came to know the quality of their commander. Called on in Java to be as much a diplomat as a soldier, the General by his wisdom and patience, his courage and remarkable refusal to be ruffled, steered us through dark days when there was room for nothing but leadership of the highest order. He knew that one slip would precipitate a catastrophe and that some governments were waiting eagerly for that slip, but neither he nor, let it be said, others in vital commands faltered.

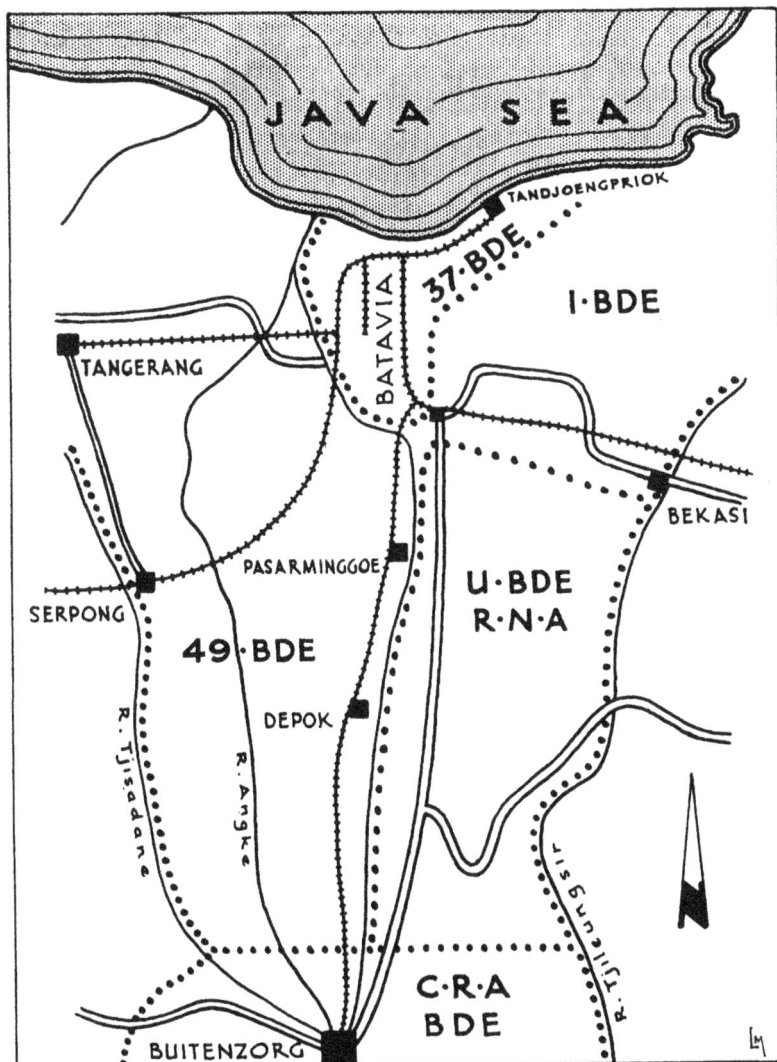

JAVA SEA

TANDJOENGPRIOK

37·BDE

I·BDE

BATAVIA

TANGERANG

BEKASI

SERPONG

PASARMINGGOE

U·BDE
R·N·A

49·BDE

DEPOK

R. Tjisadane

R. Angke

R. Tjiliwong

C·R·A
BDE

N

BUITENZORG

MAP DRAWN DIAGRAMMATICALLY FOR CLARITY

APPROXIMATELY ⊏━ ━ ━ ━ ⊐ TWENTY MILES

RAILWAYS ┼┼┼┼┼┼┼┼┼┼

BOUNDARIES •••••••••   LEGEND   ROADS ══

RIVERS ──

BATAVIA BRIDGEHEAD
BEFORE "EXODUS"

This was a period of farewells—of farewells to our guns which we bequeathed to the Dutch; of farewells to those very good friends, Major John Greeter and Capt. Jimmy Lucht, the Dutch liaison officers at Div. H.Q.; but above all it was a time when the Division said good-bye to itself. We were destined for Malaya, but we were to go there as a shadow of ourselves, for many of our units were recalled to India, where there was need of their presence. Through October and November the transports steamed slowly out of Tandjoengpriok until on November 28th, 1946, the last ship left and our deeds in Java passed into history.

We had left behind 407 killed in action and 162 who were missing; these, with 808 wounded, made a total of 1,377 casualties and are a measure of our effort. We came to Java as soldiers, as soldiers we went away, and we cherished the thought that in performing our duty with steadfast courage and disciplined restraint we had played our part in averting what was so nearly a great human tragedy and had, perhaps, helped a little to bring peace to a troubled land.

After we had gone, Dr. van Mook, in an official order of the day to the Dutch forces, said that the British had "performed a difficult task to the best of their ability," and Dr. Sjahrir too paid his "unofficial" tribute to their services; but the "Fighting Cock" can point to something better than the studied and carefully guarded utterances of politicians, and cherishes as its reward the spontaneous and warm words in which the Dutch commander answered General Hawthorn's Christmas message:

"My dear General,

"The officers and men under my command are deeply touched by your Christmas message to your officers and men.

"We have never felt so strongly how hard fate really was when it sent your Division to Java, once the most peaceful island in the world. We share your sadness when thinking of your dead and wounded, fallen after V.J. Day, when the war should have been over. We have heard of deeds of gallantry and self-sacrifice done by your troops in order to save our men, women and children from death and starvation, deeds that we believe have never been surpassed in any other theatre of war.

"We are extremely grateful for the words of deep sympathy with our men, women and children who are suffering from this aftermath of the war and for your effort to make them as happy as you can.

"On behalf of all officers and men under my command I wish you and all officers of the 23rd Indian Division a Happy Christmas and the best of luck through the coming year.

"Yours very sincerely,

"W. Schilling."

CHAPTER 26

Closing Time

WHEN the skeleton of the old "Fighting Cock" arrived in North Malaya, our new commander, Major-General B. H. Chappel, D.S.O., was awaiting us. H.Q. 1 Ind. Inf. Bde. had been disbanded, and of our battalions, all but the Seaforths, the three Gurkha units and 6 Mahratta had gone; besides these we had retained 24 Ind. Fd. Amb., our R.I.A.S.C. units and the three I.E.M.E. workshops. To fill the gaps we were allotted units from 7 Ind. Div., which we relieved, and other formations, and this "new" Division settled down to policing North Malaya with H.Q. at Taiping.

It was not a light task. We had come hoping for a rest, but the civil police were not numerous enough to maintain order by themselves, and the old job of patrolling began once more, with smugglers and bandits substituted for Pemoedas and Black Buffaloes. Units were separated from each other by tens of miles, and the unfortunate 3/5 R.G.R., with Lieut.-Colonel G. P. V. Saunders still at their head, ended up on the north-eastern coast, where they were linked to the rest of the world by an inferior railway which passed through lower Thailand.

This return to Malaya forms the epilogue to our story. We lasted long enough to welcome General Roberts, who, as Vice-Adjutant-General, was accompanying the C.I.G.S. on a tour of the Far East, and we had the pleasure of his company at dinner on the night in November, 1946, when our first reunion dinner was held in London; we lasted long enough to celebrate our fifth birthday in the New Year of 1947, but our identity was further destroyed by the departure of the Seaforths and Mahrattas to Singapore and of 3/10 G.R. to India.

The end was in sight. Malaya was reorganized into two sub-districts, one in the north with H.Q. at Taiping, one in the south with H.Q. at Port Dickson. Brigadier de Burgh

Morris and his staff went to Taiping, Brigadier MacDonald to Port Dickson, where the homing instinct took him to the quarters he had occupied after the "Zipper" landing, but he no longer wore the "Fighting Cock" on his sleeve. Quietly, without the least pain, H.Q. 23rd Indian Division evaporated over the last days of March and the beginning of April, 1947, aged five years and three months, but very experienced for its age.

This has been a plain tale, as old as the hills, a tale of the courage, endurance and self-sacrifice which war, for all its horror, evokes in men animated by a sense of purpose and united by comradeship in arms. We, who wore the "Fighting Cock," felt the strength of that unity and knew the happiness it brings, and out of that inner strength and happiness in service came this tale of ordinary men who did their duty.

At the close, there is a toast to be drunk in which all in these islands who served with the Division will join with their whole hearts. The toast is—"Our Indian sepoys," whose devotion to duty is the backbone of our story. Truly, the Indian Army that has now passed away was an achievement at which to marvel. Somehow, almost miraculously, the sense of justice, the courage, the kindliness and humour in the British character overcame the deepest prejudices and brought men of different creeds voluntarily together in common service for generation after generation. The vigour and soundness of a great tradition was finely shown in the record of the 23rd Indian Division, where many a war-born unit proved worthy heirs to this noble legacy. The link which sustained that tradition is broken, but the toast can be honoured by handing on the story of the men who made the "Fighting Cock" and the Army of which it was a part so potent a force for victory in the Second World War.

x

Appendix A

23RD INDIAN DIVISION—IMPHAL, JUNE, 1944

1st Indian Infantry Brigade
 1 Seaforth Highlanders (1 Seaforth)
 1/16 Punjab Regiment (1/16 Punjab)
 1 Patiala Infantry (Indian States Forces)

37th Indian Infantry Brigade
 3/3 Gurkha Rifles (3/3 G.R.)
 3/5 Royal Gurkha Rifles (3/5 R.G.R.)
 3/10 Gurkha Rifles (3/10 G.R.)

49th Indian Infantry Brigade
 4/5 Mahratta Light Infantry (4 Mahratta)
 6/5 Mahratta Light Infantry (6 Mahratta)
 5/6 Rajputana Rifles (5/6 Rajrif)

Artillery
 158 Field Regiment, R.A. (158 Fd. Regt.)
 3 Indian Field Regiment, R.I.A. (3 Ind. Fd. Regt.)
 28 Mountain Regiment, R.I.A. (28 Mtn. Regt.)
 2 Indian Anti-Tank Regiment, R.I.A. (2 Ind. A.Tk. Regt.)

Engineers
 68 Indian Field Company, Bengal Sappers & Miners
  (68 Ind. Fd. Coy.)
 71 Indian Field Company, Bengal Sappers & Miners
  (71 Ind. Fd. Coy.)
 91 Indian Field Company, Bombay Sappers & Miners
  (91 Ind. Fd. Coy.)
 323 Indian Field Park Company, Madras Sappers & Miners
  (323 Ind. Fd. Pk. Coy.)

Divisional Defence Battalion
 2/19 Hyderabad Regiment (2/19 Hybad)

Supplies & Transport (S. & T.)—Royal Indian Army Service
  Corps (R.I.A.S.C.)
 121, 122, 123 Indian General Purpose Transport Companies
  (Ind. G.P.T. Coys.)
 21, 24, 50, 61 Animal Transport Companies (A.T. Coys.)
 7, 10, 18 Field Ambulance Troops (Fd. Amb. Tps.)
 12, 13, 14, 15 Indian Composite Issue Sections

Medical

24, 47, 49 Indian Field Ambulances (Ind. Fd. Ambs.)
23rd Indian Division Field Hygiene Section

Ordnance

23rd Indian Division Ordnance Sub-Park

Indian Electrical & Mechanical Engineers (I.E.M.E.)

38, 61 Indian Mobile Workshops Companies (Ind. Mob. Wksp. Coys.)
23rd Indian Division Recovery Company

Provost

23rd Indian Division Provost Unit

Postal

23rd Indian Division Postal Unit

Appendix B

23RD INDIAN DIVISION—"ZIPPER"
SEPTEMBER, 1945

1. The following units remained in Burma when the Division left for India in 1944:
   R.I.A.S.C.   122 Ind. G.P.T. Coy., 61 A.T. Coy.

2. The following units were deleted from the "Zipper" order of battle and remained in India:
   Artillery   28 Mtn. Regt., R.I.A.
   R.I.A.S.C.   21, 24, 50 A.T. Coys., 7, 10, 18 Fd. Amb. Tps.

   The following unit was disbanded before "Zipper":
   Artillery   158 Fd. Regt., R.A.

4. The following units joined the Division for "Zipper" and went on from Malaya to Java:
   Artillery   178 Field Regiment, R.A. (178 Fd. Regt.)
   Reconnaissance Battalion 5/8 Punjab Regiment (5/8 Punjab)
   Machine Gun Battalion   6/8 Punjab Regiment (6/8 Punjab)
   I.E.M.E.   135 Indian Infantry Workshop Company (Ind. Inf. Wksp. Coy.)

5. *Changes of Nomenclature*:
   (a) *R.I.A.S.C.* G.P.T. Coys. were now styled Indian Companies, R.I.A.S.C. (Ind. Coys., R.I.A.S.C.)

   (b) *I.E.M.E.* Ind. Mob Wksp. Coys. were now styled Indian Infantry Workshop Companies.

Appendix C

GENERAL OFFICERS COMMANDING

Jan., 1942–Jun., 1943	Major-General R. A. Savory, C.B., D.S.O., M.C.
Aug., 1943–Mar., 1945	Major-General O. L. Roberts, C.B.E., D.S.O.
Mar., 1945–Oct., 1946	Major-General D. C. Hawthorn, C.B., D.S.O.
Oct., 1946–end	Major-General B. H. Chappel, D.S.O.

BRIGADE COMMANDERS

1st Indian Infantry Brigade

[1]May, 1942–May, 1943	Brigadier F. V. R. Woodhouse
Jun., 1943–Mar., 1944	Brigadier R. C. McCay, C.B.E., D.S.O.
Mar., 1944–Jan., 1946	Brigadier R. C. M. King, D.S.O., O.B.E.
Feb., 1946	Brigadier K. T. Darling, D.S.O. (transferred shortly after appointment to Command 5 Parachute Brigade)
Feb., 1946–Oct., 1946	Brigadier N. D. Wingrove, C.B.E.

37th Indian Infantry Brigade

[1]Mar., 1942–Jun., 1944	Brigadier H. V. Collingridge, D.S.O., O.B.E.
Jun., 1944–Jul., 1944	Brigadier J. F. Marindin, D.S.O.
Aug., 1944–end	Brigadier N. MacDonald, C.B.E., D.S.O.

49th Indian Infantry Brigade

[1]May, 1942–Oct., 1942	Brigadier R. D. Whitehouse
Oct., 1942–Mar., 1943	Brigadier W. B. Thomas, D.S.O.
Mar., 1943–Jun., 1944	Brigadier F. A. Esse, O.B.E.
Jul., 1944–Sept., 1944	Brigadier C. H. B. Rodham, D.S.O., O.B.E., M.C.
Sept., 1944–Oct., 1945	Brigadier A. W. S. Mallaby, C.I.E., O.B.E.

---

[1] The dates are those when the Brigades first came under command of the Division. All three officers had held their appointments before these dates.

Officiating
    Oct.–Nov., 1945   Colonel L. H. O. Pugh, D.S.O.
    Nov., 1945–end   Brigadier A. de Burgh Morris, D.S.O., O.B.E.

COMMANDERS ROYAL ARTILLERY

Mar., 1942–Dec., 1942   Brigadier Goulder, D.S.O., M.C.
Dec., 1942–Apr., 1945   Brigadier R. W. Andrews, D.S.O., M.C.
Apr., 1945–Jun., 1946   Brigadier R. B. W. Bethell, D.S.O.
Jun., 1946–end   Brigadier F. C. Scott, C.B.E.

Note.—Decorations shown are those gained prior to or during service with the Division.

Appendix D

SUMMARY OF HONOURS AND AWARDS GAINED BY THE 23RD INDIAN DIVISION

	Burma	Malaya & Java	Total
C.B.		1	1
C.B.E.	1	2	3
D.S.O.	9	3	12
Bar to D.S.O.	1	1	2
O.B.E.	7	2	9
M.B.E.	19	6	25
M.C.	70	23	93
Bar to M.C.	4	1	5
O.B.I.	4		4
I.O.M.	8		8
D.C.M.	4		4
M.M.	100	38	138
Bar to M.M.	3	2	5
I.D.S.M.	51	7	58
Bar to I.D.S.M.	1		1
B.E.M.	1	1	2
M.S.M.	3		3
Mentioned in Despatches	477	159[1]	636
Certificates of Gallantry ...	44	10	54
C.-in-C.'s Commendation Cards	4		4
	811	256	1067

[2] Figure does not include "Mentions" in the final gazette for Java.

"WHEN YOU GO HOME
TELL THEM OF US AND SAY
FOR YOUR TOMORROW
WE GAVE OUR TODAY"

THE ASSAM-BURMA FRONT

Map labels:

Nandat, Pantha, Indaw, Mawku, Mawlaik, Kalewa, Kalemyo, Pyingang, Kinbin, L. Maddocks, Chindwin R., Manipur R., Minthami, Athizn, Khampat, Yazagyo, Okkan, Kennedy Peak, Nalchaung, Fort White, Tiddim, Falam, CHIN HILLS

LEGEND

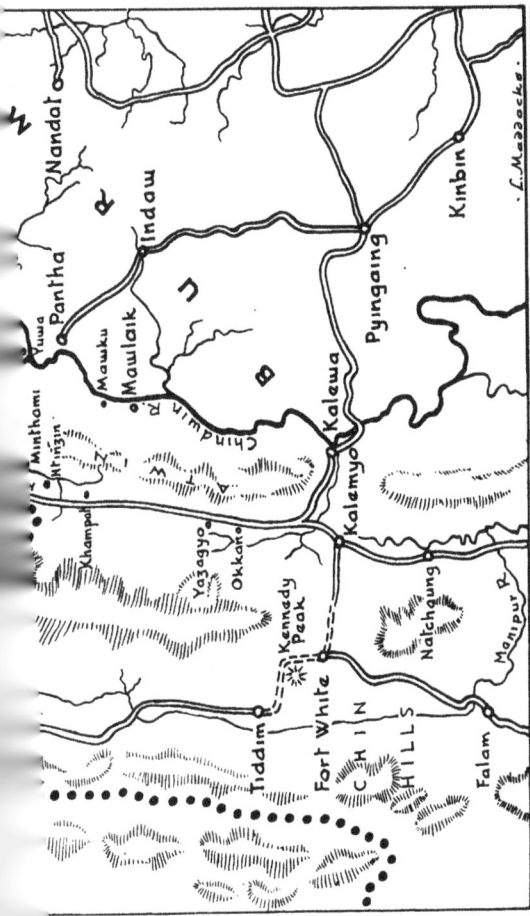

Roads usually fit for all classes of vehicles.	•——• Assam-Burma Boundary.
	Jeep tracks constructed on alignment of hill tracks, Sept. 1942 – Feb. 1944.

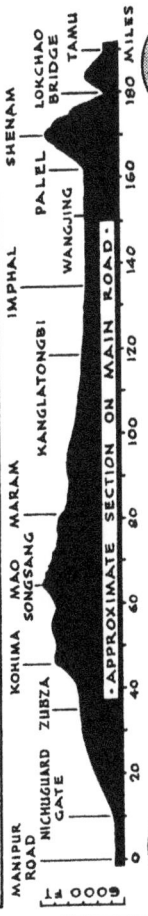

Elevation profile (• APPROXIMATE SECTION ON MAIN ROAD •):

MANIPUR ROAD, NICHUGUARD GATE, ZUBZA, KOHIMA, MAO SONGSANG, MARAM, KANGLATONGBI, IMPHAL, PALEL, WANGJING, SHENAM, LOKCHAO BRIDGE, TAMU

Scale: 6000 FT

Distance axis: 0, 20, 40, 60, 80, 100, 120, 140, 160, 180 MILES

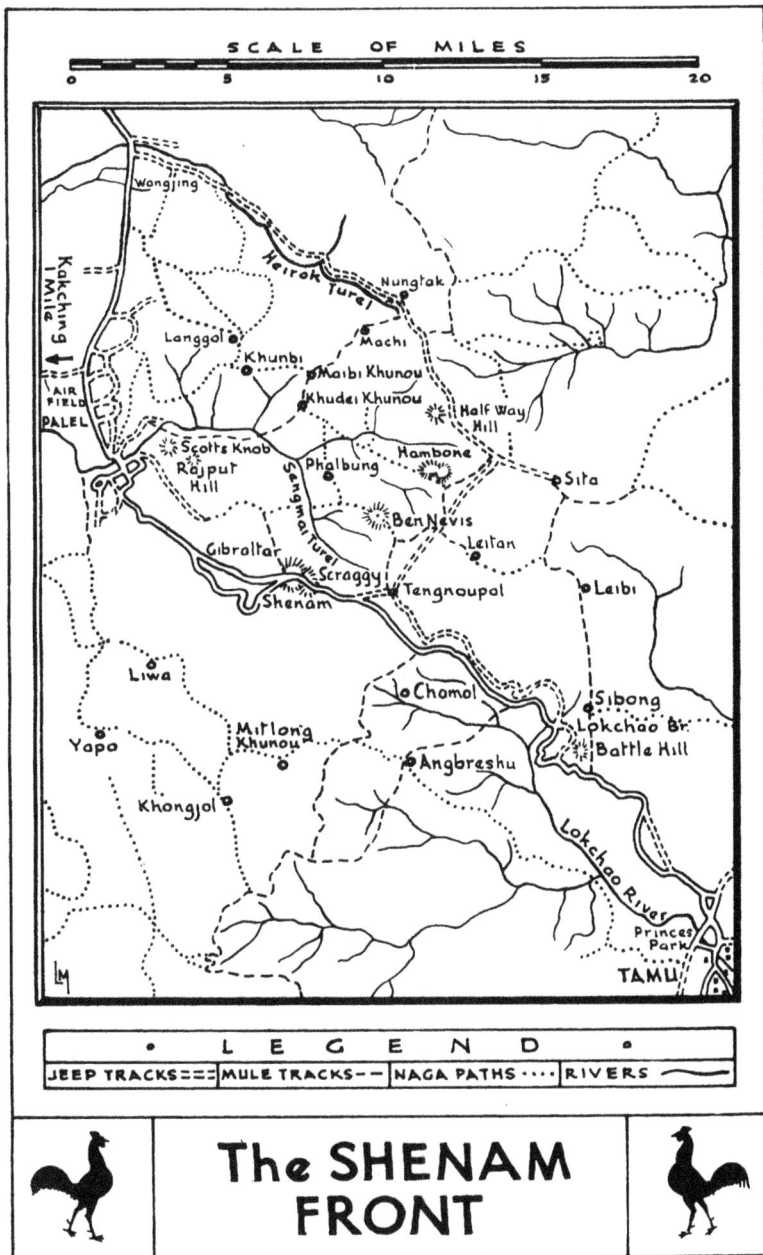

SCALE OF MILES

0 ... 5 ... 10 ... 15 ... 20

Kakching 1 Mile

Wangjing

Heirok Turel

Nungtak

Langgol

Khunbi

Machi

Maibi Khunou

Khudei Khunou

AIR FIELD

PALEL

Half Way Hill

Scotts Knob

Rajput Hill

Phalbung

Hambone

Sita

Sengmai Turel

Ben Nevis

Gibraltar

Scraggy

Leitan

Shenam

Tengnoupal

Leibi

Liwa

Chomol

Sibong

Lokchao Br

Battle Hill

Yapo

Mitlong Khunou

Angbreshu

Khongjol

Lokchao River

Princes Park

TAMU

LM

LEGEND

JEEP TRACKS === MULE TRACKS -- NAGA PATHS .... RIVERS ~~~

The SHENAM FRONT

Index

(Ranks of officers are as at the time of the events in which they were concerned)

www.ingramcontent.com/pod-product-compliance
Lightning Source LLC
Chambersburg PA
CBHW030945150426
42814CB00030B/356/J